Work Smarter with

Change the Way You Work

Kiet Huynh

Table of Contents

CHAPTER I Introduction to Slack.. 6

1.1 What is Slack? 6

1.2 Why Use Slack? 10

1.3 Key Features of Slack.. 16

    1.3.1 Channels and Direct Messages.. 16

    1.3.2 File Sharing and Integrations... 21

    1.3.3 Search and Message History 26

    1.3.4 Notifications and Customization 31

1.4 Setting Up Your Slack Workspace 37

    1.4.1 Creating a Slack Account 37

    1.4.2 Joining or Creating a Workspace 43

    1.4.3 Navigating the Slack Interface 48

CHAPTER II Mastering Slack Channels & Conversations 57

2.1 Understanding Slack Channels... 57

    2.1.1 Public vs. Private Channels 57

    2.1.2 Creating and Managing Channels 61

    2.1.3 Best Practices for Organizing Channels 70

2.2 Sending and Managing Messages 77

    2.2.1 Formatting Messages and Using Emojis....................................... 77

    2.2.2 Replying in Threads vs. Direct Messages 81

    2.2.3 Pinning, Bookmarking, and Saving Messages............................... 86

2.3 Using Mentions, Reactions, and Threads Effectively............................. 95

    2.3.1 Tagging People with @Mentions 95

    2.3.2 Using Reactions to Acknowledge Messages.................................. 99

2.3.3 Keeping Conversations Organized with Threads 105

CHAPTER III Optimizing Collaboration with Slack Features 110

3.1 File Sharing and Storage 110

3.1.1 Uploading and Sharing Files in Channels 110

3.1.2 Integrating with Google Drive and OneDrive 114

3.1.3 Managing File Permissions and Downloads 120

3.2 Using Slack Integrations and Bots 125

3.2.1 Connecting Third-Party Apps (Trello, Zoom, Asana, etc.) 125

3.2.2 Automating Tasks with Slack Bots 130

3.2.3 Setting Up Workflow Builder for Automation 137

3.3 Slack Calls and Huddles 144

3.3.1 Starting and Managing Voice & Video Calls 144

3.3.2 Using Slack Huddles for Quick Meetings 149

3.3.3 Best Practices for Remote Collaboration 153

CHAPTER IV Managing Notifications and Productivity 159

4.1 Customizing Notifications for Efficiency 159

4.1.1 Setting Notification Preferences 159

4.1.2 Using Do Not Disturb Mode 164

4.1.3 Managing Mobile and Desktop Notifications 168

4.2 Organizing Work with Slack Tools 174

4.2.1 Using Slack Reminders and To-Do Lists 174

4.2.2 Scheduling Messages for Later Delivery 180

4.2.3 Creating and Using Bookmarks 186

4.3 Enhancing Productivity with Slack Workflows 193

4.3.1 Using Shortcuts and Slash Commands 193

4.3.2 Setting Up Automated Workflows 198

4.3.3 Avoiding Information Overload in Slack 205

CHAPTER V Advanced Slack Techniques for Teams 211

5.1 Managing Team Collaboration 211

5.1.1 Best Practices for Team Communication 211

5.1.2 Creating a Knowledge Hub in Slack 216

5.1.3 Using Custom Emojis and Reactions 222

5.2 Security and Privacy in Slack 228

5.2.1 Managing Permissions and Roles 228

5.2.2 Handling Sensitive Information in Slack 234

5.2.3 Setting Up Two-Factor Authentication 240

5.3 Using Slack for Cross-Company Collaboration 247

5.3.1 Understanding Slack Connect 247

5.3.2 Collaborating with External Partners 252

5.3.3 Managing Multi-Workspace Accounts 259

CHAPTER VI Slack for Remote and Hybrid Work 265

6.1 Creating a Remote-Friendly Slack Culture 265

6.1.1 Best Practices for Remote Team Communication 265

6.1.2 Using Slack to Build Team Engagement 270

6.1.3 Setting Boundaries Between Work and Life 276

6.2 Managing Projects in Slack 283

6.2.1 Using Slack with Project Management Tools 283

6.2.2 Creating Dedicated Project Channels 288

6.2.3 Tracking Progress and Deliverables in Slack 294

6.3 Hosting Virtual Events and Meetings in Slack 300

6.3.1 Running Polls and Surveys 300

6.3.2 Organizing Company Announcements 305

6.3.3 Hosting Q&A Sessions and AMAs 309

CHAPTER VII Troubleshooting and Best Practices 315

7.1 Common Slack Issues and Fixes 315

7.1.1 Troubleshooting Notifications and Messages.................................... 315

7.1.2 Fixing Connectivity and Syncing Issues 320

7.1.3 Managing Too Many Channels and Alerts....................................... 324

7.2 Best Practices for Slack Power Users 330

7.2.1 Reducing Distractions and Staying Focused.................................... 330

7.2.2 Creating a Slack Etiquette Guide for Your Team 334

7.2.3 Keeping Slack Organized and Efficient... 340

7.3 Future of Slack and Emerging Features 346

7.3.1 What's New in Slack?.. 346

7.3.2 Upcoming AI and Automation Features 350

7.3.3 How to Keep Up with Slack Updates 353

Conclusion 359

8.1 Recap: The Key Takeaways from This Book 359

8.2 How to Keep Improving Your Slack Experience................................... 363

8.3 Final Thoughts and Next Steps 368

Acknowledgments 372

CHAPTER I
Introduction to Slack

1.1 What is Slack?

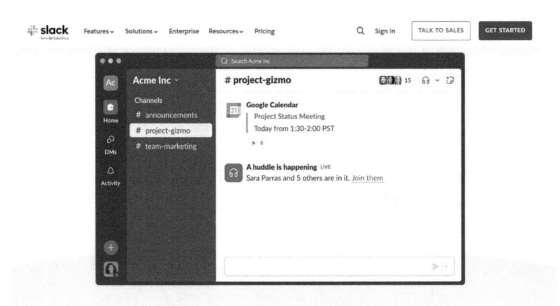

Bring your people, projects, apps, and AI agents together.

Slack is a powerful messaging and collaboration tool designed for teams to communicate, share files, and work efficiently in a digital workspace. Unlike traditional email, Slack organizes conversations into channels, enabling teams to stay focused and manage their projects more effectively. Since its launch in 2013, Slack has become one of the most widely used workplace communication platforms, with millions of active users worldwide.

The Evolution of Workplace Communication

Before Slack, teams primarily relied on emails, phone calls, and in-person meetings to collaborate. While these methods are still in use today, they often lead to inefficiencies:

- **Emails** can be slow and cluttered, making it difficult to track conversations.
- **Phone calls and meetings** require immediate attention and may interrupt workflow.
- **Multiple tools** (such as file-sharing apps, project management software, and messaging platforms) create fragmentation and reduce productivity.

Slack was created to solve these issues by offering a **centralized** and **real-time** communication hub that integrates with other work tools, reducing dependency on email and enhancing team productivity.

How Slack Works

At its core, Slack functions as a team collaboration hub where users can:

- Send messages in real-time to individuals or groups.
- Organize discussions into channels based on topics, projects, or teams.
- Share files and documents seamlessly.
- Integrate with third-party apps like Google Drive, Zoom, Trello, and Asana.
- Search past conversations and files easily using advanced search functionalities.
- Customize notifications to reduce distractions and enhance focus.

Slack is available on desktop and mobile devices, ensuring that users can stay connected no matter where they are.

Key Differences Between Slack and Traditional Communication Methods

Feature	Slack	Email	Phone Calls	Meetings
Real-time messaging	✓	✗	✓	✓
Organized discussions (Channels)	✓	✗	✗	✓
File Sharing	✓	✓	✗	✓

Feature	Slack	Email	Phone Calls	Meetings
Integrations with Work Apps	☑	Limited	✗	✗
Searchable Message History	☑	☑	✗	✗
Reduces Inbox Clutter	☑	✗	☑	☑

As seen in the table, Slack combines the benefits of multiple communication tools into one platform, making it a more **efficient** and **structured** way for teams to collaborate.

The Benefits of Using Slack

1. **Improved Team Communication:** Slack enables instant messaging, reducing the need for long email threads. By organizing discussions into channels, teams can focus on specific topics without unrelated distractions.

2. **Enhanced Collaboration with Channels:** Channels allow teams to create dedicated spaces for projects, departments, or interests. This ensures that information is structured and easy to find.

3. **Integration with Other Tools:** Slack connects with hundreds of third-party apps, including file-sharing services, project management platforms, and automation tools, streamlining workflows.

4. **Flexibility and Remote Work Support:** Whether in the office, at home, or on the go, Slack ensures team members stay connected. The mobile app allows users to communicate from anywhere.

5. **Efficient File Sharing and Search:** Slack makes it easy to upload and share files directly in conversations. Its advanced search function helps users find past messages, files, and links quickly.

6. **Customizable Notifications**: Slack provides users with the ability to manage notifications, reducing distractions and increasing productivity.

Real-World Use Cases of Slack

- **Startups and Small Businesses**: Many small teams use Slack to maintain clear and quick communication, ensuring seamless project management.

- **Large Enterprises**: Corporations integrate Slack with tools like Jira and Salesforce to enhance workflow efficiency.

- **Remote and Hybrid Teams**: Slack helps remote workers stay connected and aligned with company goals.

- **Educational Institutions**: Universities use Slack for class discussions, faculty collaboration, and student projects.

Conclusion

Slack has transformed how modern teams communicate by providing an organized, real-time, and integrated workspace for collaboration. Whether you're working on a small project or managing a large team, Slack helps keep conversations focused, efficient, and productive.

1.2 Why Use Slack?

COLLABORATION

Communicate in countless ways from one place.

Slack is built for bringing people and information together. Type things out. Talk things out. Invite external organizations into the conversation.

80% of the Fortune 100 use Slack Connect to work with partners and customers[1]

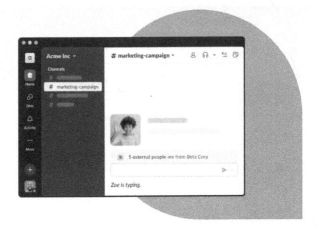

In today's fast-paced and digitally connected world, effective communication and collaboration are the cornerstones of success in any organization. Whether you're part of a small startup or a large enterprise, the need to stay connected with your team, streamline workflows, and boost productivity is more critical than ever. This is where Slack, a popular team collaboration platform, comes into play. Slack isn't just a messaging app; it's a powerful tool designed to revolutionize how teams work together, both in real-time and asynchronously.

So, why should you use Slack? Let's explore some compelling reasons why Slack has become an indispensable tool for millions of businesses around the world.

Centralized Communication Hub

Before the advent of collaboration tools like Slack, teams relied on emails, phone calls, in-person meetings, and a mix of other communication tools. While these methods still have their place, they often lead to fragmented communication that's hard to track, especially in large teams. Slack solves this problem by providing a single platform where all communication can be organized, easily accessible, and searchable.

Slack uses channels to organize conversations. Channels are essentially digital rooms where team members can communicate about specific topics, projects, or departments. Whether you're discussing a marketing campaign, coding bugs, or weekly team meetings, each conversation has its own space. This organizational structure ensures that team members never miss important information and that conversations are always on-topic.

Direct messages (DMs) in Slack allow for private, one-on-one conversations, but Slack takes it further by allowing group chats, making it a versatile communication tool. The ability to create both public and private channels, along with DMs, allows for clear organization of communication, ensuring that messages are only seen by the right people at the right time.

Real-Time Collaboration

One of the biggest advantages of Slack is its real-time communication capabilities. Unlike email, which can introduce delays between messages, Slack allows team members to engage in instant conversations. Whether it's a quick clarification on a project or a real-time brainstorming session, Slack helps ensure that no communication is delayed.

Real-time collaboration doesn't just apply to text messaging—it extends to file sharing, video calls, and interactive discussions. Team members can share documents, spreadsheets, presentations, and other files instantly within channels or direct messages, making it easy to provide feedback, make edits, or even collaborate on the spot.

Slack's integration with tools like Google Drive, Dropbox, and OneDrive allows users to share and edit documents directly within the Slack platform, eliminating the need to switch between different apps. This integration streamlines workflows and boosts productivity, as everything can be done without leaving the platform.

Enhanced Team Productivity

Slack promotes enhanced productivity by reducing the time spent searching for information, reducing unnecessary meetings, and simplifying the decision-making process. The platform has several features that contribute to a more productive team environment.

First, Slack allows users to organize and categorize information. With channels, users can easily access past messages, files, and conversations, all of which are searchable. The search functionality is incredibly powerful, allowing users to find past messages, even those from months ago. Whether you're looking for an important document, a specific conversation, or a keyword, Slack's search bar makes it easy to retrieve information instantly.

Additionally, the use of threads in Slack ensures that conversations stay organized. Instead of bombarding a channel with responses that may clutter the main discussion, users can reply directly within threads, keeping the primary channel focused and organized. This makes it easier to track discussions on specific topics and maintain clarity, even during long-running projects.

Slack also helps eliminate unnecessary meetings. When a team member needs quick feedback or an answer, Slack allows them to reach out and get a response without needing to schedule a formal meeting. The ability to have quick, efficient exchanges without disrupting the flow of the workday ensures that team members stay focused and productive.

Cross-Functional Collaboration

In many organizations, teams work in silos, with each department or function working independently. While this structure may have worked in the past, it often leads to missed opportunities for collaboration and innovation. Slack breaks down these silos by encouraging cross-functional collaboration in a seamless way.

One of the standout features of Slack is its integration capabilities. Slack connects with numerous third-party apps and services, such as Trello, Zoom, Asana, Salesforce, and many more. By connecting these apps to Slack, team members from different functions can share insights and work together without needing to switch between multiple tools.

For example, a marketing team can create a campaign plan in Trello and share it directly in a Slack channel where both the marketing and sales teams can comment, ask questions, and provide feedback. Similarly, the customer support team can integrate their help desk software into Slack, enabling the development team to quickly respond to customer issues and prioritize bug fixes.

This level of cross-functional collaboration enables teams to work more efficiently and ensures that everyone has access to the information they need to make decisions quickly and effectively.

Flexibility for Remote and Hybrid Teams

Slack's flexibility is especially valuable for remote and hybrid teams. As the world increasingly shifts to remote work, teams need tools that can support collaboration across time zones and geographic locations. Slack is designed to meet the needs of remote teams by providing a platform where teams can stay connected and continue to collaborate, regardless of where they are located.

Slack's asynchronous communication capabilities allow teams to communicate even when they're not all online at the same time. This is particularly helpful for teams working across different time zones, as team members can leave messages and updates for others to pick up when they log in. By using Slack's threads, team members can easily follow up on ongoing conversations without the need to be present at the same time.

Moreover, Slack's mobile app ensures that team members can stay connected, even when they're away from their desks. Whether you're on the go or working from home, the mobile app allows you to stay on top of conversations, participate in discussions, and get work done no matter where you are.

Building a Culture of Transparency and Accountability

One of the most valuable aspects of Slack is its ability to foster a culture of transparency and accountability within teams. By keeping all conversations in channels (with the option to create private discussions as needed), Slack ensures that information is openly shared and easily accessible to everyone who needs it.

This transparency is essential for team alignment, as it allows everyone to stay on the same page regarding project updates, feedback, and important announcements. For example, if a team member misses a meeting or is out sick, they can catch up on the entire conversation by reviewing the Slack channel, ensuring they don't miss any critical updates.

Additionally, the use of channels for specific projects, teams, or departments promotes accountability. Team members are able to clearly see who is working on what, the progress of various tasks, and who is responsible for what deliverables. Slack's reminder and task-tracking features further support accountability, ensuring that nothing falls through the cracks.

Scalability for Growing Teams

As teams grow, the complexity of communication and collaboration also increases. Slack is highly scalable and designed to grow with your team. Whether you're a small startup or a large enterprise, Slack's organizational structure can accommodate your evolving needs.

With features like shared channels, which allow teams to collaborate with external partners or other departments, and the ability to manage a vast number of channels, Slack ensures that communication remains organized even as the team grows. The platform also offers administrative controls to ensure that the right people have the right permissions, maintaining security and data integrity as your team scales.

Additionally, Slack's integrations and third-party apps allow you to extend its capabilities as your team's needs evolve. You can add more tools as required and customize your Slack experience to suit your organization's unique workflows.

Conclusion

In conclusion, Slack is a versatile and powerful tool that can transform how teams communicate and collaborate. Whether you're looking to centralize your team's communication, enhance real-time collaboration, improve productivity, foster cross-functional teamwork, or support remote work, Slack has the features and flexibility to meet your needs.

By adopting Slack, teams can streamline their communication, reduce misunderstandings, and ensure that important information is always accessible. It helps businesses grow and thrive by improving collaboration and increasing overall productivity, ultimately changing the way you work for the better.

As we move forward, Slack is continually evolving, offering new features and improvements to further enhance team collaboration. Whether you're just starting with Slack or looking to deepen your usage, there's no better time to start using this powerful platform and experience the difference it can make in your workday.

1.3 Key Features of Slack

1.3.1 Channels and Direct Messages

Slack is a powerful communication platform designed to improve collaboration in teams of all sizes. At the core of Slack's functionality are Channels and Direct Messages (DMs), which serve as the foundation for organizing conversations, sharing information, and maintaining efficient communication.

This section will explore how Channels and Direct Messages work, their key differences, best practices for using them effectively, and how they contribute to better teamwork and productivity.

Understanding Slack Channels

What Are Slack Channels?

Slack Channels are virtual spaces where teams can communicate, share files, and collaborate on projects. They function like dedicated chat rooms, allowing users to focus discussions on specific topics, projects, or teams.

Every Slack workspace consists of multiple channels that serve different purposes, such as:

- **General team communication** (e.g., #company-updates, #team-marketing)

- **Project-specific discussions** (e.g., #project-alpha, #website-redesign)

- **Social or non-work-related discussions** (e.g., #random, #book-club)

By organizing conversations into channels, Slack ensures that discussions remain focused and easy to navigate.

Types of Channels in Slack

Slack offers two main types of channels:

1. **Public Channels**

   o Anyone in the workspace can join and view the conversation.

   o Messages and files are searchable by all members.

   o Ideal for company-wide announcements, general team discussions, and cross-functional projects.

2. **Private Channels**

   o Only invited members can see and participate in the conversation.

   o Great for sensitive discussions, confidential projects, or smaller working groups.

Additionally, Slack provides **Shared Channels** (via Slack Connect), which allow different organizations to collaborate securely within a single channel. This is particularly useful for companies working with external partners or clients.

Understanding Direct Messages (DMs)

What Are Direct Messages?

Choose the communication style that works for you

Collaboration isn't limited to just text. Use voice, video and more to help get your message across.

While **Channels** are designed for group discussions, **Direct Messages (DMs)** are used for one-on-one or small group conversations. DMs function like private chats, allowing users to discuss matters that don't require the entire team's attention.

Slack DMs can be used for:

- Quick, private conversations between colleagues.

- Addressing urgent questions without disrupting a channel.

- Sharing confidential information.

Types of Direct Messages

1. **One-on-One DMs**

   o A private conversation between two individuals.

   o Great for quick check-ins, asking questions, or discussing sensitive matters.

2. **Group DMs**

   o Conversations with up to **eight** people.

   o Useful for temporary discussions that don't require a dedicated channel.

Beyond this limit, Slack encourages using a **private channel** instead of a group DM to keep conversations structured and searchable.

How to Use Direct Messages Effectively

- **Use DMs sparingly** to avoid information silos—important conversations should happen in channels.

- **Keep DMs concise and to the point** to respect the recipient's time.

- **Use reactions and emoji acknowledgments** to confirm messages without unnecessary replies.

- **Avoid excessive notifications** by considering whether a DM is necessary or if the question can be posted in a relevant channel.

Best Practices for Using Channels and DMs

When to Use a Channel vs. a Direct Message

Scenario	Use a Channel	Use a Direct Message
Sharing company-wide updates	☑	✕
Discussing a project with a team	☑	✕
Sending a private message to a colleague	✕	☑
Asking a question relevant to multiple people	☑	✕
Addressing a personal or confidential issue	✕	☑

Using **Channels** instead of **DMs** whenever possible ensures transparency, better information flow, and reduced message duplication.

Etiquette for Slack Communication

1. **Use Threads in Channels**

   o Instead of replying in the main conversation, use **threads** to keep discussions organized.

2. **Avoid Overloading with DMs**

o   If the topic is relevant to multiple people, post it in a channel rather than sending individual DMs.

3. **Respect People's Time**

o   Use **status updates** (e.g., "Away" or "Do Not Disturb") to indicate availability.

o   Avoid sending urgent DMs outside of working hours unless necessary.

4. **Use Reactions to Acknowledge Messages**

o   Instead of responding with "Okay" or "Got it," use ✅, 👍, or 🎉 reactions.

5. **Use Proper Naming Conventions** for Channels

o   Prefix project-based channels with #proj- (e.g., #proj-new-website).

o   Use clear names that indicate the channel's purpose.

Advanced Features for Channels and DMs

Using Slack Connect for External Collaboration

Slack Connect allows different organizations to collaborate securely within shared channels. This is particularly useful for:

- Working with external vendors, clients, or contractors.
- Avoiding long email threads by keeping discussions in one place.
- Managing cross-company projects efficiently.

Setting Up Automated Notifications in Channels

Slack allows teams to integrate bots and workflows to automate notifications, such as:

- Sending daily stand-up reminders.
- Notifying teams of updates from project management tools like Trello or Jira.
- Alerting users when tasks are assigned to them.

Using Search in Channels and DMs

Slack's powerful search functionality helps users quickly find:

- Specific messages within a channel.

- Files shared in past conversations.

- Messages from a particular user or containing certain keywords.

Example search commands:

- in:#marketing strategy → Searches for "strategy" in #marketing.

- from:@john → Shows messages from John.

- has:link → Finds messages that contain links.

Conclusion

Channels and Direct Messages are the backbone of Slack's communication system, enabling teams to collaborate efficiently while keeping conversations structured.

By leveraging channels for group discussions and using DMs for private conversations, teams can maintain **transparency**, **reduce message clutter**, and **increase productivity**.

Key takeaways:
- Use **public channels** for company-wide discussions.
- Use **private channels** for confidential projects.
- Use **DMs** only for private or urgent matters.
- Keep conversations **organized** with threads and proper channel naming.

In the next section, we will explore **File Sharing and Integrations**, another essential feature that enhances Slack's functionality. 🚀

1.3.2 File Sharing and Integrations

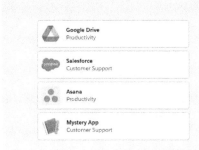

Bring context into the conversation

Get important updates, discuss them, and take action – all without switching tabs. By connecting other work tools to Slack, you can have richer, more informed conversations.

See the Slack Marketplace →

Slack is more than just a messaging platform; it's a powerful hub for collaboration, allowing users to share files effortlessly and integrate third-party tools to streamline workflows. Whether you need to share documents, images, spreadsheets, or even code snippets, Slack provides multiple ways to keep your team connected. Additionally, with its vast ecosystem of integrations, Slack can be customized to fit the needs of any organization, making it a true productivity powerhouse.

Understanding File Sharing in Slack

File sharing in Slack is designed to be quick, intuitive, and highly accessible. Users can drag and drop files directly into a channel, upload them from their computer or cloud storage, and even attach them to messages. Slack supports a variety of file types, including:

- Documents (PDF, Word, Google Docs)
- Spreadsheets (Excel, Google Sheets)
- Presentations (PowerPoint, Google Slides)
- Images (JPEG, PNG, GIF)
- Code snippets and text files
- Compressed files (ZIP, RAR)

Each file uploaded to Slack remains within the workspace, making it easy to retrieve, reference, and collaborate on shared content.

Uploading and Sharing Files

There are multiple ways to share files in Slack, depending on the source and the context of the collaboration.

1. Drag-and-Drop Uploads

Slack allows users to simply drag a file from their desktop and drop it into a Slack channel or direct message. This is the fastest way to share files on the go.

2. Uploading from Your Device

Users can also manually upload files by clicking the **"+" (Add) button** in the message box and selecting **"Upload a file"** from their computer.

3. Sharing Files from Cloud Storage

Slack supports direct integrations with major cloud storage services, such as:

- Google Drive
- Dropbox
- OneDrive
- Box

Instead of uploading a file, users can share a cloud link. This keeps Slack's storage optimized and ensures that the latest version of a document is always accessible.

4. Attaching Files to Messages and Threads

Users can attach files to messages or threads to keep conversations organized. This is particularly useful for discussions about specific reports, project plans, or client feedback.

Managing Shared Files

Finding Previously Shared Files

Slack provides an easy way to retrieve past files. Users can:

- Click on the **"Files"** tab in a channel or DM to see a list of all shared files.
- Use Slack's search bar and enter keywords or file types to locate specific documents.

Pinning Important Files

To ensure that crucial documents don't get lost in long conversations, files can be **pinned** to a channel for quick access.

Setting File Permissions

While Slack itself doesn't restrict file access, integrated cloud storage solutions allow users to manage permissions directly from Slack. This means you can share a file with viewing or editing permissions while maintaining control over who can access it.

Slack Integrations: Expanding Functionality

Slack's real strength lies in its **integrations**—tools that allow users to connect their favorite apps and automate repetitive tasks. These integrations enhance productivity, reducing the need to switch between multiple applications.

Popular Slack Integrations

Slack supports thousands of third-party integrations across various categories, including:

1. Productivity and Collaboration

- **Google Drive**: Share, preview, and manage documents directly from Slack.
- **Microsoft 365**: Access files from OneDrive and collaborate on Word, Excel, and PowerPoint.
- **Trello**: Manage projects and track progress within Slack.
- **Asana**: Create tasks and receive notifications on project updates.

2. Development and IT Tools

- **GitHub**: Get updates on code commits, pull requests, and issues.
- **JIRA**: Track bug reports and development sprints.
- **Zapier**: Automate workflows by connecting Slack to thousands of apps.

3. Communication and Video Conferencing

- **Zoom**: Start video calls directly from Slack.
- **Google Meet**: Share a Google Meet link for instant meetings.
- **Microsoft Teams**: Cross-platform communication for hybrid teams.

4. Customer Support and CRM

- **Zendesk**: Receive customer service tickets and respond quickly.

- **Salesforce**: Get real-time updates on sales activities.

- **HubSpot**: Track leads and manage customer interactions.

How to Set Up and Use Slack Integrations

Integrating third-party apps with Slack is straightforward. Follow these steps to get started:

1. Finding and Adding an Integration

- Click on **Apps** in the left sidebar.

- Search for the desired app in the Slack App Directory.

- Click **"Add to Slack"** and follow the authentication process.

2. Authorizing Permissions

Most integrations require permission to access Slack data. Depending on the app, you may need to:

- Sign in to your account (e.g., Google Drive, Dropbox, Trello).

- Grant Slack permission to send notifications or pull information.

3. Configuring Notifications and Automations

Once installed, you can customize how Slack interacts with the integration. For example:

- Set **Trello** to send Slack notifications when a task is assigned.

- Configure **Google Drive** to post updates when a file is modified.

- Automate workflows using **Zapier** to trigger actions across multiple apps.

Best Practices for File Sharing and Integrations

To maximize efficiency, consider the following best practices:

1. Use Cloud Storage Instead of Local Uploads

Instead of uploading large files directly to Slack, use Google Drive, OneDrive, or Dropbox. This prevents storage overload and ensures that team members always access the latest version.

2. Limit Notifications from Integrations

While integrations improve efficiency, excessive notifications can be distracting. Customize alerts to ensure only essential updates appear in Slack.

3. Keep Channels Organized

- Create dedicated channels for integrations (e.g., #project-updates, #sales-notifications).

- Use **Slack Connect** to collaborate with external partners securely.

4. Regularly Audit and Remove Unused Integrations

Too many integrations can slow down workflows. Review and disable outdated apps that no longer serve a purpose.

Conclusion

Slack's file-sharing capabilities and integrations make it an indispensable tool for modern workplaces. Whether you're collaborating on documents, managing projects, or tracking customer interactions, Slack streamlines communication and centralizes resources. By leveraging cloud storage, automating tasks, and keeping integrations well-organized, teams can significantly boost productivity and reduce inefficiencies.

Ready to take your Slack experience to the next level? The next chapter will dive into mastering channels and conversations—helping you build an efficient and structured communication flow.

1.3.3 Search and Message History

Slack is a powerful communication tool designed for teams to collaborate efficiently. One of its most underrated yet highly valuable features is **Search and Message History**. As conversations flow rapidly in Slack channels, finding critical information can become challenging without an effective search mechanism. This section will explore how Slack's search functionality works, best practices for using it efficiently, and how message history is maintained and managed.

1. The Importance of Search and Message History in Slack

In fast-paced work environments, conversations in Slack can move quickly. Unlike emails, which have structured subject lines and threading, Slack messages can get buried in active channels. Without a robust search system, retrieving past discussions, shared files, or key decisions would be time-consuming.

The **Search and Message History** feature in Slack ensures that users can:

- Quickly retrieve past messages, files, and links shared in conversations.
- Find specific discussions based on keywords, timestamps, or people involved.
- Save time by avoiding the need to scroll through long chat histories.
- Maintain transparency by keeping a record of all discussions.

2. Understanding Slack's Search Interface

Slack provides a powerful search interface that is accessible in multiple ways:

- **Search Bar**: Located at the top of the Slack window, the search bar allows users to type queries and filter results.
- **Advanced Filters**: Users can refine searches based on channels, people, dates, file types, and keywords.
- **Search Modifiers**: Slack offers specific search commands that make finding information more precise.

To access search:

1. Click on the search bar at the top of the Slack interface.
2. Enter a keyword or phrase.
3. Use search filters (such as messages, files, or people) to narrow down results.

3. How to Search for Messages Effectively

3.1 Basic Search Queries

Typing a keyword in the search bar will return messages containing that term. However, Slack's search goes beyond simple keyword matching. It ranks results based on relevance, showing the most recent and frequently mentioned messages first.

3.2 Using Search Modifiers

Slack allows users to refine searches using modifiers. Here are some essential ones:

Modifier	Function	Example
from:	Search messages sent by a specific person	from:@john
in:	Search messages within a specific channel	in:#marketing
before:	Find messages sent before a certain date	before:2024-01-01
after:	Find messages sent after a certain date	after:2024-02-01
on:	Find messages on an exact date	on:2024-03-15
has:	Search messages that contain specific elements (e.g., links, files, images)	has:link
is:pinned	Find messages that have been pinned in a channel	is:pinned
from:me	Find messages that you have sent	from:me

Using these modifiers together can help refine searches. For example, to find a file sent by John in the #sales channel after January 1, 2024, you can search: from:@john in:#sales after:2024-01-01 has:file

3.3 Searching for Files and Links

Slack allows users to search for specific files shared in conversations. To do this:

1. Click on the search bar.

2. Select the **"Files"** filter.

3. Enter keywords related to the file name or content.

If you remember the person who sent the file, you can combine search modifiers: from:@maria has:pdf (Find all PDF files sent by Maria).

4. Message History and Retention in Slack

How Message History Works

Slack stores all conversations within a workspace. However, access to message history depends on the workspace's settings:

- **Free Plan**: Only allows access to the most recent 90 days of messages.

- **Paid Plans (Pro, Business+, Enterprise Grid)**: Offer unlimited message history.

Organizations using Slack for long-term record-keeping should consider upgrading to a paid plan to ensure all messages remain accessible.

Deleting and Editing Messages

Slack allows users to edit or delete their messages based on workspace permissions. To do so:

- **Editing a Message**: Hover over the message → Click the three dots (⋮) → Select **Edit message** → Modify and save.

- **Deleting a Message**: Hover over the message → Click the three dots (⋮) → Select **Delete message**.

Admins can restrict editing/deleting privileges, ensuring critical conversations remain unchanged.

5. Best Practices for Managing Message History

To maintain an organized and efficient workspace, consider the following best practices:

Pinning Important Messages

Pinned messages help highlight key discussions or frequently referenced information. To pin a message:

1. Hover over the message.

2. Click the three dots (⋮).

3. Select **Pin to channel**.

Pinned messages can be accessed from the channel's details panel.

Bookmarking Important Messages

For personal reference, users can save messages using Slack's "Save for later" feature:

- Hover over a message.

- Click the **bookmark icon**.

- Access saved messages by clicking on **"Saved items"** in the left sidebar.

Using Threads to Keep Conversations Organized

To prevent clutter in a channel, use threads:

1. Hover over a message.

2. Click **"Reply in thread"**.

3. Type your response and choose whether to also send it to the channel.

---

6. Leveraging Slack Search for Team Efficiency

Slack's **Search and Message History** feature is more than just a way to find old messages—it enhances productivity by:

- Helping teams retrieve project discussions without delay.

- Improving transparency by ensuring past decisions are accessible.

- Reducing repetitive questions by allowing users to search before asking.

Integrating Slack Search with Workflows

Organizations can optimize Slack's search by:

- **Standardizing naming conventions** for files and discussions.

- **Encouraging proper channel usage** (e.g., using #announcements for key updates).

- **Utilizing Slack bots** that help retrieve frequently needed information.

By making search efficiency a priority, teams can **reduce time wasted looking for information and focus on productive work.**

---

7. Conclusion: Mastering Search and Message History

The **Search and Message History** feature in Slack is an essential tool for keeping workplace communication streamlined and accessible. By understanding how to search effectively, leveraging advanced filters, and managing message history, users can significantly improve their Slack experience.

To maximize efficiency:

- ☑ Use search modifiers to refine results.
- ☑ Pin and save messages for quick reference.
- ☑ Organize conversations using threads and bookmarks.
- ☑ Encourage team members to use proper channels and naming conventions.

With these best practices, Slack can become a powerful knowledge repository that helps teams collaborate seamlessly.

1.3.4 Notifications and Customization

Slack has become an indispensable tool for teams and organizations, revolutionizing communication and collaboration across different industries. One of the most powerful features of Slack is its notification system, which ensures that you never miss out on important messages, updates, or alerts. However, with the constant influx of messages, notifications, and alerts in a busy workspace, managing them effectively becomes a crucial part of using Slack productively. This section will explore how Slack notifications work, and how you can customize them to fit your specific needs, ensuring you stay informed without becoming overwhelmed.

Understanding Slack Notifications

At its core, Slack notifications are designed to alert users to important messages, mentions, and activities within channels or direct messages (DMs). The notifications aim to keep you updated on relevant conversations without requiring you to check your Slack constantly. They serve as reminders, keeping you in the loop with important updates from coworkers, teams, or projects.

Notifications come in several forms within Slack:

1. **Push Notifications**: These notifications are sent to your device (either mobile or desktop) when something happens that is relevant to you. This could be a new message, a mention in a channel, or a direct message.

2. **In-App Notifications**: These notifications appear within the Slack interface when you're actively using the app. They might show up as a small badge or popup alert on the screen.

3. **Email Notifications**: Slack can send you email notifications for important events, like when you're mentioned or receive a direct message, ensuring that you don't miss anything even when you're not in the app.

4. **Desktop Notifications**: If you're using Slack on your computer, desktop notifications will show up outside of the Slack interface, alerting you to messages in real-time.

Each type of notification has its own set of preferences and settings, which gives you flexibility in managing how and when you're notified.

How to Customize Slack Notifications

With the volume of messages and alerts Slack can generate, it's important to tailor notifications to suit your workflow. By customizing notifications, you can control the level of interruption you experience throughout your day, ensuring that you're not bombarded by unnecessary alerts while still staying informed on the important messages. Slack offers a wide range of customization options for notifications, from the sounds they make to how often you receive them.

Let's dive into how you can set up and manage your Slack notifications for optimal productivity:

Notification Preferences

To access and adjust your notification settings, click on your profile picture in the top-right corner of Slack, then select **Preferences**. Here, you'll find the **Notifications** section, where you can tailor settings to meet your needs.

1. **Notify Me About...**

   o **All New Messages**: This setting will notify you whenever a new message is posted in any channel or direct message. It's useful if you're in a critical role where being informed of everything is necessary.

   o **Mentions and Keywords**: Slack allows you to be notified only when someone mentions you directly, or when certain keywords are used in conversations you're part of. This is an excellent option if you want to minimize distractions but still stay on top of relevant conversations.

   o **Nothing**: If you prefer not to receive notifications for messages in channels you're a part of, you can opt for this setting to avoid all interruptions.

2. **Sound and Badge Preferences**

   o Slack lets you adjust the sound notification settings. You can enable or disable sounds for messages and mentions, allowing you to either be alerted audibly or keep the notifications silent.

   o You can also choose whether or not you want to see notification badges on the Slack icon in your taskbar. If you're someone who prefers a less distracting experience, turning off badges might help you focus better.

3. **Mute Channels and Conversations**

   o For channels or conversations that aren't immediately relevant to you, Slack allows you to mute them. Muted channels won't send any notifications, and messages will appear grayed out in your sidebar. This is a great way to stay organized and limit interruptions, particularly in larger teams or channels where non-essential chatter might distract you.

   o You can mute a channel by clicking the **bell icon** next to the channel name. You'll still be able to see new messages, but you won't get notifications for them. If a message in a muted channel requires your attention, you'll see a badge indicating a new message, but it won't trigger a sound or pop-up alert.

4. **Customizing Mobile Notifications**

- o Mobile notifications are especially useful when you're away from your desk or working remotely. Slack gives you full control over mobile notifications, allowing you to manage them separately from your desktop settings.

- o Within the **Preferences** section, you can enable or disable mobile notifications, and even choose to receive push notifications only for certain events, such as mentions or direct messages. This ensures you're not overwhelmed by updates while on the go.

- o Slack also allows you to control **Do Not Disturb** hours for mobile devices. You can set "quiet hours" to avoid receiving notifications during your personal time or outside of working hours. This feature is particularly valuable for maintaining a work-life balance.

Notification Frequency and Priority

Slack gives users the ability to fine-tune the frequency and priority of notifications, allowing you to stay informed on the most critical messages without being overwhelmed.

1. **Set Notification Frequency for Channels**:

   - o **Every Message**: If you want to be notified every time a message is posted in a particular channel, this setting can be enabled. This is useful for channels where you need to be in the loop at all times.

   - o **Only Mentions**: For less urgent channels, you can choose to receive notifications only when you're mentioned. This is often used in channels that aren't critical for your immediate attention but where you still need to be alerted when something directly pertains to you.

   - o **Customizable Alerts**: Slack allows you to set different notification settings for each individual channel. This means you can adjust the frequency of notifications based on the importance of each channel.

2. **Setting Up Keyword Alerts**:

   - o Slack offers a powerful feature that allows you to set custom **keyword alerts**. For example, if you're working on a specific project and need to stay up to date with discussions around certain terms, you can create keyword alerts.

- When someone types in your chosen keywords, Slack will notify you, even if you're not directly mentioned. This feature is especially helpful for monitoring critical topics without needing to follow every message in every channel.

Managing Notification Overload

Notification overload can easily become a problem, especially in fast-paced Slack workspaces. Slack has a number of features designed to help you manage this overwhelming influx of messages, ensuring that you stay productive and focused.

1. **Do Not Disturb (DND) Mode**:

    - The **Do Not Disturb** mode is one of the most useful features for blocking out distractions. When enabled, Slack will suppress all notifications (both push and desktop notifications). You can set specific times for DND, such as during meetings or focused work sessions.

    - Additionally, you can schedule DND periods, which is great for keeping your notifications in check during after-work hours or lunch breaks.

2. **Customizable Quiet Hours**:

    - If you find it challenging to disconnect from work, Slack allows you to set up **quiet hours** to automatically silence notifications during off-hours. This helps you create boundaries between work and personal time, ensuring you're not disturbed by messages after hours.

3. **Summary Notifications**:

    - Slack introduced **summary notifications** to give you an overview of what you missed when you weren't active in the app. This allows you to catch up on important updates without getting lost in every small detail. It's a great way to stay informed while avoiding real-time distractions.

Managing Notifications for Large Teams

For large teams or organizations, managing notifications effectively becomes even more important to avoid information overload. Slack helps in this context by allowing administrators to set rules and guidelines for notifications.

1. **Admin Controls for Notification Settings**:

   o Workspace administrators can enforce certain notification settings to ensure that all members are aligned with the communication culture of the organization. Admins can require team members to configure specific settings for consistency, such as the use of certain notification types, to avoid disruption and maintain smooth workflows.

2. **Organization-Wide Notifications**:

   o Slack allows organizations to send broadcast messages or announcements to all members via the **@channel** or **@everyone** mentions. This is useful when there's critical information that needs to be shared with all team members at once.

Final Thoughts on Notifications and Customization

Slack notifications and customization options are powerful tools for enhancing your productivity, reducing distractions, and ensuring that you're always up to date on the most important conversations. By taking the time to fine-tune your settings, you can create a Slack experience tailored to your work habits and priorities, ultimately leading to a more organized and efficient communication process. Whether you're working on a team of a few people or managing an entire organization, Slack's notification and customization features provide the flexibility to make communication seamless and stress-free.

Remember, the key to effectively managing Slack notifications is finding the right balance between staying informed and avoiding overload. With the right configurations, you can work smarter, not harder, and ensure that Slack remains a valuable tool for collaboration and communication.

1.4 Setting Up Your Slack Workspace

1.4.1 Creating a Slack Account

Slack has become a powerhouse for team communication and collaboration, particularly in today's fast-paced, remote, and hybrid work environments. Whether you're managing a small startup, part of a remote team, or leading a large organization, Slack provides a unified platform where all your communication needs can be met. In this section, we'll walk you through the step-by-step process of creating a Slack account, ensuring that you're equipped to hit the ground running and set up your workspace with ease.

Why You Need a Slack Account

Before diving into the setup process, it's essential to understand why Slack is so effective for businesses and teams. Slack's primary purpose is to facilitate communication. It brings together conversations, tools, files, and other important resources in a centralized platform, which helps teams collaborate more effectively, stay organized, and maintain productivity. In addition to instant messaging, Slack offers voice and video calls, file sharing, integrations with third-party apps, and automation tools that make workflows smoother.

To take full advantage of these features, you first need to create an account. The process is simple, straightforward, and free for teams that want to start with a basic workspace. Let's get started.

Step-by-Step Guide to Creating Your Slack Account

1. Visit the Slack Website

To create an account, the first thing you need to do is visit the official Slack website at www.slack.com. You'll be greeted by a simple, clean homepage that prompts you to sign up for an account.

- **Direct Link**: You can also go directly to the signup page at https://slack.com/get-started.

2. Choose How You Want to Sign Up

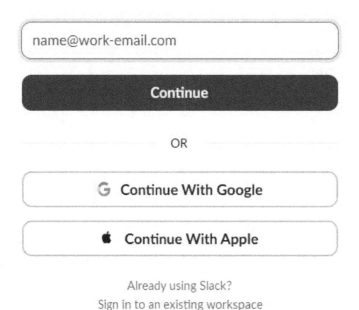

Once you're on the signup page, you will see several options for creating an account:

- **Sign Up with Email**: This is the most straightforward method. If you prefer to use your email, simply enter your email address and click "Continue."

- **Sign Up with Google**: If you're already signed into your Google account, Slack allows you to sign up using your Google credentials. This eliminates the need to create a new password, making the process faster.

- **Sign Up with Apple**: Slack also supports Apple's "Sign in with Apple" feature. If you have an Apple ID, you can create your Slack account using that, too.

Select your preferred method, and proceed to the next step.

3. Enter Your Email Address

If you chose to sign up with an email address, you'll be prompted to enter your email. After inputting your email, click **Continue**. Slack will send a verification email to the address you provided.

- **Check Your Inbox**: Go to your email inbox and open the verification email from Slack. If you don't see it in your primary inbox, check your spam or promotions folder.

- **Verify Your Email**: Click on the **Verify Email** button within the email, which will redirect you to Slack's website to confirm your email address.

Once your email is verified, you can proceed to the next step.

4. Set Up Your Slack Workspace

Confirmed as ▉▉▉▉▉▉ ▉▉▉▉▉ n Change

Get started on Slack

It's a new way to communicate with everyone you work with. It's faster, better organized, and more secure than email — and it's free to try.

Create a Workspace

☑ It's okay to send me marketing communications about Salesforce, including Slack. I can unsubscribe at any time.

By continuing, you're agreeing to our Main Services Agreement, User Terms of Service, and Slack Supplemental Terms. Additional disclosures are available in our Privacy Policy and Cookie Policy.

After verifying your email, Slack will guide you through setting up your workspace. A "workspace" in Slack is where your team will collaborate. Think of it as your team's digital office space, where all communication, projects, and files are housed.

Here's how to set up your workspace:

- **Enter Your Workspace Name**: The first step is to give your workspace a name. It's best to choose a name that reflects your organization or team. For instance, if you're setting it up for a project, you might call it "Project X Team." For companies, names like "Company Name Workspace" work well.

- **Create Your Slack URL**: Slack will then prompt you to create a custom URL for your workspace. This will be the address you'll use to access your Slack workspace. For example, if you name your workspace "DesignTeam", the URL could be "designteam.slack.com." Keep it short, easy to remember, and reflective of your workspace.

- **Choose Your Time Zone**: Select your time zone from the dropdown menu to ensure that Slack accurately tracks timestamps and schedules.

5. Invite Team Members

Once your workspace is created, Slack will prompt you to invite others to join. You can add team members by:

- **Inviting by Email**: If you have the email addresses of the people you want to add to your workspace, enter them in the email field and send invitations.

- **Share a Join Link**: If you don't want to manually invite members, you can simply share a unique invite link with your team. Anyone with this link can join your workspace.

- **Skip for Now**: If you're setting up your workspace for personal use or want to complete setup before inviting others, you can skip this step and add members later.

It's important to remember that while inviting team members early is beneficial for collaboration, you can always add more people at any time.

Customizing Your Slack Workspace

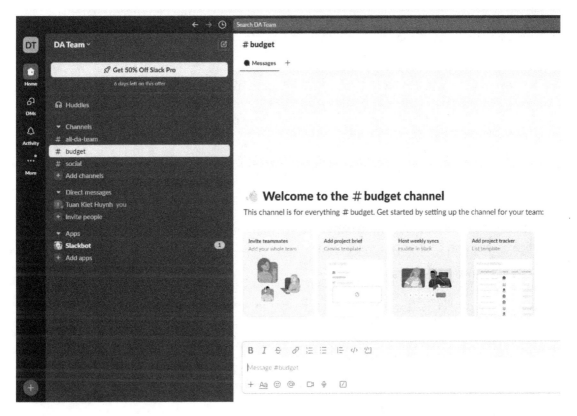

Now that your workspace is up and running, it's time to personalize it to suit your team's needs. Slack provides several customization options, which include adjusting the workspace theme, uploading logos, and adding integrations with third-party tools. Here's how you can make your Slack workspace more unique and suited to your organization:

1. Workspace Settings

- **Branding and Logo**: You can upload your company logo to make your workspace feel more official and aligned with your brand. This logo will appear in various parts of the interface, helping your workspace feel professional and cohesive.

- **Workspace Theme**: Slack offers light and dark themes for the workspace interface. You can choose the one that suits your team's aesthetic preferences. If you want, you can also customize colors to make Slack feel even more personalized.

2. Adding Integrations

One of the biggest advantages of Slack is its integration capabilities. Slack can connect with over 2,200 apps, including Google Drive, Trello, Zoom, Asana, and many others. To add these integrations:

- Go to your workspace settings and navigate to **Apps & Integrations**.

- From there, you can browse available integrations or search for the apps your team uses the most.

- Add the apps to your Slack workspace by following the on-screen instructions. Many apps can be configured to send notifications or updates directly into Slack channels.

By adding integrations, you'll streamline workflows, making it easier to manage tasks, track projects, and collaborate without leaving Slack.

3. Customizing Channel Settings

Slack uses channels as the primary way to organize conversations. Channels are spaces where specific teams or groups within the organization can communicate, collaborate, and share updates. You can create both public and private channels.

- **Public Channels**: These are open to everyone within your workspace. Any member can join a public channel and participate in discussions.

- **Private Channels**: These channels are invite-only and are ideal for sensitive discussions or specific teams within your organization.

When creating channels, you can specify the channel's name, description, and set permissions for who can join or view the channel.

What's Next?

Once your Slack account is set up and your workspace is configured, you can start using it right away. Now that you understand how to create your Slack account and customize your workspace, it's time to dive deeper into Slack's features and explore how it can help you work smarter.

In the next chapters, we'll go into more detail about Slack channels, communication best practices, managing notifications, using integrations, and much more. By the end of this guide, you'll be equipped with all the tools and knowledge necessary to leverage Slack for maximum productivity.

Conclusion

Creating your Slack account and setting up your workspace is a straightforward yet vital first step in transforming the way your team communicates. With the right setup, you can unlock the full potential of Slack, ensuring that your team stays organized, communicates effectively, and remains productive.

By following this guide, you're laying a solid foundation for a seamless, collaborative work environment where everyone can stay connected, no matter where they are located. The next steps are just as crucial — so keep reading to discover how to get the most out of Slack's powerful features!

1.4.2 Joining or Creating a Workspace

Slack is an incredibly powerful tool that has transformed the way teams and companies communicate. Whether you're part of a large corporation, a small team, or a solo entrepreneur, setting up a Slack workspace is an essential step to start leveraging its full potential. In this section, we will guide you through the process of joining an existing workspace or creating a new one, ensuring you can begin using Slack effectively from day one.

What is a Slack Workspace?

A **Slack workspace** is essentially a digital hub where you can communicate, collaborate, and share resources with others. It's the foundational unit of Slack, and within a workspace, you'll find channels (where conversations happen), direct messages (for one-on-one chats), and integrations with other tools (like Google Drive, Zoom, and many others). Every workspace is independent and separate from others, and you can be a part of multiple workspaces if needed.

In this section, we'll cover:

- How to join an existing Slack workspace

- How to create a new workspace

- Differences between personal workspaces and organizational workspaces

- Tips for managing multiple workspaces

Joining an Existing Slack Workspace

Joining an existing Slack workspace can be a quick and straightforward process, but you need to follow the right steps to ensure you're properly added and have access to everything you need.

Step 1: Receive an Invitation

To join an existing workspace, the first thing you'll need is an **invitation**. You cannot simply search for a workspace and join without permission. Invitations are typically sent by a workspace administrator, who will invite you via your email address.

If you are joining a workspace in your company, the HR team or your manager will likely send you an invitation to join the company's Slack workspace. If you're joining a community workspace, the workspace owner or community manager will send you the invitation.

When you receive the invitation email, make sure to check your spam folder in case it gets filtered there. If you don't see the invitation, reach out to the administrator for assistance.

Step 2: Accept the Invitation

Once you've received the invitation, open the email and click the **Join Now** or **Accept Invitation** button. This will redirect you to a page where you'll be asked to either sign in to Slack or create a new account if you don't already have one.

Step 3: Sign In or Create an Account

If you already have a Slack account, you can sign in using your credentials (email and password). If you don't have an account, click on the option to **Create an Account**. You'll be prompted to enter your name, email address, and create a password. Make sure to use your work or professional email address if you're joining an organizational workspace.

Slack will send a verification code to your email address, which you'll need to enter to confirm your identity. Once you've verified your email address, you'll be successfully logged in.

Step 4: Select Your Workspace

After logging in, you'll be directed to the workspace you've been invited to. If you've been invited to multiple workspaces, you will be able to select which workspace you want to enter.

If it's your first time using Slack, you'll be greeted with a quick **onboarding tutorial** that walks you through the basics of Slack, including how to navigate channels, send messages, and join conversations. Take the time to complete the tutorial, as it will give you a solid understanding of Slack's core features.

Step 5: Personalize Your Profile

Once you're inside the workspace, you'll want to personalize your Slack profile. Click on your profile picture or initials in the top right corner and select **Profile & Account**. Here, you can:

- **Upload a Profile Picture**: Choose a photo or avatar that represents you.
- **Add a Display Name**: This can be your real name or a nickname, depending on your workspace's culture.
- **Set Your Time Zone**: This ensures that your colleagues know when you are available.

Additionally, you can customize your **notification preferences** and make other adjustments that will improve your user experience on Slack.

Step 6: Explore the Workspace

Once you've joined the workspace and personalized your profile, take some time to explore. Join channels, introduce yourself in the #introductions channel (if there's one), and start engaging in conversations.

You can also search for specific channels or conversations using the search bar at the top of the Slack interface. Slack's powerful search function allows you to quickly find messages, files, and people across all your workspaces.

Creating a New Slack Workspace

Creating a new workspace in Slack is a relatively simple process, whether you're starting a new team within an organization, setting up a group for a project, or creating a workspace for personal or community purposes.

Step 1: Start the Setup Process

To create a new workspace, go to Slack's website and click on **Get Started** or **Create a New Workspace**. Slack will ask you to enter your email address, and it will send a verification code to that address. Once verified, you'll be able to proceed.

Step 2: Set Up Your Workspace Name

Choose a name for your workspace. This will be the name that identifies your Slack space, so make sure it's relevant to your team, organization, or community. For example, a workspace for a marketing team could be named "Marketing Team," while a workspace for a personal project might be called something like "Project XYZ."

If you're creating a workspace for a company or organization, make sure the name aligns with the company's brand and structure.

Step 3: Choose Your Workspace Domain

The next step is choosing a domain for your workspace. This domain is what will follow after "slack.com/" and will be part of your unique Slack URL (e.g., slack.com/your-workspace-name).

Be mindful that the domain name must be unique, so try several variations if the one you want is already taken.

Step 4: Invite Members

After setting up your workspace, you'll be asked to invite people to join. You can invite team members using their email addresses. If your team uses Slack frequently, they might already have Slack accounts, in which case you can just search for their usernames or email addresses to invite them.

You can also skip this step and choose to invite people later, but it's a good idea to start building your team in the workspace right away to begin collaboration.

Step 5: Set Up Channels

Once your workspace is ready and you've invited your team, you'll want to create channels for various topics or teams. Slack encourages organizing work around channels, and each channel can be dedicated to a specific subject, project, or team. You can create public or private channels depending on the needs of your group.

Here are a few examples of channels you might set up:

- #general – For all company-wide or workspace-wide announcements

- #marketing – For team discussions around marketing

- #project-xyz – For project-specific communication

Step 6: Customize Your Workspace Settings

To make sure your workspace runs smoothly, you'll want to customize its settings. This includes setting permissions for who can create channels, who can invite new members, and other administrative tasks. You can access workspace settings by clicking on your workspace name in the top-left corner and selecting **Workspace Settings**.

Personal vs. Organizational Workspaces

It's important to understand the difference between personal workspaces and organizational workspaces:

- **Personal Workspaces**: These are typically for individual users or small teams. They are often used for personal projects, freelancing, or community groups.

- **Organizational Workspaces**: These are designed for larger companies or organizations. They often come with additional administrative controls, integrations, and security features. Larger teams or companies might have multiple workspaces, depending on how they structure their teams and projects.

Managing Multiple Workspaces

If you're part of several workspaces, managing them efficiently is crucial. Slack allows you to switch between workspaces seamlessly. Here are some tips:

- Use the **Workspace Switcher**: At the top-left corner of the Slack interface, you can easily switch between different workspaces by clicking on your workspace name.

- **Customize Notifications**: For each workspace, you can customize your notification preferences to avoid overload.

- **Use the Mobile App**: On mobile, Slack allows you to easily switch between workspaces with a swipe or tap, keeping all your teams and projects within reach.

Conclusion

Joining or creating a Slack workspace is the first step to transforming your work and communication. Whether you're joining an existing workspace or starting your own, understanding the steps involved will help you get set up quickly and effectively. By following the right steps to personalize your Slack workspace, invite the right people, and create channels for your team, you're ready to maximize the productivity and efficiency Slack offers.

With this foundation in place, you can move on to mastering the features of Slack, setting up a collaborative environment, and streamlining your workflow. Let's dive deeper into Slack's core functionalities in the following chapters!

1.4.3 Navigating the Slack Interface

Slack is more than just a messaging platform—it's a central hub for collaboration, information sharing, and team communication. Once you've set up your Slack workspace, it's time to dive into the interface. The ease of use and customization available within Slack make it one of the most efficient tools for team collaboration. In this section, we'll walk through the essential components of the Slack interface to help you navigate the platform with ease.

The Left Sidebar: Your Command Center

The left sidebar is the heart of Slack's interface. It houses the most essential tools and sections of the platform, offering quick access to your messages, channels, and important settings. Here's a breakdown of the key elements within the left sidebar:

1. **Workspace and Channels**: At the very top of the sidebar, you'll see the name of your workspace, along with the icon representing your team. If you're part of multiple workspaces, you can switch between them by clicking the workspace name and selecting the one you want to use. Directly beneath the workspace name, you'll find a list of channels, both public and private, that you're a member of.

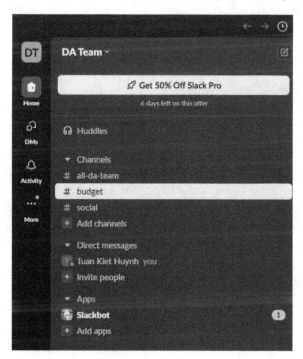

2. **Channels**

   Channels are the core of Slack's organizational system. Channels group conversations by topics, projects, or departments. By default, Slack shows your starred channels at the top of the list, making it easier to access the ones you need most frequently. Slack allows you to join or create new channels as needed, ensuring you have a dedicated space for every aspect of your work.

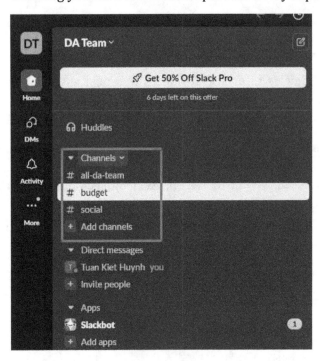

3. **Direct Messages (DMs)**

   Just below the channel list, you'll find your Direct Messages (DMs), which are private, one-on-one conversations. These are where you'll have private chats with individual team members. DMs also support group conversations, so you can collaborate privately with a small team without the need for a dedicated channel. You can even create custom DM groups for specific projects or tasks.

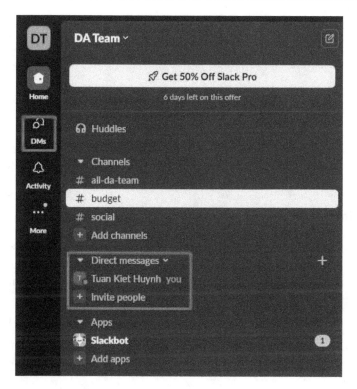

4. **Mentions & Reactions**

This section provides a quick overview of all your @mentions (when someone tags you in a message) and reactions (emojis you've received). It's an easy way to track important messages and stay on top of conversations where your input is needed. This notification list is often updated in real-time, helping you stay responsive and organized.

5. **Apps and Integrations**

If your workspace uses integrations or third-party apps (e.g., Google Drive, Trello, or GitHub), they will appear in this section. You can interact with these apps directly through the sidebar, allowing you to manage tasks, receive alerts, and get work done without switching between different tools. To make the most of your workspace, ensure that the apps you use are properly integrated into Slack.

6. **Starred Items**

To keep important channels, messages, or DMs easily accessible, you can "star" them. Starred items appear at the top of your sidebar, making it quick and convenient to access frequently referenced conversations or files. Star channels or DMs that are relevant to your current work, so you never miss out on vital communication.

The Main Window: Your Active Workspace

The main window of Slack is where all your active conversations take place. This section is broken down into different panels and sections that enable seamless communication and organization.

1. **Channel or DM Window**

   When you click on a channel or a DM, the window will display all messages within that conversation. Slack uses a chronological flow for messages, so the most recent messages will be at the bottom. You'll also notice threaded messages—these are responses to a specific message and allow for more focused conversations without clogging up the main thread. In Slack, threads are an essential tool to keep conversations organized.

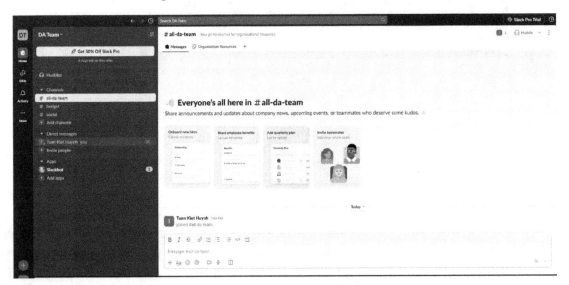

2. **Message Input Box**

   At the bottom of the main window, you'll find the message input box. This is where you type and send your messages. But it's not just a text box—it comes with a variety of tools to enhance your communication. You can:

- o Attach files and images by clicking the "+" icon on the left side of the input box.

- o Use rich text formatting like bold, italics, and strikethrough by using markdown syntax or clicking on the formatting toolbar.

- o Add emojis, gifs, and files directly into your message using quick actions and shortcut keys.

- o Use slash commands for quick actions (e.g., /remind for reminders, /poll for creating polls).

3. **Threads**

A significant feature in Slack's interface is the **Threads** panel. When someone replies to a message in a thread, it can be viewed in a side panel without cluttering the main conversation. Threads help maintain a clean, organized workspace. By simply clicking on any message with a reply icon, you can view the full thread and participate in the conversation directly.

4. **File Sharing**

Slack makes it easy to share files with your team. You can drag and drop files into the message input box, or click the "+" icon to select files from your computer or cloud services like Google Drive or Dropbox. Once uploaded, files appear as thumbnails within the conversation, making it easy for team members to download or view them.

The Top Bar: Quick Access Tools

The top bar of Slack provides various tools and settings that allow you to personalize your experience and ensure smooth communication.

1. **Search Bar**

   Slack's search bar is one of its most powerful features. Located at the top of the interface, it allows you to quickly search through all messages, files, channels, and even DMs. It's an essential tool for finding important information in real-time or going back to past conversations. Slack's search function is highly flexible, enabling you to search for keywords, dates, specific users, and even use advanced search filters like from: or in: to narrow down results.

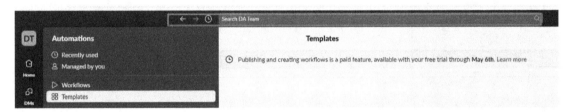

2. **Workspace Name & Settings**

   Clicking on your workspace name at the top left opens up a menu where you can access various settings and preferences. Here, you can adjust everything from your notification preferences to your account settings. Additionally, you can invite new members to your workspace, manage integrations, and configure team preferences for the workspace.

3. **Slack Status & Profile**

   Slack allows you to set a custom status and display your availability. Clicking on your profile picture at the top-right corner lets you set your status (e.g., "In a meeting," "Out for lunch," or "Available"). You can also customize your notification preferences from here, control how others view your profile, and adjust privacy settings.

4. **Help & Support**

   In the top bar, you'll also find a help menu that links to Slack's support articles, FAQs, and troubleshooting resources. If you encounter any issues or need to learn how to use specific features, Slack's comprehensive support section is just a click away.

Conclusion: Navigating Slack with Ease

Navigating the Slack interface is all about familiarity and personalization. By understanding the layout and customizing Slack to fit your preferences, you can make the platform work for you and your team. Slack's intuitive interface and powerful features make it a valuable tool for effective communication and collaboration. Whether you're working in a small team or across a large organization, mastering Slack's interface will improve your efficiency and help you work smarter.

As you get comfortable with Slack, take the time to explore the various tools and features available in the interface. Slack is a dynamic platform that evolves with each update, so staying up to date and continuously discovering new ways to work within it will help you maximize its full potential.

CHAPTER II
Mastering Slack Channels & Conversations

2.1 Understanding Slack Channels

2.1.1 Public vs. Private Channels

Slack channels are the foundation of communication and collaboration within a Slack workspace. They help teams organize discussions, share information, and streamline workflows efficiently. Understanding the difference between **public** and **private** channels is crucial to ensuring that information is shared with the right people while maintaining security and confidentiality where needed.

What Are Slack Channels?

Slack channels act as virtual rooms where teams can collaborate on specific topics, projects, or departments. Instead of having scattered conversations across different platforms, emails, or meetings, Slack channels centralize discussions and provide a structured way to organize workplace communication.

There are two primary types of channels in Slack:

1. Public Channels – Open for everyone in the workspace to join and view messages.

2. Private Channels – Restricted to invited members only, ensuring privacy for sensitive discussions.

Both types serve different purposes and are essential for maintaining effective communication within an organization.

Public Channels: Open Communication and Transparency

Definition

A public channel in Slack is accessible to anyone within the workspace. All members of the organization can see the discussions, join the conversation, and search through its messages.

Public channels are marked with a # symbol and can be found in the channel directory of the workspace.

Key Features of Public Channels:

- Anyone in the workspace can join without needing an invitation.

- Messages and files are searchable by all workspace members.

- They promote transparency and open discussions across teams.

- They help reduce redundant conversations by keeping important information in one place.

- Ideal for company-wide announcements, general topics, and knowledge sharing.

When to Use Public Channels

Public channels are best used when discussions need to be accessible to a broad audience or when transparency is beneficial. Here are some ideal use cases:

1. General Team Communication: Channels like #general, #company-updates, and #team-announcements allow open communication within an organization.

2. Project Collaboration: If multiple teams are working on a shared project, a public channel such as #project-launch ensures everyone stays informed.

3. Company-Wide Knowledge Sharing: Channels like #tech-support, #HR-guidelines, or #best-practices provide an open space for employees to ask and answer questions.

4. Cross-Department Discussions: Public channels facilitate collaboration between different teams, ensuring visibility and reducing silos.

Pros and Cons of Public Channels

Pros	Cons
Encourages transparency across teams	Too many messages can cause distractions
Easy to onboard new employees (they can view past discussions)	Some discussions may not be relevant to everyone
Helps avoid duplicate efforts across teams	Information overload if not organized properly
Open to all, reducing the need for direct messages	Misuse can lead to off-topic discussions

Best Practices for Public Channels

- Use clear and descriptive names (e.g., #marketing-strategy instead of #marketing).

- Pin important messages so new members can quickly get up to speed.

- Encourage engagement but set communication norms to avoid spam.

- Create a channel guide in Slack to help users understand the purpose of each public channel.

Private Channels: Secure and Focused Discussions

Definition

A **private channel** in Slack is restricted to invited members only. These channels are not visible to anyone outside the group, and messages are confidential.

Private channels are marked with a **lock symbol** (🔒) next to the channel name, indicating restricted access.

Key Features of Private Channels:

- Only invited members can join and see the messages.

- Messages and files are NOT searchable by non-members.

- Used for confidential discussions such as financial matters, HR concerns, or leadership meetings.

- Can be created for focused project teams to keep work organized.

- Ensures privacy and security for sensitive topics.

When to Use Private Channels

Private channels should be used when discussions involve sensitive or restricted information. Some common use cases include:

1. **Confidential HR Matters:** Channels like #salary-discussions, #executive-decisions, or #HR-issues protect employee privacy.

2. **Leadership and Executive Teams:** Senior management may have channels like #board-meetings or #strategy-team for high-level discussions.

3. **Client-Specific Projects:** If an agency or consultant is working with a specific client, a private channel like #client-ABC-project ensures confidentiality.

4. **Security and IT Discussions:** IT and cybersecurity teams may need a channel for internal security issues, which should not be open to all employees.

5. **Legal and Compliance Discussions:** Channels like #contract-reviews help teams manage legal matters without public exposure.

Pros and Cons of Private Channels

Pros	Cons
Ensures privacy and security for sensitive information	Can create silos within the company
Limits access to only relevant team members	Harder for new employees to access past discussions
Reduces distractions by focusing on essential discussions	Less transparency compared to public channels
Helps maintain confidentiality for HR, finance, or legal teams	Can become redundant if too many private channels exist

Best Practices for Private Channels

- Only create private channels when necessary to avoid unnecessary silos.

- Regularly review channel members to ensure only the right people have access.

- Keep discussions relevant and avoid turning private channels into personal chat rooms.

- Maintain proper documentation elsewhere if needed, so important decisions aren't lost in private conversations.

Public vs. Private Channels: Choosing the Right One

Criteria	Public Channel	Private Channel
Visibility	Open to all workspace members	Restricted to invited users
Searchability	Messages and files are searchable by everyone	Only searchable by channel members
Purpose	General discussions, transparency, company-wide topics	Sensitive discussions, confidential projects
Access	Anyone can join without approval	Only invited members can participate
Examples	#company-news, #product-launch, #helpdesk	#HR-team, #finance-strategy, #client-X

Before creating a new channel, ask yourself:

☑ Does the information need to be widely accessible? → Use a public channel.

🔒 Is the conversation confidential or team-specific? → Use a private channel.

By understanding the difference between public and private channels, teams can create a well-organized Slack workspace that promotes effective communication, transparency, and productivity.

Final Thoughts

Mastering the use of public and private channels is key to streamlining communication and reducing workplace noise. Public channels foster open collaboration, while private channels help maintain confidentiality and security.

In the next section, we'll dive into how to create and manage channels effectively, ensuring that your Slack workspace remains organized and efficient.

2.1.2 Creating and Managing Channels

Slack channels are the backbone of communication in a workspace. They help organize discussions, ensure clarity, and make information easily accessible. In this section, we will explore how to create and manage channels effectively to maximize collaboration and efficiency.

Creating a Slack Channel

A well-structured channel system helps teams stay organized and communicate efficiently. Here's how to create a new channel in Slack:

Step-by-Step Guide to Creating a Channel

1. **Open Slack** – Launch Slack and navigate to the left sidebar where your channels are listed.

2. **Click on the "+" Icon** – Next to "Channels," click on the "+" button to add a new channel.

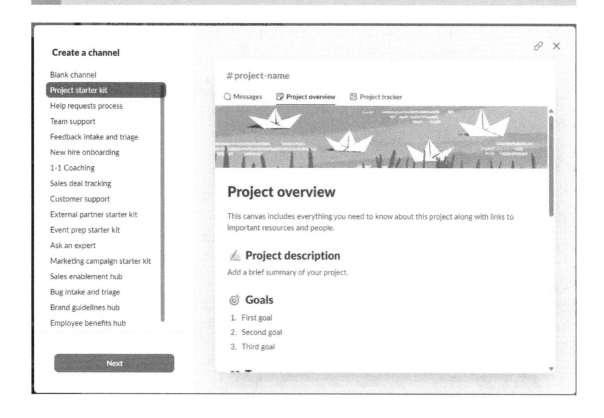

3. **Choose a Name for Your Channel**

   o Keep the name **descriptive and concise** (e.g., #marketing-strategy, #project-alpha).

   o Use **hyphens instead of spaces** (Slack automatically enforces this).

   o Follow **naming conventions** if your organization has one (e.g., department-based prefixes like #hr-recruitment).

4. **Set the Channel Type**

   o **Public Channel** – Anyone in the workspace can see and join.

   o **Private Channel** – Only invited members can see and participate.

5. **Add a Channel Description** (Optional but Recommended)

- o Explain the purpose of the channel (e.g., "A channel for discussing marketing strategy for Q3").

- o Keep it clear so new members understand the channel's function.

6. **Invite Members**

- o Add relevant team members immediately, or allow them to join later.

7. **Click "Create"** – Your channel is now active and ready for use.

Pro Tip: If you are creating a **temporary project channel**, consider adding a prefix like #temp- and setting a reminder to archive it once the project is complete.

Managing Channels Effectively

Creating a channel is just the beginning—proper management ensures that discussions remain organized and useful.

Setting Channel Guidelines

To maintain productivity, establish channel guidelines:

- **Define the Purpose** – Make it clear what type of content belongs in the channel.

- **Encourage Threaded Replies** – This helps keep conversations organized and prevents clutter.

- **Use Pinned Messages** – Pin important information such as guidelines, key resources, or deadlines.

- **Moderate Discussions** – Assign moderators or admins to ensure the channel stays on topic.

Editing Channel Settings

Once a channel is created, you may need to modify its settings. To do this:

1. Open the channel.

2. Click on the channel name at the top of the screen.

3. Select "Settings."

4. Here, you can:

   o Change the channel name or topic.

   o Update the description.

   o Adjust permissions (for example, restricting who can post).

Best Practices for Channel Organization

A poorly organized Slack workspace can lead to confusion. Here are best practices for managing your channels effectively:

1. Maintain a Clear Naming System

- Use **consistent prefixes** (e.g., #team-marketing, #proj-launch2024).

- Avoid vague names like #general-discussion unless necessary.

2. Limit the Number of Channels

- Too many channels can overwhelm users.

- Instead of creating new channels for every topic, consider **reusing existing ones**.

- If a discussion grows beyond the scope of a channel, then create a new one.

3. Archive Inactive Channels

- Unused channels clutter the workspace.

- Go to "Channel Settings" → "Additional options" → "Archive this channel" to remove inactive ones.

4. Assign Channel Owners

- Every channel should have at least one responsible person who:

    o   Ensures that discussions stay on topic.

    o   Updates channel settings when necessary.

    o   Cleans up old or irrelevant content.

5. Use Integrations to Enhance Channels

- Add relevant **Slack apps** such as Google Drive, Trello, or Asana.

- Automate workflows using **Slack bots** (e.g., sending reminders).

Managing Large Channels

1. Using Threads to Keep Discussions Organized

Large channels often become chaotic with multiple conversations happening at once. Encourage team members to use threaded replies instead of replying directly in the channel.

2. Breaking Up Large Channels into Sub-Channels

If a channel grows too large, consider creating sub-channels with a more specific focus. For example:

- Instead of #marketing, break it into:

    o #marketing-content (for blog posts, videos, etc.)

    o #marketing-social (for social media campaigns)

    o #marketing-ads (for paid advertising strategies)

3. Using Announcements Channels

For company-wide updates, use read-only channels where only admins can post. Examples:

- #company-announcements

- #hr-updates

- #security-alerts

This prevents important messages from getting lost in general discussions.

Moderating Channels

1. Assigning Moderators

In large workspaces, moderators help keep discussions relevant. Moderators can:

- Remove off-topic discussions.

- Mute or restrict disruptive users.

- Enforce Slack etiquette.

2. Setting Posting Permissions

For official communication channels, limit who can post:

- Navigate to "Channel Settings."

- Under "Posting Permissions," choose:

    o "Everyone" (default)

    o "Only Admins and Owners"

3. Handling Channel Conflicts

If conflicts arise:

- Direct users to **DMs or private channels** for resolving issues.

- Establish **clear community guidelines** for behavior.

- Mute or remove disruptive users if necessary.

Archiving and Deleting Channels

Sometimes, a channel is no longer needed. You have two options:

1. Archiving a Channel

- Keeps the chat history but prevents new messages.

- Users can still access past discussions.

- Ideal for completed projects or old discussions.

To archive a channel:

1. Open the channel.

2. Click the **channel name** → "Settings" → "Additional options" → "Archive this channel."

2. Deleting a Channel

- Permanently removes all messages and files.

- Should only be done if the information is no longer needed.

To delete a channel:

1. Archive the channel first.

2. Click on "Delete this channel."

3. Confirm deletion (this action **cannot be undone**).

Conclusion

Creating and managing channels in Slack is crucial for maintaining an efficient and organized workspace. By following best practices, teams can:

- ✔ Keep conversations structured.
- ✔ Reduce unnecessary noise.
- ✔ Improve team collaboration.
- ✔ Maximize productivity in Slack.

By implementing these techniques, you can transform Slack from a simple chat tool into a powerful collaboration platform.

2.1.3 Best Practices for Organizing Channels

Slack channels are the backbone of efficient communication and collaboration within a workspace. Properly organizing channels ensures that conversations remain structured, information is easy to find, and team members can work more effectively. Without an organized approach, Slack can quickly become chaotic, with messages scattered across numerous channels, making it difficult to track important discussions.

In this section, we'll explore best practices for organizing Slack channels, covering strategies for structuring channels, naming conventions, managing inactive channels, and maintaining a clear and efficient workspace.

1. Establish a Clear Channel Structure

The first step to organizing Slack effectively is creating a well-defined channel structure. Without a structured approach, teams might create redundant or unnecessary channels, leading to confusion and communication gaps.

Here's how to establish a structured channel system:

1.1 Categorize Channels by Function

Divide your Slack channels into different **categories** based on their purpose. Some common categories include:

- **Project-Based Channels**: Channels for specific projects or initiatives (e.g., #project-website-redesign, #product-launch-2024).

- **Departmental Channels**: Channels for teams within the company (e.g., #marketing, #engineering, #sales).

- **Company-Wide Channels**: Channels for general announcements and company-wide discussions (e.g., #general, #announcements).

- **Social & Fun Channels**: Non-work-related channels to build culture and engagement (e.g., #random, #fun-memes, #coffee-break).

By grouping channels into logical categories, employees can **easily find the right place to communicate** and avoid creating unnecessary duplicate channels.

1.2 Use Parent-Child Channel Organization

For larger organizations, using **parent-child relationships** in channel naming can help create a more structured approach.

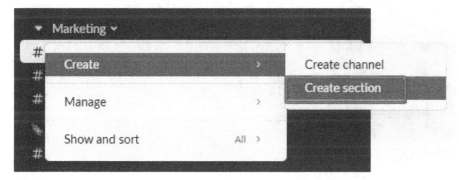

For example:

- **Parent Channel:** #marketing

  - **Child Channels:** #marketing-socialmedia, #marketing-content, #marketing-events

- **Parent Channel:** #project-alpha

  - **Child Channels:** #project-alpha-dev, #project-alpha-design, #project-alpha-qa

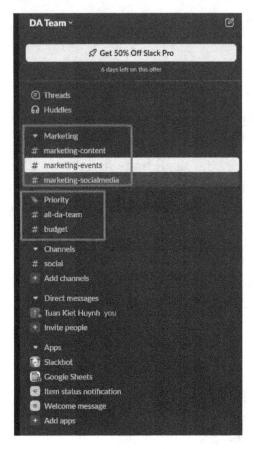

This hierarchical approach ensures that subteams within a department or project have dedicated spaces while still being connected to the broader group.

2. Implement a Consistent Naming Convention

A **consistent naming convention** is crucial for keeping channels organized and easy to navigate. Without a structured naming system, Slack workspaces can become cluttered, making it difficult to find the right channels.

2.1 Use Standardized Prefixes

Prefixes help categorize channels and make them more recognizable at a glance. Here are some common prefixes used in Slack:

- #ann- → Announcement channels (e.g., #ann-company-updates, #ann-policy-changes).

- #team- → Team-specific channels (e.g., #team-hr, #team-finance).

- #proj- → Project-based channels (e.g., #proj-new-website, #proj-product-launch).

- #help- → Support channels (e.g., #help-it, #help-hr).

- #fun- → Social channels (e.g., #fun-memes, #fun-music).

Having a consistent structure allows users to **quickly identify** what each channel is for without having to guess.

2.2 Keep Names Short and Descriptive

Slack has a 21-character limit for channel names, so keeping names concise is essential.

☑ **Good examples:**

- #proj-new-website (instead of #project-new-website-redesign-2024).

- #team-sales (instead of #sales-team-internal).

🚫 **Avoid:**

- Overly long names that are hard to read.

- Ambiguous names like #stuff, #work, or #discussions.

2.3 Use Hyphens for Readability

Instead of using underscores or spaces (which Slack does not support in channel names), use **hyphens** to improve readability:

☑ #customer-support
🚫 #customersupport

---

3. Regularly Review and Archive Inactive Channels

Over time, Slack workspaces can become cluttered with **inactive channels** that are no longer relevant. Regularly reviewing and archiving old channels ensures that employees aren't overwhelmed with too many options.

Identify Unused Channels

Use Slack's built-in analytics or manual checks to find channels that:

- Have low activity (e.g., no messages for several months).

- Were created for one-time projects that have been completed.

- Have members who left the company or project.

Archive Unused Channels

Instead of deleting old channels, archive them so that past discussions remain accessible if needed. Archiving channels:

- Prevents further messages from being sent.

- Keeps the workspace clean without losing historical data.

If necessary, team members can still search archived channels or reactivate them later.

Encourage Users to Leave Unneeded Channels

Educate team members on leaving channels that are no longer relevant to them. A cluttered Slack sidebar can reduce efficiency, so periodically remind users to review their channel memberships.

---

4. Set Clear Channel Descriptions and Pinned Messages

A well-defined channel description helps new members understand the purpose of a channel without having to ask.

Add Channel Descriptions

When creating a new channel, always add a clear description. For example:

✅ #proj-marketing-strategy → "Discussing marketing strategies for 2024 campaigns. All team members welcome to contribute."
✅ #help-it → "IT support channel. Report technical issues and get assistance here."

These descriptions help team members quickly determine whether they should join a channel.

Use Pinned Messages for Important Information

Pin key messages at the top of a channel for quick reference. This is useful for:

- Important links (e.g., Google Drive folders, project trackers).

- Team guidelines and meeting schedules.

- Frequently asked questions (FAQs).

Pinned messages prevent repetitive questions and make sure crucial details are always accessible.

5. Encourage Good Channel Etiquette

Even with a well-structured Slack workspace, maintaining good communication habits is essential to keep conversations productive.

Set Expectations for Each Channel

Clearly communicate the purpose and usage rules for each channel. This can be done through:

- Channel descriptions (as discussed earlier).

- A welcome message when someone joins a channel.

- Pinned guidelines for proper use.

For example, a #random channel might have a rule like:
"This channel is for casual, non-work conversations. Keep discussions respectful and inclusive."

Avoid Overloading Channels with Off-Topic Discussions

Encourage employees to keep conversations relevant to the channel's topic. For general chats, create a dedicated space like #off-topic or #watercooler.

Use Threads to Keep Discussions Organized

When responding to a message in a busy channel, use threads instead of sending separate messages. This prevents long conversations from cluttering the main discussion.

Conclusion

Organizing Slack channels effectively leads to better communication, improved productivity, and a more structured workflow. By establishing a clear channel structure, using consistent naming conventions, regularly archiving inactive channels, and promoting good etiquette, teams can maximize the efficiency of their Slack workspace.

By following these best practices, your Slack workspace will remain clear, organized, and easy to navigate, helping teams collaborate more effectively and reduce communication friction.

2.2 Sending and Managing Messages

Effective messaging is at the core of communication in Slack. Whether you're chatting in a channel or sending a direct message, understanding how to format your messages, use emojis, and manage conversations effectively will improve collaboration and make your messages clearer and more engaging.

2.2.1 Formatting Messages and Using Emojis

When sending messages in Slack, proper formatting ensures readability, clarity, and emphasis. Slack provides several text formatting options to structure messages, highlight important information, and make conversations more effective. Additionally, emojis are a powerful way to add context, tone, and engagement to conversations.

Formatting Messages in Slack

Slack allows users to format their text using a simple markup system. Proper formatting helps messages stand out and improves overall communication in a workspace. Below are the key formatting techniques you can use in Slack:

Bold, Italics, and Strikethrough

- **Bold**: To emphasize text, use asterisks (*) around the word or phrase.

    o   Example: *Important Update:* → **Important Update:**

- *Italics*: To italicize text, use underscores (_) around the word or phrase.

    o   Example: _Reminder:_ → *Reminder:*

- ~~Strikethrough~~: To cross out text, use tildes (~) around the word or phrase.

    o   Example: ~Outdated Information~ → ~~Outdated Information~~

Block Quotes and Code Blocks

- **Block Quote**: Use > at the beginning of a line to create a block quote. This is useful for highlighting key information or referencing previous messages.

- o Example:

- o > This is an important announcement.

→

This is an important announcement.

- **Inline Code**: Use backticks (`) around a word or phrase to display it as inline code.

  - o Example: Use `Ctrl + C` to copy → Use Ctrl + C to copy

- **Code Blocks**: Use triple backticks (```) before and after a block of text to create a multi-line code snippet.

  - o Example:

def hello_world(): print("Hello, Slack!")

  - o This is useful for sharing programming code or structured data in Slack.

Lists and Bullet Points

- **Numbered Lists**: Use numbers followed by a period to create ordered lists.

  - o Example:
  - o 1. First item
  - o 2. Second item
  - o 3. Third item

→

  1. First item
  2. Second item
  3. Third item

- **Bullet Points**: Use asterisks (*), plus signs (+), or dashes (-) to create unordered lists.

  - o Example:
  - o * Task 1

    o   * Task 2

    o   * Task 3

→

    ▪   Task 1

    ▪   Task 2

    ▪   Task 3

Line Breaks and Paragraphs

- Press Shift + Enter to insert a line break within a message without sending it immediately.

- Use multiple lines for clarity, especially in longer messages or announcements.

Using Emojis in Slack

Emojis are a fun and effective way to add emotion, clarity, and engagement to messages in Slack. They help make conversations more expressive and dynamic.

Using Emojis in Messages

Slack supports thousands of standard emojis, which you can add to your messages by typing : followed by the emoji name.

- Example: Great job! :tada: → Great job! 🎉

- Example: Let's meet at 3 PM :clock3: → Let's meet at 3 PM 🕒

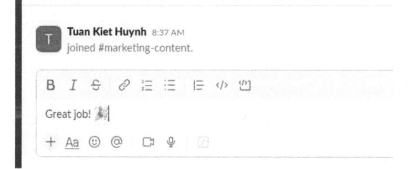

You can also browse and insert emojis using the emoji picker by clicking on the smiley face icon in the message field.

Emoji Reactions

Instead of replying with text, you can use emoji reactions to acknowledge messages, show approval, or categorize responses. This helps reduce clutter in conversations while still providing feedback.

- Example:
  - (:thumbsup:) – Shows agreement or approval
  - (:white_check_mark:) – Indicates task completion
  - (:fire:) – Highlights something exciting or important
  - (:question:) – Requests clarification

To add a reaction:

1. Hover over a message.
2. Click the emoji reaction button (smiley face with a +).
3. Select an emoji or search for one using keywords.

Custom Emojis

Slack allows users to upload custom emojis, which can represent company branding, inside jokes, or team-specific symbols.

To add a custom emoji:

1. Click on your workspace name in the top-left corner.
2. Select Customize Slack.
3. Click Add Custom Emoji and upload an image.
4. Assign a name to the emoji (e.g., :teamlogo:).

Now, team members can use the new emoji in their messages and reactions.

Emoji Shortcuts and Productivity Tips

- Use :wave: to greet colleagues in a friendly way.

- Use :eyes: to indicate that you're reviewing something.

- Use :hourglass_flowing_sand: to show that you're waiting on a response.

- Use :heavy_check_mark: to confirm task completion.

Best Practices for Formatting and Emojis

To use formatting and emojis effectively in Slack, follow these best practices:

☑ **Keep messages clear and structured** – Use headings, bullet points, and bold text to improve readability.

☑ **Use emojis to enhance tone, but don't overuse them** – Too many emojis can make messages hard to read.

☑ **React with emojis instead of sending unnecessary replies** – This keeps channels less cluttered.

☑ **Leverage custom emojis for team culture and branding** – Use inside jokes and team-related symbols for engagement.

Conclusion

Mastering Slack's formatting and emoji features allows you to communicate more effectively, keep conversations engaging, and reduce misunderstandings. By using bold text, bullet points, and emojis wisely, you can ensure that your messages are clear and impactful. In the next section, we'll explore how to reply effectively in Slack using threads and direct messages, ensuring that discussions remain organized and easy to follow.

2.2.2 Replying in Threads vs. Direct Messages

Effective communication in Slack relies on understanding when to use threads versus direct messages (DMs). Both serve distinct purposes and, when used correctly, can enhance team collaboration, prevent message overload, and keep conversations organized. This section will explore the differences between threads and direct messages, when to use each, best practices, and potential pitfalls.

Understanding Threads and Direct Messages

Slack offers multiple ways to communicate, but **threads** and **direct messages** are among the most commonly used. They help organize discussions and reduce clutter in shared channels.

- **Threads**: Keep conversations focused and contained within a single message. They are especially useful for group discussions that don't require a new channel or multiple notifications.

- **Direct Messages (DMs)**: Facilitate private conversations between two or more people. They are useful for sensitive discussions, quick clarifications, or casual check-ins.

Let's break down the differences in greater detail.

What Are Threads?

A **thread** is a structured conversation that stems from an original message. Instead of cluttering a channel with multiple responses, Slack allows users to reply **inside** the original message, creating a neat conversation that can be expanded or minimized as needed.

How Threads Work

1. **Starting a Thread**:

   o   Hover over a message in a channel.

   o   Click on the **Reply in thread** button.

   o   Type your response and hit enter.

   o   The reply remains attached to the original message and does not appear in the main channel feed unless explicitly shared.

2. **Viewing and Following Threads**:

   o   Users can choose to follow a thread and receive notifications when there are new replies.

   o   The **Threads** tab in the left sidebar keeps track of active and recent threads.

3. **Sharing a Thread Reply in the Channel**:

     o   If the response is important to the entire channel, users can click **Also send to channel** before posting their reply.

When to Use Threads

- To keep lengthy discussions **organized** and avoid flooding the channel with multiple responses.

- When discussing **specific details** related to a message without diverting the main topic of the channel.

- To ensure that **relevant people** are notified without disrupting the entire team.

Benefits of Using Threads

✅ **Keeps channels clean** – Reduces clutter and makes it easier to scan conversations.

✅ **Improves focus** – Allows team members to engage in discussions without overwhelming others.

✅ **Organizes responses** – Ensures that related messages stay together, preventing confusion.

✅ **Reduces unnecessary notifications** – Alerts only those involved in the discussion.

Pitfalls of Using Threads

✖ **Hidden conversations** – If not followed, important discussions might go unnoticed.

✖ **Delayed responses** – Unlike channel messages, threads don't always catch immediate attention.

✖ **Limited visibility** – Only those who engage in the thread see ongoing updates, which can sometimes exclude relevant participants.

What Are Direct Messages (DMs)?

A **direct message (DM)** is a private chat between individuals or small groups. Unlike threads, DMs are **not tied to channels** and do not appear in public spaces.

How Direct Messages Work

1. **Starting a DM:**

     o   Click the **Messages** section in the sidebar.

     o   Search for the recipient's name.

     o   Type and send your message.

2. **Group DMs:**

     o   You can add multiple people to a DM conversation.

     o   However, group DMs are not as structured as Slack channels and do not support threaded replies.

3. **Notification Settings:**

     o   DM notifications are prioritized and usually more immediate than channel messages.

     o   Users can mute DMs if necessary.

When to Use Direct Messages

- When discussing **confidential or private matters** (e.g., HR issues, personal concerns).

- For **quick, informal check-ins** that don't require a channel discussion.

- When you need an **urgent response** from a specific individual.

- When working on **one-on-one tasks** that don't involve the broader team.

Benefits of Using DMs

☑ **Private and secure** – Great for sensitive discussions.
☑ **More direct** – Ensures immediate attention.
☑ **Reduces distractions for others** – Only relevant parties are notified.

Pitfalls of Using DMs

✕ **Lack of visibility** – Others in the organization cannot benefit from the discussion.
✕ **Lost context** – Important decisions made in DMs may not be recorded in shared spaces.
✕ **Encourages siloed communication** – Overusing DMs can reduce team transparency.

Threads vs. Direct Messages: Key Differences

Feature	Threads	Direct Messages
Visibility	Public (within a channel)	Private

Notification Control	Only participants in the thread receive updates	Recipients always get notified
Best Used For	Organizing conversations within a channel	One-on-one or private discussions
Accessibility	Others in the channel can view and participate	Only invited members can see messages
Long-Term Reference	Easily searchable within a channel	Harder to retrieve, especially in large conversations

Best Practices for Using Threads and DMs Effectively

☑ **Use Threads When:**

✓ You need to keep a conversation organized within a channel.

✓ The discussion is relevant to a specific message.

✓ You don't want to disrupt the main channel with multiple responses.

☑ **Use Direct Messages When:**

✓ You need to discuss private or confidential matters.

✓ You require a quick response from an individual.

✓ The topic is not relevant to the entire team.

🚫 **Avoid These Mistakes:**

✘ Starting a DM when the conversation should be in a channel – This reduces transparency.

✘ Using a thread for an entirely new topic – This makes it harder to find relevant information later.

✘ Replying in the channel when the discussion should be in a thread – This can clutter conversations.

Conclusion: Choosing the Right Tool for the Right Context

Both threads and direct messages play crucial roles in Slack communication. Threads help keep channel conversations organized, while DMs are best for private discussions. Using them effectively can lead to better collaboration, fewer distractions, and improved team efficiency.

The key takeaway is to choose the appropriate method based on who needs to see the message, how urgent it is, and whether it should be easily referenced later. By following best practices, teams can avoid confusion and create a more productive Slack experience.

2.2.3 Pinning, Bookmarking, and Saving Messages

Effective communication in Slack involves not only sending and receiving messages but also efficiently managing important information. Slack provides several features that help users keep track of critical messages, ensuring that key discussions, files, or decisions do not get lost in the continuous flow of conversations. The three primary tools for message management in Slack are pinning, bookmarking, and saving messages.

These tools allow individuals and teams to quickly retrieve important messages without having to scroll endlessly through chat history. Understanding how to use these features effectively can significantly enhance productivity, collaboration, and organization within Slack.

1. Pinning Messages in Slack

1.1 What is Pinning?

Pinning a message in Slack keeps it easily accessible within a channel or direct message (DM) conversation. When a message is pinned, it appears in a dedicated "Pinned Items" section, allowing users to find and reference it quickly.

Pinning is particularly useful for:

- Highlighting important announcements or decisions.

- Keeping track of meeting notes or key action points.

- Ensuring critical documents and links remain easily accessible.

Unlike bookmarking and saving, which are personal tools, pinning messages affects the entire channel or DM group, making it a **team-wide** feature.

1.2 How to Pin a Message in Slack

To pin a message in a Slack channel or DM:

1. Hover over the message you want to pin.

2. Click on the **three-dot menu (More actions)** that appears.

3. Select **"Pin to channel"** or **"Pin to conversation"** (if it's a DM).

4. The message is now pinned and can be accessed by clicking the **channel name** and selecting **"Pinned"** from the sidebar.

Tip: Only **workspace members with the appropriate permissions** can pin or unpin messages in a channel. If you cannot pin a message, check with the workspace administrator or channel owner.

1.3 Managing Pinned Messages

To view all pinned messages in a channel or DM:

- Click on the **channel or DM name** at the top of the screen.

- Select **Pinned** from the dropdown menu.

- A list of all pinned messages will appear.

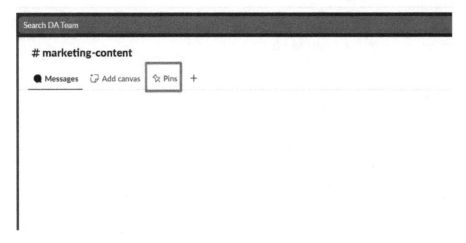

To unpin a message:

1. Hover over the pinned message.

2. Click on the **three-dot menu (More actions)**.

3. Select **"Unpin from channel"** or **"Unpin from conversation"**.

💡 **Best Practice:** Limit the number of pinned messages to **5-10 key items** to avoid cluttering the pinned messages section.

2. Bookmarking Messages in Slack

2.1 What is Bookmarking?

The **bookmark feature** in Slack (also known as "Channel Bookmarks") is a way to keep important links, files, or messages visible at the top of a channel. Unlike pinned messages, which are stored in a list, bookmarks appear as a persistent toolbar at the top of the channel for easy access.

Bookmarks are ideal for:
- Frequently used documents (e.g., Google Docs, spreadsheets, project plans).
- Links to external tools or resources.
- Reference documents such as team guidelines or onboarding materials.

2.2 How to Add a Bookmark in Slack

To add a bookmark to a Slack channel:

1. Click on the **Bookmark bar** at the top of the channel.

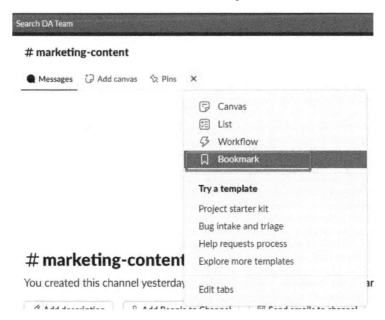

2. Select **"Add a bookmark"**.

3. Paste a **link, message, or file** you want to bookmark.

4. Click **Save**, and it will appear in the bookmark bar for all channel members.

To remove or edit a bookmark:

1. Click on the **bookmark bar**.

2. Find the bookmark you want to remove/edit.

3. Click the **three-dot menu** next to the bookmark.

4. Select **Edit or Remove**.

💡 **Best Practice:** Regularly update bookmarks to ensure they remain relevant and useful for the team.

---

3. Saving Messages in Slack

3.1 What is Saving Messages?

The **Save Message** feature in Slack is a personal tool that allows individual users to flag important messages for later review. Unlike pinning (which is visible to everyone in a channel), saved messages are private and can only be accessed by the individual user.

Saving messages is useful for:

- Marking messages that require follow-up actions.

- Keeping personal reminders of important information.

- Storing messages for future reference without notifying others.

3.2 How to Save a Message in Slack

To save a message:

1. Hover over the message you want to save.

2. Click the **"Save for later" (bookmark icon)** next to the message.

3. The message will now appear in the **Saved items** section.

To view saved messages:

- Click on your **profile picture** in the top-right corner.

- Select **Saved items (Later)** from the dropdown menu.

- All your saved messages will be listed.

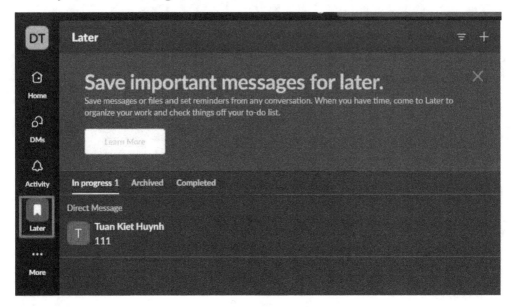

To unsave a message:

1. Open the **Saved items** section.

2. Find the message you want to remove.

3. Click the **"Remove from Later (Unsave)" (bookmark icon)** to remove it from the list.

💡 **Best Practice:** Use saved messages as a temporary reminder system and clear them out once they are no longer needed.

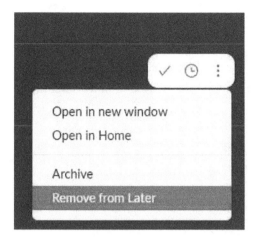

4. Best Practices for Managing Messages in Slack

To maximize efficiency in Slack, follow these best practices when using pinning, bookmarking, and saving messages:

When to Use Each Feature?

Feature	Purpose	Visibility	Best Use Case
Pinning	Team-wide reference	Visible to all channel members	Key announcements, meeting notes, critical messages
Bookmarking	Channel-wide reference	Visible to all channel members	Important links, external tools, frequently used documents
Saving	Personal reference	Private (only visible to the user)	Messages for later review, reminders, personal action items

Keeping Slack Organized

✔ **Limit pinned messages** to 5-10 critical items per channel.

✔ **Regularly review and update bookmarks** to ensure they are relevant.

✔ **Use saved messages for short-term tracking**, but clean them up regularly.

✔ **Encourage team members to use these tools effectively** to prevent information overload.

5. Conclusion

Pinning, bookmarking, and saving messages in Slack are powerful tools that improve communication efficiency and keep important information easily accessible. By implementing best practices, users can reduce information overload and streamline workflows.

Key Takeaways:

- ☑ **Pin important messages** that benefit the whole team.
- ☑ **Bookmark critical links and documents** for quick access.
- ☑ **Save messages privately** to track tasks and reminders.
- ☑ **Regularly clean up and update pinned, bookmarked, and saved items** to maintain an organized workspace.

By mastering these message management features, you can **work smarter in Slack**, ensuring that essential information is always at your fingertips!

2.3 Using Mentions, Reactions, and Threads Effectively

2.3.1 Tagging People with @Mentions

In a busy Slack workspace, one of the most powerful tools for ensuring your message gets the attention it deserves is using the @mention feature. Tagging someone with an @mention in a message or comment alerts them to your specific communication, ensuring they are informed, whether they are active or offline. Understanding how and when to use @mentions effectively can greatly enhance your communication and collaboration, reducing misunderstandings and increasing productivity across your team.

What is an @Mention?

An @mention is a way to tag someone directly in a Slack message, making sure they are notified about the message. When you type the @ symbol followed by a person's name (e.g., @JohnDoe), Slack automatically highlights the name and notifies that individual. This is an effective way to grab someone's attention, whether you're posting in a channel, direct message, or even within a thread.

Mentions can be particularly useful in group conversations where numerous people are involved, ensuring that your communication doesn't get lost amidst the chaos of a busy Slack channel. Furthermore, Slack also allows mentions in private messages, making it versatile for both public and private communications.

How to Tag People in Slack

To tag someone in Slack, simply type the @ symbol followed by their username. As you begin typing, Slack will suggest names based on the letters you've entered, making it easy to quickly find the person you want to tag. Once their name appears in the dropdown list, click on it, and it will be inserted into your message. When the message is sent, Slack will notify the person you tagged with an alert in their Slack app.

You can also mention a group of people by tagging roles. For example, @team or @marketing will notify everyone who is in that group. This is particularly useful for addressing a whole department or team without needing to list every individual's name.

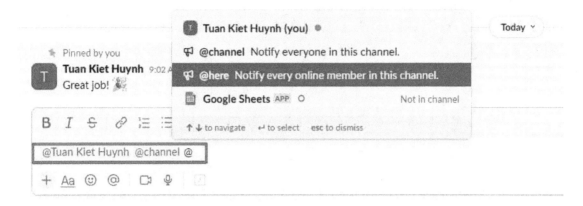

Types of Mentions in Slack

There are a few variations of mentions in Slack that can be used in different situations. Let's break them down:

1. **@username**: The standard mention where you tag a specific person by their Slack username. This ensures they are notified of your message.

2. **@here**: This mention alerts all members who are currently online or active within the channel. It's a good option when you want to get the attention of those available right now but don't need to notify those who are offline or inactive.

3. **@channel**: This is a more robust notification method. @channel alerts all members of a channel, whether or not they are currently online. It's a great way to notify everyone in a channel about an important update or announcement. However, use this mention sparingly as it can be disruptive when overused.

4. **@everyone**: Similar to @channel, but it's more commonly used in a multi-channel or workspace-wide context. It notifies all members in a workspace, not just those in a specific channel. It's reserved for very important or urgent communications.

When to Use @Mentions

Knowing when and how to use @mentions is key to effective communication on Slack. Overusing mentions can lead to notification fatigue, where team members become desensitized to the alerts. However, using them strategically can increase engagement and ensure that messages are not overlooked.

Here are some guidelines on when to use @mentions:

1. **Direct Communication**: When you need to get the attention of an individual, @mentioning someone in a channel or direct message makes sure they see the message and can respond promptly.

2. **Accountability and Follow-up**: If you've discussed something with someone, and you need them to take action or follow up on a task, tagging them with an @mention makes your request clear and direct. It creates a sense of accountability for that person to respond or act accordingly.

3. **Team Announcements or Updates**: When there's a critical announcement or update for a group, using @here, @channel, or @everyone ensures that the relevant people are informed, even if they're in different time zones or not actively watching the channel.

4. **Feedback Requests**: When you need feedback or an answer from a particular person, it's best to @mention them specifically, so they know their input is needed. It's an easy way to make sure that no questions go unanswered.

5. **Collaborative Efforts**: When working on a shared project, tagging specific teammates in a message about the project ensures that the right people are aware of the latest developments. This helps to keep everyone aligned and encourages active participation.

Best Practices for @Mentions

Although @mentions are a powerful communication tool in Slack, they should be used carefully to avoid spamming team members with unnecessary notifications. Here are some best practices for using @mentions effectively:

1. **Be Specific**: Tag only the people who absolutely need to see or respond to the message. Avoid using @channel or @everyone for non-urgent updates, as it can overwhelm people with notifications.

2. **Context is Key**: When tagging someone, especially if you're addressing a particular task or request, provide enough context so the person understands why they are being tagged. A simple "@JohnDoe Can you review this document?" is more effective than just tagging someone without any explanation.

3. **Tagging in Threads**: If you're replying to a message or continuing a conversation within a thread, make sure to tag the person you're responding to. This not only ensures they're notified, but it also keeps the conversation organized.

4. **Use @here and @channel Sparingly**: While @here and @channel are useful, they should be used selectively. Tagging everyone unnecessarily can lead to notification overload and result in people ignoring future alerts. It's important to consider the urgency and relevance of your message before using these mentions.

5. **Respect Time Zones**: If you work with a global team, be mindful of time zones when using @mentions. Avoid tagging people late at night or early in the morning unless the message is extremely urgent. Slack allows you to schedule messages, which can help you avoid disturbing people outside of working hours.

6. **Tagging Roles and Teams**: Rather than tagging individuals, consider tagging roles or teams when you want to communicate with a group. This allows you to engage the appropriate audience without having to tag every individual separately. For example, instead of tagging multiple people, you could use @marketing or @dev-team to notify the entire team.

7. **Avoid Overuse of Notifications**: While it's tempting to tag people frequently, overusing @mentions for every message can be counterproductive. Use @mentions only when the message requires direct attention or action from the person tagged.

How @Mentions Improve Communication in Slack

Effective communication is crucial in any workspace, and Slack's @mention system helps ensure that messages don't go unnoticed. By tagging people directly, it's easier to get responses and manage workloads. This feature improves transparency by clearly assigning tasks and requests to individuals.

The @mention feature also helps to foster collaboration. When multiple people are tagged in a conversation, everyone involved can easily jump in, contribute their thoughts, and work together to move things forward. This is especially useful in team channels, where everyone might have a role to play in responding to a project update or a shared task.

Furthermore, Slack's ability to filter notifications based on @mentions makes it easier to focus on what's important. Rather than wading through an endless stream of general messages, you can prioritize and focus on the ones where you've been specifically tagged. This not only saves time but ensures that you don't miss any critical updates.

Tagging and Notification Settings

While @mentions are helpful, they can sometimes lead to notification overload, especially in large, active teams. Thankfully, Slack offers ways to customize your notification settings to strike the right balance between staying informed and avoiding unnecessary distractions.

1. **Personal Notification Preferences**: You can customize how you receive notifications based on @mentions. This includes deciding whether you want to be notified for @mentions in threads, channels, or direct messages. For example, you might want to get a mobile push notification when you're @mentioned in a direct message but only desktop notifications for mentions in channels.

2. **Do Not Disturb Mode**: When you need to focus or step away from Slack, you can enable Do Not Disturb mode to mute notifications, including @mentions. This allows you to prevent interruptions while still receiving important alerts once you return.

3. **Highlighting @Mentions in the App**: Slack also lets you configure how @mentions are highlighted within the app. By enabling features like bolding or color-coding @mentions, you can visually prioritize these messages, helping you quickly identify when you've been tagged in a conversation.

Conclusion

Mastering the use of @mentions in Slack is a fundamental skill for effective communication within any workspace. By strategically tagging individuals or groups, you ensure that the right people are notified about the right tasks, making collaboration more efficient and transparent. However, it's important to use @mentions thoughtfully and selectively to avoid notification fatigue and maintain a balance between staying informed and minimizing disruptions.

By following best practices and customizing your Slack notifications, you can optimize your workflow, stay focused on what matters most, and foster a collaborative, productive environment within your team.

2.3.2 Using Reactions to Acknowledge Messages

Slack reactions are a simple yet powerful way to communicate efficiently without cluttering conversations with unnecessary messages. By using emoji reactions, teams can acknowledge, approve, or respond to messages in a way that is quick, clear, and nondisruptive. In this section, we will explore the benefits of using reactions, the different ways they can be applied in Slack, best practices for using them effectively, and how they contribute to a productive and engaging workspace.

1. The Role of Reactions in Slack Communication

What Are Slack Reactions?

Slack reactions are emoji-based responses that users can attach to any message. Instead of sending a separate message to confirm receipt or express approval, users can react with an emoji, reducing the number of messages in a channel while keeping communication clear and effective.

Why Use Reactions?

Reactions serve multiple functions, including:

- **Acknowledgment:** A simple (thumbs-up) or (checkmark) can indicate that a message has been seen or agreed upon.

- **Feedback:** Users can react with emojis like (fire) for enthusiasm, (clapping hands) for appreciation, or ? (question mark) to request clarification.

- **Prioritization:** Reactions can be used to signal importance, such as (red light) for urgent matters or (eyes) to indicate that someone is reviewing the message.

- **Engagement:** Fun reactions like (party popper) or (laughing face) help build a friendly and engaging work culture.

2. How to Use Reactions in Slack

2.1 Adding a Reaction to a Message

To add a reaction:

1. Hover over the message you want to react to.

2. Click the "Add a reaction" button (smiley face icon).

3. Select an emoji from the list or search for a specific one.

4. Click the emoji to attach it to the message.

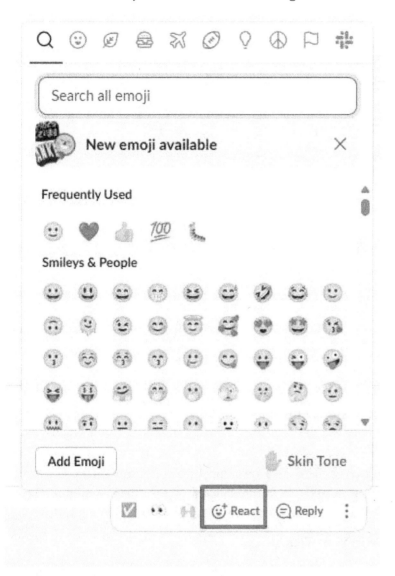

2.2 Removing a Reaction

If you accidentally add the wrong reaction or want to change it:

1. Click on the emoji reaction you added.

2. It will disappear from the message.

3. If needed, select a new reaction following the steps above.

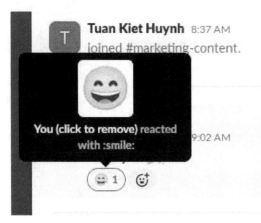

2.3 Viewing and Managing Reactions

To see who reacted to a message:

1. Hover over the reaction.

2. Slack will display the list of users who added that reaction.

3. This helps in understanding who has acknowledged or engaged with a message.

---

3. Best Practices for Using Reactions Effectively

Keep It Professional and Clear

While reactions can be fun, they should also be appropriate for the workplace. Using standard acknowledgment reactions like 👍 for approval or ✅ for task completion keeps communication clear. Avoid excessive or inappropriate emojis in professional settings.

Standardize Reaction Usage in Your Team

To ensure consistency, teams can establish guidelines for common reactions. For example:

- ✅ = Task completed

- 👀 = Reviewing in progress

- ? = Needs clarification

- 🔵 = Important update

- 🚀 = Exciting new idea

Use Reactions Instead of Unnecessary Replies

Instead of replying with "Got it" or "Thanks," using a reaction like 👍 or 🙏 (hands in gratitude) keeps channels clean and reduces notification overload.

Be Mindful of Reaction Overuse

While reactions are useful, too many can create confusion. Avoid adding multiple conflicting reactions to a message, and ensure that your reaction conveys the intended meaning.

Leverage Custom Emojis for Team-Specific Needs

Slack allows workspaces to create custom emojis that fit their company culture. For example:

- A company logo reaction to approve internal branding decisions

- A custom "urgent" emoji to flag high-priority tasks

- Fun team-specific reactions to build engagement

---

4. Advanced Uses of Slack Reactions

Using Reactions for Decision-Making

Instead of multiple replies in a thread, teams can vote using reactions:

- 👍 for yes, 👎 for no

- 🚀 for the best idea

- 🎯 for a final decision

This method speeds up discussions and makes decision-making more efficient.

Automating Tasks with Emoji Reactions

Slack integrations allow reactions to trigger actions. For example:

- Adding a ☑ reaction automatically marks a task as complete in project management tools like Asana or Trello.

- Reacting with 📅 can create a calendar event.

- Using 🎫 can convert a message into a support ticket in Jira or Zendesk.

To set up automated reactions:

1. Use Slack Workflow Builder to create automation.

2. Connect it with third-party apps like Zapier.

3. Define specific emojis to trigger automated actions.

Tracking Engagement and Employee Sentiment

Slack reactions can help measure engagement levels within a team:

- Checking how many people reacted with 🎉 to a company announcement.

- Gauging sentiment using 😄 (happy) vs. 😞 (sad) reactions.

- Using 📊 to mark messages containing important metrics or data.

---

5. Case Studies: Reactions in Real-World Slack Workspaces

Case Study 1: Reducing Notification Overload in a Marketing Team

A marketing team adopted a structured reaction system, using ☑ for approval and ❓ for clarification. This reduced unnecessary replies and improved workflow efficiency.

Case Study 2: Automating IT Support Tickets with Reactions

An IT department integrated Slack reactions with Jira, allowing employees to react with 🎫 to create a support ticket. This streamlined issue tracking and response times.

Case Study 3: Enhancing Team Culture with Custom Emojis

A remote company used custom Slack emojis to celebrate milestones, such as a custom 🎉 emoji with an employee's face for birthday wishes. This boosted team engagement.

---

6. Conclusion: Making the Most of Slack Reactions

Reactions are more than just fun emojis—they are a powerful tool for workplace communication, decision-making, and workflow automation. By following best practices and leveraging reactions effectively, teams can enhance collaboration, reduce unnecessary messages, and create a more engaging Slack experience.

Key Takeaways:

- Use reactions to acknowledge, approve, and prioritize messages.

- Standardize reactions within your team for clarity.

- Automate tasks by linking reactions with workflows.

- Use custom emojis to enhance engagement and team culture.

By incorporating Slack reactions strategically, teams can work smarter, communicate better, and create a more productive workspace.

2.3.3 Keeping Conversations Organized with Threads

Slack has revolutionized workplace communication, but one challenge that many teams face is managing the constant influx of messages and conversations. While channels and direct messages are essential for team communication, they can quickly become overwhelming if not managed properly. Threads are one of Slack's most powerful features for keeping conversations organized and ensuring that messages are easier to follow, especially in busy channels.

In this section, we will explore how to use threads effectively to maintain clarity, reduce noise, and create a more organized, efficient workspace.

Understanding Threads in Slack

At its core, a thread is a way to group all replies to a specific message in a channel or direct message. This allows team members to respond directly to a message without cluttering the main conversation stream. Threads keep your main channels focused and organized by ensuring that responses are relevant to the message they address.

The thread feature is useful for maintaining order in busy channels where multiple conversations might be happening simultaneously. Without threads, important discussions can get lost among all the other messages, creating confusion and delays. Threads allow you to engage in deep, focused discussions without interrupting the flow of the channel.

How to Start and Use Threads

To start a thread in Slack, simply hover over a message in the channel, and you will see the "Reply" button appear. Clicking this button opens the thread sidebar where you can type your response. Any responses you or others make in the thread will be displayed there, keeping them separate from the main conversation in the channel.

When replying in a thread, Slack will notify you of any new replies to the thread, keeping you updated without having to constantly monitor the channel. This also prevents you from having to sift through unrelated messages to find what is important to you.

Threads allow for the following functionality:

- **Replies to a Message**: You can respond directly to a message, whether it's a question, comment, or idea. This keeps conversations contextualized.

- **Collaborative Discussions**: Team members can continue a discussion or brainstorm without derailing the main topic of the channel.

- **Streamlined Communication**: By using threads, the main conversation in the channel remains focused on the general topic, while threads provide a space for more specific dialogue.

Best Practices for Using Threads

While threads are incredibly useful, they can also become difficult to manage if not used correctly. Here are some best practices to ensure you are using Slack threads to their full potential:

1. **Use Threads for Specific Discussions**: Threads are meant to contain discussions that are closely related to a particular topic. If you have something to say that is relevant only to the original message or a specific point, a thread is the best place to reply. If your comment is broader and relevant to the entire channel, it might be better to post a new message in the channel itself.

2. **Stay Focused and Concise**: Avoid long, winding conversations in threads. Instead, keep your responses short and to the point, ensuring that everyone involved can easily read and engage. If your discussion turns into an ongoing conversation, it

may be a good idea to take it to a private channel or direct message to avoid overwhelming others.

3. **Reply in Threads Instead of Posting in the Main Channel**: If you're replying to someone else's comment, always consider replying in a thread instead of posting a new message in the main channel. This keeps the main feed free from tangential discussions. It also ensures that the person who posted the original message is notified of your reply, keeping the conversation linked together.

4. **Use Threads to Handle Action Items and Questions**: When working on action items or responding to questions, threads are a great way to keep track of tasks and follow-ups. For example, if someone posts a question in a channel, you can respond with more details in a thread and even tag people who need to follow up. This way, everyone knows exactly what's happening without cluttering the main conversation.

5. **Organize Threads with Emojis or Reactions**: Emojis are a great way to visually organize conversations. You can use certain emojis to signify the status of a thread, like adding a "thumbs up" emoji when you have acknowledged a task or using a "checkmark" emoji to indicate that a discussion has been resolved. These small visual cues make it easier to scan a thread and determine the conversation's status at a glance.

6. **Pin Important Threads for Easy Access**: Slack allows you to pin important threads to the top of your channel or workspace. This is useful for keeping critical discussions or ongoing projects easily accessible. Pinning threads ensures that nothing gets lost in the shuffle, and team members can quickly refer back to essential conversations.

7. **Use Threaded Replies to Avoid Overloading Your Channel**: If a message requires more detailed discussion, especially if it involves a larger group of people, it's better to continue the conversation in a thread rather than posting directly in the main channel. By doing so, you avoid overwhelming others with notifications and ensure that the main channel remains relevant to the broader team. For example, if someone posts a detailed status update or question, you could reply in the thread to ask for more specifics, share your insights, or contribute to the conversation without interrupting others.

8. **Set Notification Preferences for Threads**: Slack lets you customize your notification preferences, including those for threads. You can opt to get notified when a thread you're involved in has new replies or set it so that you only get

notifications for threads you directly follow. These settings help you avoid notification overload while ensuring that you stay updated on the most important conversations.

9. **Use Threaded Conversations for Structured Feedback**: When giving feedback on work or a project, threads provide a more structured and organized approach. Instead of sending multiple separate messages or email chains, gather all feedback within one thread. This keeps everything related to the feedback in one place and helps track progress.

Managing Thread Overload

While threads can help reduce noise in Slack, it's still possible for a large team to get overwhelmed by too many threads. This can lead to some challenges in keeping everything organized, especially when there are dozens of active threads happening at once.

Here are a few strategies to manage thread overload:

- **Prioritize Important Threads**: Prioritize threads that are most relevant to your work and mute or snooze less critical ones. By marking threads that require your attention, you can easily focus on what matters most.

- **Archive Inactive Threads**: If a thread has been inactive for a while and no further action is required, consider archiving it. This reduces the clutter and allows you to focus on active, relevant threads.

- **Use Slack's Search Functionality**: If you're trying to find a particular thread, use Slack's powerful search feature to locate conversations quickly. You can search by keywords, users, and more. This is especially helpful when you need to refer to an older thread but can't remember exactly where it was posted.

Keeping Track of Actionable Items in Threads

Threads can become particularly useful for tracking action items, deadlines, and follow-ups. When you're part of a thread that involves tasks or actionable items, you can easily refer back to the conversation when needed. Here are a few strategies to help you stay on top of tasks discussed in threads:

1. **Tag Actionable Items with Reminders**: Use Slack's built-in reminder feature to set a reminder for a task discussed within a thread. Simply click on the three dots next to a message and select "Set a reminder" to receive a notification at a later time.

2. **Use Threads for Project Milestones**: When working on larger projects, create threads around major milestones. These threads can be used to share updates, discuss roadblocks, and confirm completion. Having all updates in one thread makes it easy to track progress over time.

3. **Reference Threads in Follow-up Conversations**: When you need to follow up on something discussed in a thread, refer back to that thread in a new message or another thread. This ensures that all the context is retained, and team members don't have to guess what was previously discussed.

Conclusion

Threads are an essential tool in Slack for maintaining organization and structure in conversations. By using threads effectively, you can keep your communication organized, improve your workflow, and minimize distractions. Slack's thread functionality enables you to have focused, actionable discussions while keeping your channels clean and relevant.

By following best practices for threads, such as staying focused, organizing threads with emojis, and using Slack's notification settings to stay updated, you can ensure that your Slack experience is efficient and effective. Whether you are managing a team or working on a personal project, mastering the art of threads will help you communicate more effectively, stay on top of important tasks, and create a more organized digital workspace.

CHAPTER III
Optimizing Collaboration with Slack Features

3.1 File Sharing and Storage

Slack is not just a tool for messaging; it's also a powerful platform for file sharing and collaboration. One of its most valuable features is the ability to share and store files, making it easier for teams to collaborate efficiently. In this section, we will dive into the best practices for uploading and sharing files in Slack channels, ensuring that your team can seamlessly exchange documents, images, presentations, and other types of files, all while staying organized and ensuring easy access.

3.1.1 Uploading and Sharing Files in Channels

Slack makes sharing files incredibly simple, whether you are sharing documents, spreadsheets, images, or videos. When you upload a file to a channel or direct message (DM), it becomes accessible to everyone within the conversation. Slack's integration with cloud storage platforms such as Google Drive, OneDrive, and Dropbox makes it even more powerful, allowing you to upload and share files directly from these sources.

How to Upload Files to Slack

Uploading files to Slack can be done in a few easy steps, making it a quick and efficient way to share documents during team conversations. Let's break it down:

1. **Direct File Upload**

    o **Step 1**: In any Slack channel or direct message, click on the **"Attach a File"** icon (+) located in the message input field.

- o **Step 2**: Choose the file you want to upload from your computer or drag and drop the file into the Slack interface.

- o **Step 3**: Once the file is selected, Slack will display a preview of the file. You can add an optional comment or description to provide context for the file.

- o **Step 4**: Click **"Send"** to share the file with the channel or person.

When you share a file this way, all members of the channel can access and download the file, making it ideal for team collaborations on reports, presentations, spreadsheets, and more.

2. **Cloud Storage Integration (Google Drive, OneDrive, Dropbox, etc.)**

- o If you're using cloud storage services like Google Drive, OneDrive, or Dropbox, you can easily upload files from these services directly into Slack without downloading them to your local device first.

- o **Step 1**: Click the **"Attach a File"** icon.

- o **Step 2**: Choose the cloud storage service where your file is stored.

- o **Step 3**: Select the file you want to share and add a message if necessary.

- o **Step 4**: Click **"Send"** to share the file.

Why use cloud storage integrations? By connecting your Slack workspace with cloud storage services, you can save space in your Slack account while still sharing large files with your team. Plus, if the file is updated in the cloud, Slack will provide an updated link to the latest version automatically.

3. **Sharing Links to Files** Sometimes, you don't need to upload the file itself; you may want to share a link to a file hosted on a cloud platform (Google Drive, Dropbox, etc.). This is particularly useful for large files or files that are updated frequently.

   o **Step 1**: Copy the link to the file from the cloud storage platform.

   o **Step 2**: Paste the link in the Slack message input box.

   o **Step 3**: Optionally, add a message to give context to the link.

   o **Step 4**: Press **Send**.

Sharing a link to a cloud file ensures that your team members are always accessing the most up-to-date version of the file, as opposed to having to manage multiple file versions within Slack itself.

Organizing Files Within Channels

While sharing files is easy, keeping them organized can be more challenging, especially in high-volume channels with lots of file exchanges. Here are some best practices for managing files in Slack:

1. **Use Descriptive File Names** When uploading files, make sure to name them in a way that is easy for your team to understand. A descriptive file name helps team members locate files quickly and reduces confusion when searching through messages. For example, instead of naming a file **"Document1.docx"**, use something more descriptive like **"Q1-2025-Marketing-Strategy.docx"**.

2. **Leverage Threads to Discuss Files** After uploading a file to a channel, it's essential to keep the conversation organized. Slack allows users to reply to specific messages or files using threads. This can be helpful for discussing the contents of the file without cluttering the main channel. You can reply directly to the file by clicking the **"Reply in Thread"** option. This helps ensure that any discussions or feedback related to the file stay grouped together and are easy to follow.

3. **Pinning Important Files** Slack allows you to **pin** important files within a channel. Pinned files will appear at the top of the channel for easy access. This is especially useful for files that are referenced frequently, like a project proposal or an important document. To pin a file, simply click the three-dot menu on the file preview and select **"Pin to Channel"**. Keep in mind that channels can only have a limited number of pinned items, so it's best to pin only the most essential files.

4. **Use the File Browser** Slack has a built-in file browser that allows you to easily search for and access all the files shared within a channel. To access the file browser, click on the **"Files"** tab at the top of any channel. This will give you an organized view of all the files that have been shared in the channel, allowing you to filter by file type or sort by date.

Best Practices for File Sharing in Slack

To make file sharing as effective as possible, here are some best practices to keep in mind:

- **Limit the Size of Files**: Large files can slow down your team's workflow, especially if multiple people are trying to download them at once. If possible, compress files or use links to share files hosted on cloud platforms to avoid cluttering your workspace with heavy attachments.

- **Set Permissions for Sensitive Files**: When sharing files that contain sensitive or confidential information, be mindful of who can access those files. Slack allows you to control file access by setting permissions for different users or groups within your workspace. You can also use integrations like Google Drive and OneDrive to manage file access directly through those platforms.

- **Use File Comments**: Whenever you upload a file, it's a good idea to add a comment explaining the contents or providing context for the file. This makes it easier for team members to understand the purpose of the file without having to open it, reducing confusion and saving time.

- **Keep Files Organized with Channels**: Create specific channels dedicated to particular projects or topics to ensure that files related to those projects are easy to find. For example, a channel for the marketing team might have files related to marketing campaigns, while a product development channel could contain files related to product design.

Searching for Files in Slack

As your Slack workspace grows and the number of files shared increases, finding specific files can become a challenge. Fortunately, Slack's search function is designed to help you quickly locate any file shared in your workspace.

To search for a file:

1. Use the **search bar** at the top of the Slack interface. You can type keywords from the file name or even use file types in your search. For example, typing **"type:pdf"** will show all PDF files shared in your workspace.

2. You can also use filters to narrow down your search by channel or by person. For example, searching for **"in:#marketing"** will show all files shared in the marketing channel.

3. If you remember specific details about the file (such as who uploaded it), you can use **"from: [username]"** to filter results.

By utilizing the search feature and filtering by keywords, type, or user, you can quickly find the files you need, even in busy workspaces.

Conclusion

Slack's file sharing and storage features are designed to streamline communication and collaboration, especially in remote or hybrid teams. By uploading files directly to channels, organizing files effectively, and integrating with cloud storage services, teams can collaborate efficiently and stay productive. Remember to maintain good practices by keeping files well-organized, utilizing threads for discussion, and using Slack's search tools to find important documents quickly.

Optimizing your file-sharing process in Slack will not only make collaboration easier, but it will also improve the flow of information, reduce confusion, and help keep all team members aligned and on the same page.

3.1.2 Integrating with Google Drive and OneDrive

In the modern workplace, cloud storage solutions have become essential for storing, sharing, and collaborating on files. Among the most widely used cloud storage platforms are **Google Drive** and **OneDrive**, both of which offer robust storage capabilities and seamless integration with many productivity tools. Slack has embraced this trend by enabling integrations with these platforms, allowing teams to easily share files, collaborate in real-time, and ensure that everyone has access to the most up-to-date documents.

In this section, we will explore how to integrate Slack with both Google Drive and OneDrive, the benefits of these integrations, and how they can enhance your team's collaboration.

Why Integrate Slack with Google Drive and OneDrive?

Before diving into the specifics of the integration process, it's essential to understand why integrating Slack with cloud storage platforms like Google Drive and OneDrive is a smart choice.

1. **Centralized Collaboration**: By connecting your Slack workspace with these cloud storage solutions, you centralize all your files and discussions in one place. Whether it's sharing a file in a Slack channel or discussing a document during a call, everything is organized and accessible in Slack.

2. **Real-Time Editing**: Both Google Drive and OneDrive offer real-time document editing, allowing multiple team members to work on the same file simultaneously. This is particularly valuable for collaborative projects, as it ensures that everyone is always on the same page, literally and figuratively.

3. **Seamless File Sharing**: Integrating these platforms with Slack makes file sharing quick and effortless. You no longer need to download files, email them, or upload them to a separate platform. Instead, you can share files directly within Slack, reducing the number of steps and saving time.

4. **Efficient Version Control**: With integrated cloud storage, version control becomes much easier. Any changes made to files are automatically saved and updated, so you don't have to worry about managing multiple versions of a document. Whether using Google Docs, Sheets, or OneDrive's Office documents, the latest version is always readily available to the team.

Integrating Google Drive with Slack

Google Drive is one of the most popular cloud storage solutions, and Slack's integration with Google Drive makes it easy to share files, collaborate on documents, and stay organized. Here's how you can integrate Google Drive with your Slack workspace:

Step 1: Add Google Drive to Slack

To integrate Google Drive with Slack, follow these steps:

1. **Go to the Slack App Directory**: In Slack, click on the "Apps" button in the left sidebar, then search for "Google Drive."

2. **Install the Google Drive App**: Click on the "Google Drive" app in the search results, then click the "Add to Slack" button. You'll be prompted to authorize the connection.

3. **Connect Your Google Account**: Once you click the "Add to Slack" button, Slack will ask you to sign in to your Google account. Follow the prompts to log in and allow Slack access to your Google Drive.

4. **Grant Permissions**: After signing in, you'll be asked to grant permissions for Slack to interact with your Google Drive account. This typically includes access to your Google Docs, Sheets, and other files stored in Google Drive.

Step 2: Share Google Drive Files in Slack

Once the integration is set up, sharing files from Google Drive into Slack is a breeze. Here's how:

1. **Choose a File from Google Drive**: In Google Drive, select the file you want to share.

2. **Copy the File's Link**: Right-click on the file, click on "Get link," and choose the link sharing settings. Make sure the file is set to "Anyone with the link" if you want to allow easy sharing within Slack.

3. **Paste the Link in Slack**: Go to the Slack channel or direct message where you want to share the file, and paste the link directly into the message field.

4. **Preview and Interact with the File**: Once the file is shared in Slack, team members can click the link to open the file in Google Drive. Slack will generate a preview of the document, so users can see a thumbnail of the file right in the conversation. You can also comment on the file, tag team members, and collaborate directly within Slack.

Step 3: Collaborating on Google Drive Files within Slack

Beyond sharing files, Slack's integration with Google Drive allows for deeper collaboration:

- **Real-Time Editing**: When a team member clicks the file link, they can open the document in Google Drive and make real-time changes. The changes are instantly visible to all collaborators, and notifications about those changes can be seen in Slack.

- **Commenting in Slack**: Slack allows you to comment directly on shared files in Slack. By typing "/drive" followed by your message, you can add comments to the document, tag team members, and discuss the file without leaving Slack.

- **Linking Slack Messages to Files**: You can link messages in Slack directly to files in Google Drive. This helps contextualize discussions and makes it easier for team members to locate relevant files when reviewing past conversations.

Integrating OneDrive with Slack

OneDrive, a cloud storage service from Microsoft, is another powerful tool for storing and sharing files. Just like with Google Drive, integrating OneDrive with Slack can significantly enhance your team's productivity. Here's how to integrate OneDrive with Slack:

Step 1: Add OneDrive to Slack

1. **Visit the Slack App Directory**: Click on "Apps" in the Slack sidebar and search for "OneDrive."

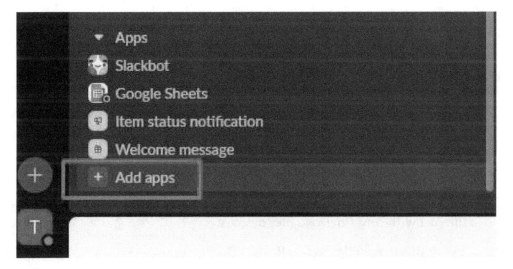

2. **Install the OneDrive App**: Select the OneDrive app and click "Add to Slack."

3. **Sign in to Your Microsoft Account**: Once prompted, sign in with your Microsoft account to allow Slack to access your OneDrive files.

4. **Grant Permissions**: Like Google Drive, you'll be asked to grant Slack permission to access your OneDrive account. These permissions allow Slack to share and interact with your OneDrive files directly.

Step 2: Share OneDrive Files in Slack

Sharing files from OneDrive into Slack is easy:

1. **Select the File in OneDrive**: Choose the file you wish to share in OneDrive.

2. **Copy the Shareable Link**: Right-click on the file and select "Copy link" to generate a shareable link.

3. **Post the Link in Slack**: Paste the link in a Slack channel or direct message. Just like Google Drive, Slack will generate a preview of the file, making it easy for your team to see the file without opening it in OneDrive.

Step 3: Collaborating on OneDrive Files in Slack

With OneDrive integration, you can also collaborate effectively:

- **Real-Time Editing**: When you share a document from OneDrive, any collaborator with access to the file can edit it in real-time using Microsoft Office Online, such as Word, Excel, or PowerPoint. All changes will be reflected immediately across all devices.

- **Comments and Feedback**: Slack enables team members to comment on OneDrive files within Slack. This provides a streamlined way for teams to communicate about a file without switching between multiple apps.

- **Search and Organize Files**: Searching for OneDrive files is just as easy as with Google Drive. You can search for shared documents or find recent files quickly within Slack, keeping everything organized and easily accessible.

Best Practices for Using Google Drive and OneDrive with Slack

To get the most out of these integrations, it's essential to implement a few best practices:

1. **Organize Files with Channels**: Create dedicated channels for specific projects or teams. This will help keep file sharing and conversations in one place, making it easier to find files when you need them.

2. **Set Clear Permissions**: Both Google Drive and OneDrive allow you to control who can view or edit your files. Make sure to set appropriate permissions for each file you share, especially if it contains sensitive information. Avoid setting files to "Anyone with the link" unless necessary.

3. **Use Slack's Search Function**: With Google Drive and OneDrive integrated, you can use Slack's powerful search function to find shared files quickly. Searching for file names, keywords, or even comments can help you locate files within seconds.

4. **Keep Files Up-to-Date**: Make sure to regularly update your shared documents to reflect the latest changes. This ensures that all team members are working from the most recent version, reducing confusion and errors.

5. **Encourage Collaboration**: Use Slack to foster collaboration around shared documents. Whether it's brainstorming in a channel or commenting on a document, Slack's features help teams stay aligned and productive.

6. **Automate with Slack Workflows**: If your team regularly works with files from Google Drive or OneDrive, consider setting up automated workflows to streamline file-sharing processes. For example, you could set up a workflow to automatically

share a file in Slack whenever a document is added to a specific folder in OneDrive or Google Drive.

Conclusion

Integrating Slack with Google Drive and OneDrive offers a powerful combination of cloud storage and team collaboration. By streamlining file sharing, enhancing collaboration, and keeping everything organized, these integrations can help your team work more efficiently and productively. Whether you're working with Google Docs, Office files, or a mix of both, Slack's seamless integration with these platforms makes it easier than ever to share, edit, and discuss files in real time.

By following best practices for managing file sharing and collaborating effectively, you can unlock the full potential of Slack's integrations with Google Drive and OneDrive, helping your team work smarter, not harder.

3.1.3 Managing File Permissions and Downloads

Managing File Permissions and Downloads in Slack

Slack is an essential tool for collaboration, and one of its standout features is its ability to handle file sharing seamlessly. Whether it's documents, images, videos, or spreadsheets, Slack allows teams to share files in various formats instantly. However, managing the permissions for these files and controlling their downloads is crucial, especially when handling sensitive information. This section will walk you through the key strategies for managing file permissions and downloads in Slack to ensure that your team remains organized and secure while collaborating effectively.

Why Managing File Permissions and Downloads Matters

When files are shared within Slack, they're typically available for members of the relevant channels or direct message (DM) threads to view and interact with. However, not all team members need the same level of access to these files. Some documents might require restricted access due to confidential information, while others might be open for everyone's editing and collaboration. Thus, understanding how to manage permissions is not only essential for maintaining security but also for ensuring the right people have the right level of access to the necessary resources.

Moreover, downloading files—especially large ones—can consume bandwidth, and unnecessary downloads could lead to clutter in the workspace or on personal devices. Efficient management of file downloads allows teams to prevent clutter and ensure that files are only downloaded when truly needed, optimizing both workflow and device storage.

File Permissions in Slack: How to Set Them

Slack offers various levels of file access control, allowing you to decide who can view, edit, or share the files you post in your channels or DMs. Here's a breakdown of how you can control these permissions:

1. Who Can See and Share Files in a Channel

The first layer of file permissions comes from the channel settings. When you upload a file to a public channel, everyone in that channel can view, comment on, and even share the file with others (depending on the workspace's settings). However, with private channels or direct messages, file permissions are automatically restricted to the members of those conversations. Here's how to manage file sharing:

- **Public Channels**: Files uploaded in public channels can be seen and shared by all members of that channel. While this ensures collaboration, it also means that sensitive files can easily be spread across the workspace. If you wish to limit access, you may consider uploading such files to a private channel or a DM.

- **Private Channels**: Files uploaded to private channels are accessible only to the members of those channels. This offers more control over who can access files, but it also means that file sharing needs to be carefully managed within those groups.

- **Direct Messages (DMs)**: Files shared in DMs are only accessible by the individuals involved in that conversation. This is the most restrictive setting, but it's useful for sharing sensitive or personal information. However, keep in mind that files shared in DMs are still subject to the same permission management for other Slack features.

2. Restricting File Downloads for Security

While Slack does not currently allow you to prevent users from downloading files in public channels, it does offer some control in the form of restricting file sharing. If you are using Slack's enterprise or business plan, you can implement more stringent controls regarding file sharing and downloading. Here are some specific features that help limit who can download files:

- **View-Only Mode for Files**: For those using Slack's enterprise grid, workspace admins can restrict members to "view-only" permissions for files that have been uploaded. This means users can view the file, but they won't be able to download or edit it. For sensitive files such as HR documents, strategic plans, or other internal resources, view-only permissions prevent accidental leaks or unauthorized sharing.

- **Shared Channels and Workspaces**: Slack's shared channels and cross-workspace features provide the opportunity to share files across different teams or organizations. However, file sharing can be customized so that only specific members or teams can download the file. This way, teams can collaborate without the risk of external parties downloading sensitive files.

- **Download Restrictions on External Files**: If you're integrating Slack with third-party apps like Google Drive or Dropbox, you can control the download permissions at the source file level. For example, in Google Drive, you can enable settings to restrict downloads, which will apply to files shared via Slack, ensuring that no one can download files without the appropriate permissions.

Using Slack's File Management Tools for Better Control

While managing file permissions is crucial, efficiently managing files within Slack is equally important. Slack provides several tools that allow you to better organize and control your files.

1. Pinning Files to Channels for Easy Access

Files pinned to channels act as bookmarks, providing easy access to important resources that everyone in the channel needs to refer back to. By pinning important files such as project documents, company policies, or reports, you ensure that they're easily accessible but not necessarily downloaded by all members unless required.

To pin a file, simply hover over the file in the channel, click on the "More Actions" button (three dots), and select "Pin to channel." This action helps organize the workspace by highlighting key documents without cluttering the channel with too many file uploads.

2. Searching for Files Within Slack

Slack's powerful search function allows you to find files quickly, whether by file type, keyword, or even file owner. For example, you can search for "type:pdf" to filter all PDF files shared within a channel, or search by keywords to find the document you're looking for. This is particularly helpful when you're working in teams and have several files shared daily.

Moreover, if files are organized into specific channels, it's easier to search within those contexts, and Slack will allow you to see file previews, download options, and related messages.

3. File Organization Using Folders and Directories

While Slack does not offer a built-in file folder system (like a traditional file management system), you can organize files more effectively using integrations. For example, Slack integrates seamlessly with Google Drive and OneDrive, enabling you to access these platforms' file management features directly from within Slack. Files shared from these platforms retain their organizational structure, making it easier to manage large sets of documents.

By integrating Slack with cloud storage services, users can continue working within Slack while having access to a more robust file storage solution. For instance, you can directly manage the file permissions on Google Drive or OneDrive to control access to files shared via Slack.

Best Practices for Managing Files in Slack

To ensure that your workspace is efficient and secure, it's important to follow best practices for managing file permissions and downloads. Here are some key tips:

1. Educate Team Members About File Permissions

One of the most critical aspects of managing file permissions is ensuring that everyone in the workspace understands how to use Slack's file-sharing features responsibly. This can be achieved by educating team members about the importance of privacy, the risks associated with unauthorized downloads, and the specific file-sharing policies of your organization.

2. Keep Files Organized by Purpose and Relevance

Slack workspaces can quickly become cluttered with files. To avoid this, create clear guidelines for what types of files should be shared in which channels. For example, administrative documents might be better suited to private channels or DMs, while general team updates can be shared in public channels.

Additionally, encourage the use of the "pinning" feature for high-priority documents, and make use of Slack's search and file management features to stay organized.

3. Use Slack's Advanced Features for Enterprise Clients

If your company uses Slack's Enterprise Grid, you can take advantage of advanced features, such as enhanced file permissions and the ability to audit file activity. These enterprise-level tools provide admins with greater control over how files are shared and downloaded across teams, ensuring that only authorized personnel have access to sensitive information.

Conclusion

Managing file permissions and downloads in Slack is an essential practice for ensuring that sensitive documents are protected while maintaining efficient workflows. By understanding and implementing the tools Slack provides for file sharing, permissions, and downloads, teams can collaborate more securely and effectively. Whether using basic settings for file access or integrating with external tools like Google Drive and OneDrive, Slack offers a range of options that help users control how their files are shared, downloaded, and accessed.

Remember, a well-managed file-sharing system can significantly enhance your team's productivity while keeping your workspace organized and secure. By following these best practices and using Slack's advanced features, you can ensure that your team works smarter and more securely in the digital workspace.

3.2 Using Slack Integrations and Bots

3.2.1 Connecting Third-Party Apps (Trello, Zoom, Asana, etc.)

In today's fast-paced and highly collaborative work environment, efficiency is key. Slack, with its powerful integrations, enables teams to connect their existing tools and streamline workflows into one cohesive platform. By connecting third-party apps to Slack, teams can communicate more effectively, stay organized, and collaborate seamlessly without having to jump between multiple platforms. This section will dive deep into how to integrate third-party apps like **Trello**, **Zoom**, **Asana**, and many others with Slack.

Why Integrating Third-Party Apps with Slack is Beneficial

Before we explore the specifics of connecting popular third-party apps, it's important to understand why this integration is so essential for modern-day teams. Slack's ability to integrate with various external tools not only centralizes communication but also simplifies the process of accessing important data. Here's why integrating apps is advantageous:

1. **Centralized Communication**: With all your tools in one place, you can avoid the back-and-forth between different platforms. Everything from task management to video calls can be initiated and tracked in Slack.

2. **Enhanced Collaboration**: Integrations bring in the relevant information from other tools directly into Slack, ensuring everyone stays up-to-date and has access to the same data, improving teamwork and collaboration.

3. **Increased Productivity**: Having notifications, updates, and key information within Slack prevents you from constantly switching between applications, which can interrupt your flow and reduce focus. This minimizes task-switching and boosts productivity.

4. **Real-Time Updates**: By connecting apps, you can receive instant notifications or updates, whether it's a new comment on a Trello card, a Zoom meeting invite, or a new task assigned in Asana. These real-time updates ensure that no information slips through the cracks.

5. **Customization and Automation**: Slack's integrations allow teams to customize the flow of information and automate repetitive tasks. For example, you can set up

rules to send messages when a task is completed in Trello, or automatically create a meeting summary after a Zoom call ends.

Now, let's dive into how to connect some of the most popular third-party apps with Slack, focusing on **Trello**, **Zoom**, and **Asana**.

1. Connecting Trello with Slack

Trello is one of the most widely used project management tools. It allows teams to organize tasks and projects visually on boards. Integrating Trello with Slack enhances the visibility of project updates and simplifies task management. Here's how you can connect Trello to Slack and leverage its functionalities:

Step 1: Install the Trello App in Slack

To connect Trello with Slack, you first need to install the Trello app from the Slack App Directory:

1. Go to the **Slack App Directory** and search for "Trello."

2. Click the **Add to Slack** button.

3. Sign in to your Trello account and grant Slack permission to access your boards.

Step 2: Link Trello Boards to Slack Channels

Once Trello is installed, you can link your Trello boards to specific Slack channels to keep your team updated:

1. In the Slack channel where you want Trello updates to appear, type /trello link.

2. Select the board you want to connect, and Slack will start receiving updates from Trello.

Step 3: Using Trello Notifications in Slack

After the integration is complete, Slack will send real-time notifications about any activity related to the linked board. These notifications can include:

- **Card updates**: When a team member adds a comment or changes the due date on a Trello card.

- **New cards or lists**: Notifications when new cards or lists are created in Trello.

- **Due dates approaching**: A reminder in Slack when the due date for a Trello card is near.

Step 4: Managing Trello Cards from Slack

Beyond notifications, Slack allows you to manage Trello cards directly from the Slack interface. For example, you can:

- Create a new Trello card by typing /trello create.
- Assign cards to team members from within Slack.
- Move cards between lists without having to open Trello.

These actions streamline your workflow and minimize the time spent switching between apps.

---

2. Connecting Zoom with Slack

Zoom is an essential tool for virtual meetings and video calls, especially in remote work environments. Integrating Zoom with Slack allows you to schedule, start, and join Zoom meetings directly from Slack. Here's how to connect Zoom with Slack:

Step 1: Install the Zoom App in Slack

To connect Zoom with Slack, follow these steps:

1. Visit the **Slack App Directory** and search for "Zoom."
2. Click the **Add to Slack** button.
3. Follow the prompts to sign in to your Zoom account and authorize Slack to access your Zoom settings.

Step 2: Scheduling Zoom Meetings from Slack

Once Zoom is installed, you can schedule Zoom meetings directly from Slack. Simply:

1. Go to the channel where you want to schedule the meeting.
2. Type /zoom schedule to open the Zoom scheduler.
3. Select the meeting date, time, and invite participants. Zoom will send an invitation and link to the Slack channel.

Step 3: Starting a Zoom Meeting in Slack

In addition to scheduling meetings, you can start an instant Zoom meeting directly from Slack. Here's how:

1. Type /zoom in any Slack channel or direct message to instantly start a meeting.

2. Slack will generate a meeting link and automatically share it with the participants in the channel or direct message.

Step 4: Joining a Zoom Meeting from Slack

If you receive a Zoom meeting invitation in Slack, you can join the meeting with a single click. Slack will display a Zoom link, and all you need to do is click on it to join the meeting.

Step 5: Zoom Notifications in Slack

Slack can also notify you when a scheduled Zoom meeting is about to begin. You'll receive reminders and direct links to the meeting in the Slack channel or private message.

---

3. Connecting Asana with Slack

Asana is a powerful task and project management tool that allows teams to organize work and track progress. By integrating Asana with Slack, you can bring task updates, project timelines, and team collaboration into your Slack workspace. Here's how you can connect Asana to Slack:

Step 1: Install the Asana App in Slack

To connect Asana with Slack:

1. Go to the **Slack App Directory** and search for "Asana."

2. Click the **Add to Slack** button.

3. Sign in to your Asana account and allow Slack to access your Asana projects and tasks.

Step 2: Linking Asana Projects to Slack Channels

Once Asana is integrated, you can link specific Asana projects to Slack channels. This allows all team members to receive updates about project tasks and milestones directly in the Slack channel. To link a project:

1. In your Slack channel, type /asana link to connect an Asana project.

2. Choose the Asana project you want to link to the channel.

Step 3: Task and Project Updates in Slack

Asana will send notifications to Slack when tasks are updated. These notifications can include:

- Task assignments.

- Due date changes.

- New comments and attachments.

You can also create tasks directly from Slack by typing /asana create and entering the task details.

Step 4: Managing Tasks from Slack

Slack also allows you to complete or update tasks without opening Asana. You can:

- Mark tasks as complete.

- Update task details such as assignees, due dates, and comments.

- Attach files from Slack directly to Asana tasks.

This integration ensures that your team stays on top of tasks and deadlines without leaving the Slack interface.

Additional Third-Party App Integrations

While **Trello**, **Zoom**, and **Asana** are among the most popular integrations, Slack offers many other useful integrations, such as:

- **Google Drive**: Share, store, and manage files from Google Drive directly in Slack.

- **GitHub**: Get notifications on commits, pull requests, and issues directly in your Slack channels.

- **Salesforce**: View and update customer data and opportunities without leaving Slack.

- **Monday.com**: Keep your team's workflows and task management in sync within Slack.

Conclusion

Integrating third-party apps into Slack significantly enhances productivity and streamlines workflows. Whether you're managing projects in **Trello**, scheduling meetings in **Zoom**, or tracking tasks in **Asana**, Slack brings all your essential tools together in one convenient place. The ability to receive real-time updates, automate tasks, and collaborate with ease makes Slack not just a communication tool, but a central hub for your team's work.

By integrating these and other tools, you create a seamless, interconnected workflow that saves time, reduces distractions, and boosts overall team productivity. The power of Slack integrations lies in its flexibility and the ability to connect to a wide range of apps that cater to your team's specific needs.

3.2.2 Automating Tasks with Slack Bots

Slack bots are an essential tool for automating repetitive tasks, reducing manual effort, and improving overall productivity. By integrating bots into your Slack workspace, you can streamline workflows, manage tasks more efficiently, and create a more organized and responsive team environment. This section will guide you through the concept of Slack bots, their functionality, and how to automate tasks using Slack bots to save time and increase efficiency.

What are Slack Bots?

Slack bots are automated programs that can perform a wide variety of functions within Slack channels and direct messages. They work by executing tasks or responding to specific commands based on predefined criteria. Bots can be used to automate both simple and complex tasks, ranging from setting reminders and responding to messages to integrating with external services and automating entire workflows.

These bots can either be built by Slack, available through third-party integrations, or developed custom-built for your workspace needs. Many bots are capable of integrating with other productivity tools, like project management software, calendars, and communication tools, which makes them incredibly powerful for streamlining business processes and daily operations.

Why Use Slack Bots for Task Automation?

Slack bots help automate repetitive tasks, saving you time and reducing the risk of errors. Instead of manually handling various processes, you can set bots to perform tasks like:

- **Task Scheduling**: Automating the scheduling of recurring meetings, reminders, and follow-ups.

- **Data Collection**: Collecting and organizing information from team members and external applications.

- **Notifications and Alerts**: Automatically sending notifications when certain conditions are met, such as when a project deadline is approaching or a new file is uploaded.

- **Customer Support**: Providing instant responses to frequently asked questions or resolving common issues.

By automating tasks, bots can also reduce the workload on team members, allowing them to focus on more important or complex work.

Setting Up Bots in Slack

Before you can begin automating tasks, you need to set up Slack bots in your workspace. Fortunately, Slack provides an easy-to-use interface for both installing and managing bots. Here's how to get started:

1. Choosing the Right Bot for Your Needs

- **Slack's Built-in Bots**: Slack offers a variety of built-in bots, like the Slackbot, which can handle simple tasks like answering FAQs and reminding team members about deadlines.

- **Third-Party Bots**: You can find bots created by third-party developers that integrate with popular tools such as Google Drive, Asana, and Trello. These bots often perform specific tasks that are directly related to the app they integrate with.

- **Custom Bots**: If you have unique needs, you can build your own Slack bot using the Slack API. Custom bots can be programmed to do anything you need, from interacting with databases to connecting Slack with internal tools and services.

2. Installing Bots

To install a bot in Slack, follow these steps:

1. **Visit the Slack App Directory**: Open the Slack App Directory and search for the bot you want to install.

2. **Install the Bot**: Once you find the bot, click "Add to Slack" and follow the instructions to complete the installation. You may need to authenticate the bot or connect it with external services.

3. **Configure the Bot**: After installation, you'll often be prompted to configure the bot settings to tailor it to your workspace needs. You might need to specify which channels the bot will operate in, the types of tasks it will handle, and what permissions it needs.

3. Managing and Customizing Bots

After installing a bot, you can manage its settings through the Slack interface:

- **Access the Bot Settings**: Navigate to the "Apps" section of Slack, find the bot, and click on "Settings" to adjust its preferences.

- **Custom Commands**: Many bots allow you to customize commands or set up triggers for specific actions. You can create workflows that trigger the bot to send messages, set reminders, or interact with other apps when certain conditions are met.

Examples of Automating Tasks with Slack Bots

Let's explore some examples of how Slack bots can automate tasks and improve productivity within your organization.

1. Automating Reminders and Follow-ups

Using Slack bots like **Reminder Bot**, you can automate reminders and follow-up messages to ensure that deadlines are met and tasks are completed on time. For example, you can set the bot to send reminders to your team every Monday morning about upcoming tasks or deadlines, or to alert individuals if they haven't responded to a message or request after a set period of time.

How it Works:

- Use the command /remind followed by the task and the time you want to set the reminder.

- Slackbot will automatically send reminders based on the schedule you set.

This is useful for regular check-ins, project timelines, or personal reminders for team members.

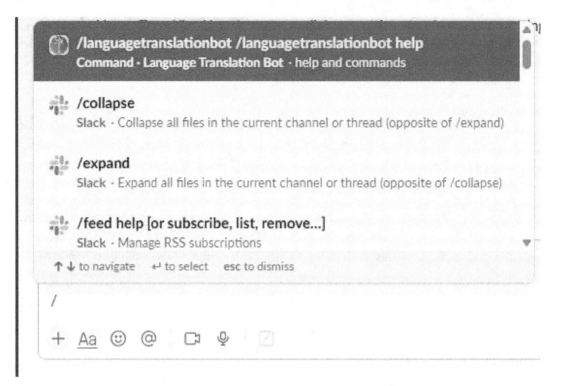

2. Automating Data Collection

SurveyBot or **Polly** are bots that allow teams to automate data collection and feedback. These bots can be set up to ask team members questions or gather feedback directly in Slack, and the responses are automatically collated.

How it Works:

- A team leader or manager creates a survey using the bot interface.

- The bot sends the survey to a specified channel or directly to team members.

- Responses are automatically collected and shared with the user who set up the survey, allowing for quick insights without manual data gathering.

This is a great way to automate employee engagement surveys, quick feedback loops, or project evaluations.

3. Managing Support and Helpdesk Requests

Bots like **Halp** allow teams to automate internal helpdesk requests. Team members can submit requests through a simple Slack message, and the bot can automatically route the requests to the appropriate person or team.

How it Works:

- Team members can submit their requests directly in Slack, for example by using a command like /help.

- The bot generates a ticket and assigns it to the relevant team or individual, keeping track of the request's progress.

- Slack will send automatic updates and notifications to both the requester and the responder, ensuring that everyone stays in the loop.

This kind of automation reduces the manual work of managing helpdesk systems, ensuring requests are handled promptly and efficiently.

4. Automating Task Management and Project Updates

If you're using project management tools like **Trello**, **Asana**, or **Jira**, you can automate the process of creating and updating tasks directly from Slack using the respective bots for these tools. These bots can monitor project progress, assign tasks, and even notify team members when a task is approaching its due date.

How it Works:

- A bot like **Trello Bot** can be set up to send notifications in Slack whenever there's an update on a card in your Trello board.

- You can create and update tasks directly from Slack, and the bot will sync those changes with your project management tool.

Automating project updates and task assignments helps teams stay organized without needing to constantly switch between different platforms.

5. Automating Routine Administrative Tasks

If you frequently have to perform routine administrative tasks like organizing meetings or setting up events, bots like **Meekan** can automate the scheduling process. Meekan uses AI to find the best time for meetings based on participants' availability.

How it Works:

- Simply tell Meekan your meeting requirements.

- The bot will analyze everyone's calendars, find suitable times, and automatically schedule the meeting.

- It will even send reminders and adjust the meeting time if there are any changes.

This kind of bot reduces the back-and-forth that often happens when scheduling meetings, allowing your team to focus on more important tasks.

Best Practices for Automating Tasks with Slack Bots

To get the most out of Slack bots, consider these best practices:

1. Start Simple

Begin with simple automation tasks and gradually expand. Don't overload your team with too many bots all at once. Start by automating one or two tasks, and then evaluate how the bots perform.

2. Integrate with Existing Tools

Slack bots work best when they are integrated with the tools your team already uses. For example, if your team uses **Google Drive**, install the Google Drive bot. This will allow for seamless file sharing and integration directly within Slack.

3. Monitor and Optimize

As with any automation tool, it's important to monitor how well the bots are performing. Are they saving time? Are team members interacting with them effectively? If certain bots aren't adding value, consider replacing or reconfiguring them.

4. Maintain a Balance

While automation is a powerful tool, don't forget the importance of human interaction. Bots should be used to handle routine tasks, but there will always be times when direct human interaction is necessary. Ensure that bots complement rather than replace team communication.

Conclusion

Slack bots are a game-changer when it comes to automating tasks and improving efficiency within your workspace. By integrating bots for reminders, data collection, project management, and communication, you can free up time for your team to focus on more valuable tasks. As Slack continues to grow and introduce new features, bots will only become more sophisticated, offering even greater opportunities for automation and productivity.

By using Slack bots wisely and strategically, you can create a smoother, more efficient workflow that boosts your team's productivity and optimizes collaboration across the board.

3.2.3 Setting Up Workflow Builder for Automation

Automation is one of the most powerful ways to increase efficiency and streamline work processes in Slack. Slack's **Workflow Builder** allows users to create automated workflows that handle repetitive tasks, gather information, and improve team communication. Whether you're automating a simple request form or integrating with third-party tools, Workflow Builder makes Slack a more dynamic and efficient workspace.

This section will guide you through setting up Workflow Builder, explain its key features, and provide examples of workflows that can improve your productivity.

Understanding Slack Workflow Builder

Workflow Builder is a built-in tool in Slack that allows users to automate tasks without needing to write any code. Workflows can be triggered by specific actions, such as a new message in a channel, a button click, or a form submission. Once triggered, the workflow follows a series of predefined steps, such as sending messages, collecting responses, or interacting with external applications.

Benefits of Using Workflow Builder

- **Time-Saving Automation**: Reduces manual work by automating repetitive tasks.

- **Consistency in Processes**: Ensures that tasks and communications follow a standardized process.

- **Improved Collaboration**: Helps teams work together more effectively by reducing communication delays.

- **No Coding Required**: Allows non-technical users to create automated processes with a simple interface.

How to Access and Use Workflow Builder

Before creating your first workflow, you need to access the **Workflow Builder** tool.

Step 1: Open Workflow Builder

1. Click on your workspace name at the top left of Slack.

2. Select **Tools & Settings > Workflow Builder**.

3. Click **Create a Workflow** to start building your automation.

Publishing and creating workflows is a paid feature, available with your free trial through May 6th. Learn more

Untitled Workflow
A brand new workflow

Never published   Finish Up   ...

Choose an event to start the workflow, and then add the steps that will follow.

Start the workflow...

⚡ Choose an event

Then, do these things

+ Add steps

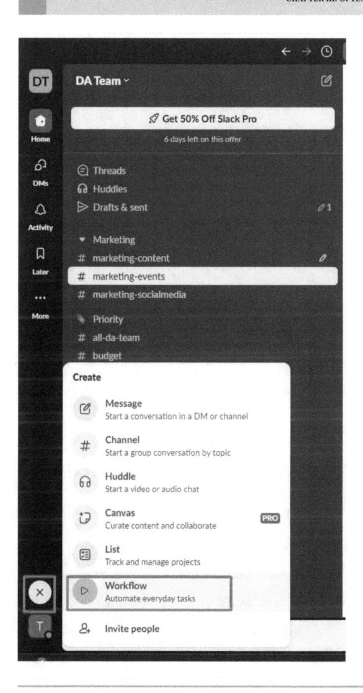

Creating a New Workflow

When setting up a workflow, you need to define three key components:

1. **Trigger** – The event that starts the workflow.

2. **Actions** – The steps the workflow performs.

3. **Outputs** – The final result or data collected by the workflow.

Step 1: Choose a Trigger

Triggers determine how a workflow starts. Slack offers different types of triggers:

- **Shortcut Trigger**: A workflow starts when a user manually selects it from the shortcut menu.

- **New Channel Message Trigger**: The workflow runs when a message containing specific keywords is posted.

- **Emoji Reaction Trigger**: Users trigger the workflow by reacting to a message with a specific emoji.

- **Scheduled Trigger**: The workflow runs at a specific time or frequency.

- **Webhook Trigger**: The workflow is triggered by an external system sending a request to Slack.

Step 2: Add Actions

Once you have chosen a trigger, you need to define the actions that will take place. Some common actions include:

- **Sending a Message**: The workflow posts a message in a channel or direct message.

- **Asking for Input**: The workflow collects responses from users via a form.

- **Creating a Reminder**: The workflow automatically reminds users about tasks.

- **Interacting with Third-Party Apps**: The workflow integrates with services like Google Drive, Trello, or Asana.

Step 3: Customize Your Workflow Steps

Each action in the workflow can be customized with dynamic placeholders. For example, if you are sending a message, you can insert:

- The **user's name** who triggered the workflow.

- A **timestamp** of when the workflow was started.

- Any **collected input** from a previous step.

Step 4: Test and Publish Your Workflow

1. Click **Preview** to test your workflow.

2. Make any necessary adjustments.

3. Click **Publish** to make the workflow available to your team.

Examples of Useful Slack Workflows

1. Onboarding New Employees

When a new employee joins, a workflow can automatically:

- Send them a welcome message.

- Add them to relevant Slack channels.

- Assign them a checklist of tasks to complete.

2. Automating Stand-Up Meetings

A daily stand-up workflow can:

- Send a message to team members every morning asking for their updates.

- Collect responses in a shared Slack channel.

- Notify managers if someone needs assistance.

3. Handling IT Support Requests

An IT support workflow can:

- Allow employees to submit IT issues using a form.

- Automatically notify the IT team in a designated channel.

- Assign the issue to the next available IT staff member.

4. Managing Approvals and Requests

A workflow for expense approvals can:

- Let employees submit expense reports in Slack.

- Notify managers for approval.

- Automatically update a tracking spreadsheet when an expense is approved.

Advanced Workflow Builder Features

1. Using Conditional Logic

Some workflows may need **if-then** logic. For example:

- If an employee selects "Urgent" in a request form, the message is sent immediately to a manager.

- If the request is "Low Priority," it is added to a queue instead.

2. Integrating with External Tools

Slack Workflows can integrate with:

- **Google Sheets** (to store collected data).

- **Jira or Trello** (to create and update tasks).

- **Zapier** (to connect with hundreds of other apps).

3. Setting Up Webhook Triggers

Advanced users can use **webhooks** to trigger workflows from an external system. For example, a customer service system can send a webhook request to Slack when a new support ticket is created.

Best Practices for Using Workflow Builder

- **Keep Workflows Simple**: Avoid overcomplicating automation.

- **Use Clear Messages**: Ensure that automated messages are easy to understand.

- **Test Before Publishing**: Always test your workflows before making them live.

- **Monitor and Optimize**: Regularly review your workflows to see if they need improvements.

Final Thoughts

Slack's **Workflow Builder** is a game-changer for teams looking to improve efficiency and collaboration. By automating repetitive tasks, teams can save time, reduce errors, and focus on more strategic work. Whether you're setting up basic message notifications or integrating Slack with third-party tools, Workflow Builder makes automation accessible to everyone—without requiring technical expertise.

By following the steps and best practices outlined in this section, you can create powerful workflows that help your team **work smarter, not harder** with Slack.

3.3 Slack Calls and Huddles

3.3.1 Starting and Managing Voice & Video Calls

Slack isn't just about messaging—it's also a powerful tool for voice and video communication. Whether you need a quick one-on-one call, a team meeting, or a spontaneous check-in, Slack's voice and video call features make it easy to connect without switching to another platform.

In this section, we'll explore:

- The types of calls available in Slack

- How to start and manage voice and video calls

- The best practices for using Slack calls effectively

Understanding Slack Calls

Slack's built-in voice and video call features allow users to communicate in real time without leaving the app. Calls can be initiated in direct messages (DMs), group DMs, and channels, making it easy to connect with colleagues quickly.

Slack provides two main ways to conduct calls:

1. **Slack Voice and Video Calls** – A standard call option available on paid plans.

2. **Slack Huddles** – A lightweight, always-on audio chat designed for quick discussions.

For voice and video calls, Slack integrates with third-party applications like Zoom, Microsoft Teams, and Google Meet for more advanced video conferencing needs. However, its built-in call feature is often sufficient for small meetings and one-on-one conversations.

Starting a Voice or Video Call in Slack

1. Starting a Call from a Direct Message (DM)

One of the easiest ways to initiate a voice or video call is through a direct message:

1. **Open Slack and navigate to a DM** – This can be with an individual or a group.

2. **Click on the phone or camera icon** at the top right of the DM window.

   o The 📞 phone icon starts a voice call.

   o The 🎥 camera icon starts a video call.

3. **Wait for the other participant(s) to join** – The recipient(s) will receive a notification.

Tip: If you're in a DM with multiple people, Slack will automatically create a group call when you initiate a call from that chat.

2. Starting a Call in a Slack Channel

Calls in channels are great for teams that need to discuss something with multiple members at once.

To start a call in a channel:

1. **Go to the desired channel** where you want to initiate the call.

2. **Type /call in the message bar and press enter** – Slack will start a call and notify channel members.

3. **Participants can join by clicking the call link** that appears in the channel.

Note: Not all team members in the channel will be automatically added to the call. They must click on the call link to join.

3. Using the Call Interface

Once a call starts, you'll see Slack's call interface, which includes:

- **Mute/Unmute button** – Useful for reducing background noise.

- **Camera toggle** – Switch between voice-only or video mode.

- **Screen sharing** – Share your screen to present documents or collaborate visually.

- **End call button** – Click this when the call is over.

Pro Tip: If you're using Slack on mobile, the interface may look slightly different, but the core functionalities remain the same.

Managing Calls Effectively

Adding More Participants to a Call

During a call, you may want to add additional team members. Here's how:

1. **Click the "Invite People" button** in the call interface.
2. **Search for and select the names** of the colleagues you want to invite.
3. **They will receive an invitation** to join the call.

This feature is especially useful when conversations naturally expand beyond the initial participants.

Screen Sharing in Slack Calls

One of the most powerful collaboration tools in Slack calls is **screen sharing**. This is particularly useful for:

- Presenting a document
- Walking a teammate through a task
- Troubleshooting issues remotely

To share your screen:

1. Click the "Share Screen" button in the call interface.
2. Select which screen or window you want to share.
3. Your team members will now see your screen in real-time.

While sharing, you can still talk and interact as usual. Slack also allows participants to annotate or comment while someone is sharing their screen.

Tip: If you experience lag while sharing, try closing unnecessary applications to free up bandwidth.

Best Practices for Using Slack Calls

1. Optimize Your Audio and Video Settings

Before joining a call, make sure:

- Your microphone and speakers are working correctly.
- You're in a quiet environment to minimize background noise.
- Your camera is positioned well for video calls.

2. Use Headphones for Better Audio Quality

Using headphones or earbuds with a built-in microphone can:

- Reduce echo and feedback.
- Improve voice clarity.
- Minimize background noise.

3. Mute Yourself When Not Speaking

To avoid background noise disrupting the conversation:

- Use the **mute button** when you're not talking.
- Unmute only when you need to contribute.

4. Keep Calls Concise and Purposeful

Slack calls are designed for quick and efficient communication. To keep calls productive:

- Set an agenda before the call.
- Keep the discussion focused on key topics.
- Use follow-up messages in Slack to summarize action items.

5. Utilize Slack's Call Integration Features

Slack integrates with Zoom, Google Meet, and Microsoft Teams. If you need advanced video conferencing features, you can:

- Type /zoom or /meet in a channel to start a Zoom or Google Meet call.

- Use Slack's integration settings to link other video call tools.

Common Issues and Troubleshooting

Even though Slack calls are reliable, users might encounter some challenges. Here's how to fix common issues:

1. Call Not Connecting

- Check your internet connection.

- Restart Slack or try switching to a different network.

2. Poor Audio or Video Quality

- Close unnecessary applications that may be using bandwidth.

- Adjust your camera and microphone settings.

3. Screen Sharing Not Working

- Ensure you have the necessary permissions enabled (especially on Mac).

- Restart Slack and try again.

Conclusion

Slack calls and video chats provide an easy way to communicate with your team without switching between multiple applications. Whether you're using it for quick check-ins, troubleshooting sessions, or team meetings, mastering Slack calls can greatly enhance your productivity and team collaboration.

By following the best practices outlined above, you'll be able to use Slack's voice and video call features effectively, ensuring smooth and efficient communication in your workplace.

3.3.2 Using Slack Huddles for Quick Meetings

In today's fast-paced work environment, the ability to communicate effectively and efficiently is essential. Slack Huddles is a powerful feature designed to facilitate quick, informal audio conversations without the need for scheduling formal meetings. This section will explore how Slack Huddles work, when to use them, their key features, and best practices for making the most of them.

What is a Slack Huddle?

A **Slack Huddle** is an audio-first, lightweight meeting feature that allows team members to jump into a quick, spontaneous conversation directly within a Slack channel or direct message (DM). Unlike traditional video calls, Huddles are designed to be low-pressure, distraction-free, and efficient, making them ideal for rapid collaboration.

Huddles differ from Slack Calls in that they:

- Are audio-based by default (although screen sharing is available).

- Do not require scheduling—anyone can start a Huddle in a channel or DM.

- Encourage informal, quick conversations rather than structured meetings.

- Allow multiple participants to join and leave as needed.

When to Use Slack Huddles?

Slack Huddles are useful in various workplace scenarios, including:

1. **Quick Check-Ins** – When you need to touch base with a team member without drafting a long message.

2. **Brainstorming Sessions** – When you want a fluid, free-flowing discussion without the rigidity of a scheduled meeting.

3. **Troubleshooting Issues** – When written messages aren't enough to resolve a problem quickly.

4. **Clarifying Tasks** – When a task needs immediate clarification, and typing back-and-forth would take too long.

5. **Remote Team Connection** – For maintaining a sense of connection in hybrid or remote work environments.

If your discussion requires note-taking, detailed decision-making, or a structured agenda, a scheduled Slack Call or video meeting may be a better alternative.

How to Start a Slack Huddle

Slack makes it incredibly easy to start a Huddle. Here's how:

On Desktop:

1. Open the **Slack channel** or **DM** where you want to start the Huddle.

2. Look at the **bottom left corner** of the Slack window. Click the **headphones icon**.

3. The Huddle begins, and you'll see a small window pop up with participant icons.

4. Others in the channel or DM will receive a notification and can **click to join**.

On Mobile:

1. Open the **Slack app** on your mobile device.

2. Navigate to the **channel or DM** where you want to start a Huddle.

3. Tap the **headphones icon** in the top right corner.

4. The Huddle will start, and other participants can join in.

Once in a Huddle, you'll have access to various interactive features to enhance collaboration.

Key Features of Slack Huddles

Slack Huddles come with several useful features that improve the communication experience:

1. Audio-Only Conversations

- By default, Huddles are audio-only, reducing video fatigue and allowing participants to focus on the conversation rather than their appearance.

2. Live Captions

- Slack offers **live captions** for Huddles, making them more accessible for people with hearing impairments or those in noisy environments.

- Captions appear in real time and help participants follow the discussion more effectively.

3. Screen Sharing

- If needed, you can **share your screen** during a Huddle to illustrate a point, review a document, or collaborate visually.

- Unlike full video calls, screen sharing in Huddles is lightweight and designed for quick explanations.

4. Floating Huddle Window

- When using a desktop, Huddles open in a small, **movable** floating window, allowing you to navigate Slack without losing access to the conversation.

5. Join and Leave Flexibility

- Unlike traditional meetings, Huddles **do not require invites**. Anyone in the channel or DM can **join or leave freely**.

Best Practices for Using Slack Huddles Effectively

To ensure that Slack Huddles remain productive and beneficial, consider these best practices:

1. Keep It Short and Purposeful

- Huddles should be used for quick discussions, not lengthy meetings.

- If a Huddle is lasting too long, consider switching to a scheduled call or meeting.

2. Use Headphones for Better Audio Quality

- Background noise can be distracting. Using headphones with a built-in microphone improves audio clarity.

3. Announce the Huddle's Purpose

- Before starting a Huddle, send a quick message in the Slack channel explaining why you're starting it. Example:
  "Hey team, let's do a quick Huddle to finalize the marketing campaign details."

4. Enable Live Captions for Accessibility

- If your team includes members with hearing impairments or non-native English speakers, enabling live captions can improve comprehension.

5. Take Quick Notes or Summarize Key Points

- After the Huddle, drop a quick summary message in the Slack channel so that everyone stays aligned.

- Example:
  "Huddle recap: We agreed to launch the email campaign on Friday. Sarah will draft the final copy by Wednesday."

6. Leverage Screen Sharing for Visual Explanations

- If explaining something complex, quickly share your screen rather than trying to describe it verbally.

7. Be Mindful of Time Zones

- If working with remote teams, check the team's availability before starting a Huddle.

Comparing Slack Huddles vs. Slack Calls

Feature	Slack Huddles	Slack Calls
Audio-Only	Yes	Optional (Audio & Video)
Video Support	No	Yes
Live Captions	Yes	Yes
Screen Sharing	Yes	Yes
Scheduled	No	Yes

Feature	Slack Huddles	Slack Calls
Best Use Case	Quick, informal discussions	Formal meetings, presentations

While Slack Calls are better suited for structured video meetings, Huddles are ideal for fast, **unplanned conversations** that need immediate attention.

Conclusion: Making Slack Huddles a Part of Your Workflow

Slack Huddles are a **powerful tool** for fostering quick, effective communication without disrupting workflow. By using Huddles strategically, teams can:

- Reduce meeting fatigue by replacing unnecessary video calls.

- Encourage real-time collaboration without lengthy text exchanges.

- Stay connected in remote work environments through informal discussions.

To maximize the benefits of Slack Huddles, teams should adopt best practices, communicate efficiently, and integrate them seamlessly into daily workflows. Whether it's a quick check-in, a brainstorming session, or a problem-solving discussion, Slack Huddles provide a flexible, lightweight solution for modern teamwork.

3.3.3 Best Practices for Remote Collaboration

Remote collaboration has become an essential part of modern workplaces, and Slack is a powerful tool to keep teams connected, productive, and engaged. However, to make the most of Slack for remote work, teams need to follow best practices to ensure seamless communication, minimize misunderstandings, and maintain efficiency.

In this section, we will cover the best practices for using Slack effectively in remote collaboration, focusing on communication clarity, meeting efficiency, team engagement, and workflow automation.

---

1. Establish Clear Communication Guidelines

1.1 Use Clear and Concise Messaging

One of the biggest challenges in remote collaboration is the lack of face-to-face communication, which can lead to misunderstandings. To avoid this:

- Keep messages clear and to the point.

- Use bullet points or numbered lists when providing detailed instructions.

- If a message is too long, consider breaking it into multiple messages or summarizing key points at the beginning.

1.2 Use Threads for Organized Discussions

Without proper message organization, important discussions can get buried in busy Slack channels. Using threads effectively can help:

- Reply to messages in threads instead of the main channel to keep discussions focused.

- Tag relevant team members so they receive notifications.

- Summarize important points when concluding a thread.

1.3 Utilize @Mentions Properly

Tagging the right people ensures messages reach the intended audience without causing notification overload:

- Use @username for direct mentions.

- Use @channel to notify everyone in a channel (use sparingly).

- Use @here to notify only those who are currently active.

1.4 Set Expectations for Response Time

Since remote teams may work in different time zones, it is important to establish expectations for response times:

- Define working hours and expected reply times for different types of messages.

- Encourage team members to use status updates (e.g., "In a meeting", "Focusing", "Out for lunch") so others know their availability.

- Use Scheduled Messages in Slack to send messages at appropriate times.

2. Improve Meeting Efficiency with Slack Calls and Huddles

When to Use Slack Calls vs. Slack Huddles

Slack provides two primary options for voice and video communication:

Feature	Best for	Key Benefits
Slack Calls	Formal meetings, presentations, client discussions	Supports video, screen sharing, and recording
Slack Huddles	Quick check-ins, brainstorming sessions, informal discussions	Lightweight, audio-first, instant collaboration

Use Slack Huddles for quick decision-making and reserve Slack Calls for more structured meetings.

Minimize Meeting Overload

Remote teams often suffer from too many meetings, which can reduce productivity. Best practices to prevent this include:

- Use Slack messages for minor updates instead of scheduling unnecessary meetings.
- Encourage asynchronous communication, allowing team members to respond when they are available.
- Use Slack polls to gather input quickly instead of scheduling a call.

Prepare for Productive Virtual Meetings

For meetings that must happen, follow these best practices:

- Share an agenda in Slack before the meeting.
- Use Slack Reminders to notify participants of upcoming meetings.
- Assign a meeting facilitator to keep the discussion focused.
- Summarize key takeaways in Slack after the meeting.

3. Foster Team Engagement and Culture in Slack

3.1 Create Dedicated Social and Fun Channels

Building a strong remote work culture requires intentional effort. Slack can be used to create a sense of community by:

- Setting up social channels (e.g., #random, #watercooler, #fun-memes) to encourage casual conversations.

- Creating interest-based groups (e.g., #book-club, #fitness, #gaming).

- Using Slackbot reminders to prompt team members to share weekly wins, gratitude, or fun facts.

3.2 Encourage Recognition and Appreciation

Remote teams can sometimes feel disconnected, so it's important to recognize team members' efforts:

- Use custom emojis for team-specific recognition (e.g., 🎉 for achievements, 🌟 for exceptional work).

- Create a #kudos or #shoutout channel for team members to publicly recognize each other.

- Use Slack integrations like Bonusly or HeyTaco to gamify peer recognition.

3.3 Organize Virtual Team-Building Activities

Slack can be used to foster team bonding through remote-friendly activities:

- Host Slack trivia games using bots like Polly.

- Run "Ask Me Anything" (AMA) sessions with team leads.

- Organize Slack Donut meetings, where employees are randomly paired for casual chats.

4. Automate and Optimize Remote Workflows

4.1 Reduce Repetitive Tasks with Slack Integrations

Slack integrates with hundreds of apps to streamline remote work:

- Use Trello, Asana, or Monday.com integrations to track tasks without leaving Slack.

- Connect Google Calendar to receive meeting reminders.

- Automate workflows with Zapier or Slack Workflow Builder.

4.2 Set Up Automated Notifications

To ensure remote teams stay updated without excessive manual follow-ups:

- Set up automatic reports (e.g., daily stand-ups, sales updates) using Slack integrations.

- Configure alerts from project management tools (e.g., "New task assigned" notifications).

- Use Slackbot reminders for recurring tasks (e.g., "Submit weekly reports by Friday").

4.3 Balance Work and Well-Being

Working remotely can lead to burnout if boundaries are not maintained. Encourage healthy work habits by:

- Setting Do Not Disturb hours in Slack to prevent late-night notifications.

- Using "Away" status to indicate personal breaks.

- Encouraging employees to log off at reasonable hours.

Conclusion: Making Remote Work Seamless with Slack

Effective remote collaboration requires clear communication, well-managed meetings, strong team engagement, and automation. By implementing these best practices, teams can maximize productivity, reduce friction, and create a positive remote work culture.

The key takeaways for using Slack in remote collaboration are:
- ✅ Use threads, mentions, and clear messaging to keep communication organized.
- ✅ Minimize unnecessary meetings by leveraging asynchronous updates.
- ✅ Foster team culture through social channels, recognition, and virtual events.
- ✅ Automate repetitive tasks with Slack integrations and notifications.
- ✅ Set work-life boundaries to prevent burnout and maintain productivity.

By following these guidelines, teams can make Slack a powerful hub for collaboration, ensuring that remote work remains efficient, engaging, and effective.

CHAPTER IV
Managing Notifications and Productivity

4.1 Customizing Notifications for Efficiency

4.1.1 Setting Notification Preferences

Slack is a powerful communication tool, but without proper notification management, it can become overwhelming. To stay productive while ensuring you don't miss important messages, it's essential to customize your Slack notifications effectively. This section will guide you through setting up your notification preferences, optimizing alert settings, and maintaining a balance between staying informed and avoiding distractions.

Understanding Slack's Notification System

Slack offers a highly flexible notification system that allows you to control when and how you receive alerts. Notifications can be customized at different levels, including:

- **Workspace-Level Notifications** – General notification settings that apply across all your Slack workspaces.

- **Channel-Specific Notifications** – Fine-tune alerts for each channel based on priority.

- **Direct Message and Mention Alerts** – Notifications for personal conversations and messages where you're tagged.

- **Device-Specific Settings** – Customize how notifications behave on desktop, mobile, and email.

By mastering these settings, you can create a tailored Slack experience that keeps you engaged without causing unnecessary interruptions.

Accessing and Configuring Notification Preferences

To access your notification settings in Slack, follow these steps:

1. Click on your **profile picture** in the top-right corner of Slack.

2. Select **Preferences** from the dropdown menu.

3. Navigate to the **Notifications** tab.

Once inside the Notifications panel, you'll see several customization options. Let's break them down one by one.

1. Choosing Your Default Notification Settings

When you open the Notifications menu, the first section allows you to set your general notification preferences. You can choose how frequently you receive notifications based on your work style.

Notification Frequency Options:

- **All new messages** – You'll get a notification for every message in any channel or conversation you're part of. Best for teams that require real-time engagement.

- **Direct messages, mentions, and keywords** – Slack only notifies you when someone directly messages you, mentions your name (@yourname), or uses a specific keyword you set up. This is the most commonly used setting as it reduces distractions.

- **Nothing (Do Not Disturb mode)** – No notifications at all. This is useful when you want complete focus time.

💡 **Tip:** If you find Slack notifications overwhelming, choosing the second option—**Direct messages, mentions, and keywords**—is a great balance between staying informed and reducing distractions.

2. Setting Up Channel-Specific Notifications

Sometimes, you may want to receive notifications only from critical channels while muting others. To customize channel notifications:

1. Open the channel you want to modify.

2. Click the **channel name** at the top of the screen.

3. Select **Notifications** from the dropdown menu.

4. Choose one of the following options:

   o **All new messages** – Get notified for every message.

   o **Mentions only** – Get notified when someone mentions you.

   o **Nothing** – Mute the channel completely.

You can also enable **mobile-only notifications** for less urgent channels to reduce desktop distractions while still staying informed when you're away from your computer.

💡 **Tip:** Pinning high-priority channels and muting less relevant ones can help declutter your Slack feed while ensuring you don't miss important updates.

---

3. Managing Direct Messages and Mentions Notifications

Direct messages (DMs) and mentions are often more urgent than general channel messages. Slack allows you to customize how and when you receive notifications for them.

Key DM and Mention Settings:

- **Sound & Display Options** – Choose a notification sound and whether alerts should appear as pop-ups.

- **Keyword Alerts** – Set specific words (e.g., "urgent," "deadline") that trigger notifications, ensuring you don't miss critical discussions.

- **Reply Reminder** – Enable notifications that remind you to respond if you haven't replied to an important DM.

💡 **Tip:** If you work on multiple projects, setting up **keyword notifications** for project names or client names can help you filter important discussions.

4. Setting Notification Preferences for Different Devices

Slack allows device-specific customization so you can control how you receive notifications on desktop, mobile, and email.

Desktop Notifications:

- **Banner vs. Silent Mode** – Choose whether notifications appear as pop-up banners or remain silent.

- **Show message preview** – Decide if the notification should display the message content or just the sender's name.

- **Snooze notifications** – Mute alerts for a specific period (e.g., 30 minutes, 1 hour).

Mobile Notifications:

- **Always send notifications to mobile** – Get notified on mobile even when active on the desktop.

- **Send notifications when inactive** – Only receive mobile alerts when away from your computer.

- **Never send mobile notifications** – Completely turn off mobile notifications.

Email Notifications:

- Enable email notifications for missed direct messages and mentions when offline for an extended period.

- Set the frequency (immediate, daily, or never) to control email overload.

💡 **Tip:** If you switch between devices frequently, enable **"Send notifications to my mobile when I'm inactive on desktop"** to ensure you never miss an urgent update.

5. Using Do Not Disturb Mode for Focus Time

Slack's **Do Not Disturb (DND)** mode helps you block notifications during deep work sessions.

To activate DND mode:

1. Click on your profile picture.

2. Select **Pause notifications** from the dropdown.

3. Choose a preset time duration (e.g., 30 minutes, 1 hour) or set a custom schedule.

Automating DND Mode:

- Set **recurring DND hours** (e.g., 10 PM – 7 AM) to avoid work notifications outside business hours.

- Allow **priority overrides** so key team members can still reach you in emergencies.

 Tip: If you work in different time zones, let your teammates know when you're available by setting a **custom status** (e.g., "Working on a project – back at 3 PM").

6. Managing Notification Overload

Even with customized notifications, Slack can still feel overwhelming if not managed properly. Here are some best practices to reduce alert fatigue:

- **Use Slack Status** – Let others know when you're available or busy to reduce unnecessary pings.

- **Turn Off Unnecessary Alerts** – If a channel isn't important, mute it.

- **Batch Check Notifications** – Instead of reacting instantly, set fixed times (e.g., every 30 minutes) to check Slack.

- **Leverage the Mentions & Reactions Tab** – Instead of scrolling through every channel, use the "@Mentions" tab to see only messages where you're tagged.

 Tip: If you're in too many Slack workspaces, prioritize the most important ones and set notifications to **only mentions and DMs** for the others.

Final Thoughts

Customizing Slack notifications is essential for maintaining a balance between staying informed and minimizing distractions. By adjusting notification preferences at the workspace, channel, and device levels, you can create a Slack environment that enhances productivity rather than disrupts it.

In the next section, we'll explore how to organize your work with Slack tools, including reminders, scheduled messages, and bookmarks.

4.1.2 Using Do Not Disturb Mode

Slack is designed to keep teams connected and facilitate seamless communication. However, constant notifications can sometimes become overwhelming, leading to distractions and reduced productivity. That's where **Do Not Disturb (DND) mode** comes in handy. This feature allows you to control when and how you receive notifications, helping you stay focused and maintain a healthy work-life balance.

In this section, we will explore **how to use Do Not Disturb mode effectively**, including how to enable and disable it, customize settings, automate schedules, and leverage best practices for different work scenarios.

Understanding Do Not Disturb Mode in Slack

Do Not Disturb (DND) mode temporarily pauses notifications, preventing them from appearing on your desktop, mobile device, or email. When enabled, Slack will mute all alerts, including direct messages, mentions, and channel updates. However, team members can still send messages, and you can check them whenever you're ready.

One important aspect of DND mode is that it provides transparency. When enabled, your status will change to a **moon icon** ᙆ , signaling to your colleagues that you are unavailable. Additionally, if someone tries to send you a direct message, Slack will inform them that you are in Do Not Disturb mode, allowing them to decide whether to notify you anyway (if urgent) or wait until you're available.

How to Enable and Disable Do Not Disturb Mode

Slack makes it simple to toggle DND mode on and off. You can do this manually or set up a recurring schedule based on your working hours.

Enabling Do Not Disturb Manually

To activate Do Not Disturb mode manually, follow these steps:

1. **On Desktop (Windows & Mac):**

   o   Click on your profile picture in the **top-right corner**.

   o   Select **Pause notifications** from the dropdown menu.

   o   Choose a duration (e.g., "30 minutes," "1 hour," "Until tomorrow").

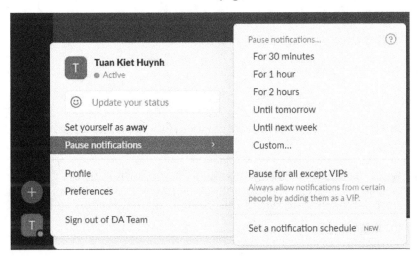

2. **On Mobile (iOS & Android):**

   o   Tap the **You** tab (profile icon in the bottom-right).

   o   Select **Pause notifications**.

   o   Choose the desired time duration.

To disable DND mode manually, simply **click or tap "Resume notifications"**, and Slack will restore normal notification settings.

Setting a Custom Do Not Disturb Schedule

For a more structured approach, you can set up **automatic DND schedules** to mute notifications during specific times, such as outside work hours or during lunch breaks.

How to Set Up a Recurring DND Schedule

1. **On Desktop:**

   o   Click your profile picture in the top-right corner.

- o Select **Preferences** > **Notifications**.

- o Scroll down to **Do Not Disturb** and set a schedule (e.g., "10:00 PM to 7:00 AM").

2. **On Mobile:**

- o Tap the **You** tab > **Notifications**.

- o Find the **Do Not Disturb Schedule** section.

- o Set your preferred quiet hours.

Why Use a DND Schedule?

- **Work-life balance:** Prevent notifications from disturbing you during evenings, weekends, or personal time.

- **Focus sessions:** Avoid distractions during deep work hours or meetings.

- **Time zone differences:** If working with international teams, set boundaries to avoid late-night pings.

Overriding Do Not Disturb for Urgent Messages

Even when DND mode is active, team members can still notify you in urgent cases. If someone tries to message you, Slack will notify them that you're in Do Not Disturb mode and give them the option to override it.

How to Send an Urgent Notification to Someone in DND Mode

- Simply type your message and include an @mention (e.g., @John, urgent update needed).

- Slack will ask: "John has Do Not Disturb on. Would you like to notify them anyway?"

- The sender can then choose to notify you if it's truly urgent.

This feature helps balance uninterrupted focus time while ensuring that critical messages can still get through when necessary.

Best Practices for Using Do Not Disturb Mode Effectively

1. Establish Clear Expectations

- Inform your team about your DND schedule so they know when you're unavailable.

- Use Slack status updates (e.g., "Deep work session, back at 3 PM") to provide additional context.

2. Use Different DND Settings for Different Workflows

- **Short breaks** → Manually enable DND for 30 minutes or 1 hour.

- **Deep focus work** → Use a recurring DND schedule during peak productivity hours.

- **End of workday** → Set an automatic DND schedule from 6 PM to 8 AM.

3. Combine DND Mode with Status Messages

- Example: If you set DND from 9 AM to 12 PM for deep work, also update your Slack status to "Working on project X – Available after 12 PM".

4. Respect Others' DND Settings

- Before overriding someone's Do Not Disturb mode, ask yourself:

  o Is this truly urgent, or can it wait?

  o Can I leave a message instead for them to check later?

- Encourage team culture where people respect each other's focus time.

Common Issues and Troubleshooting

Even though DND mode is straightforward, there are some common issues that users might face:

1. "I'm still getting notifications even when DND is on."

- Check if the notification is from an app integration or bot, as some third-party apps might bypass Slack's DND settings.

- Double-check if you've manually enabled "Notify anyway" for certain channels.

2. "My DND schedule isn't working as expected."

- Ensure your Slack app is updated to the latest version.

- Verify that your time zone is set correctly in Slack's settings.

3. "I forgot to turn off DND and missed important messages."

- Consider setting up automated workflows to disable DND at a certain time.

- Ask team members to use the "notify anyway" option for urgent matters.

Conclusion: Do Not Disturb as a Productivity Tool

Do Not Disturb mode is more than just a notification blocker—it's a tool to help you stay focused, improve productivity, and maintain work-life balance. By using it strategically, you can:

- Reduce distractions during deep work sessions.
- Set healthy boundaries between work and personal time.
- Ensure that urgent messages still get through when necessary.

By integrating DND mode into your Slack workflow, you can create a more organized and efficient work environment, allowing you to work smarter, not harder.

Would you like to explore additional tips on using Slack efficiently? Check out the next section on Slack Reminders and To-Do Lists to supercharge your productivity!

Key Takeaways:

✓ **Activate DND mode manually** for short breaks.
✓ **Set a recurring DND schedule** to protect work-life balance.
✓ **Use urgent notifications wisely** to respect teammates' focus time.
✓ **Combine DND with status messages** for better communication.

4.1.3 Managing Mobile and Desktop Notifications

Effective notification management is crucial for maintaining productivity while using Slack. Without proper customization, excessive notifications can lead to distractions, while too few may result in missed important updates. This section will guide you through managing notifications on both mobile and desktop versions of Slack, ensuring that you receive only the most relevant alerts at the right time.

Understanding Slack Notifications

Slack notifications serve to keep users informed about messages, mentions, and updates within workspaces. They are customizable at multiple levels, including:

- Workspace-wide notifications: General settings for all messages across Slack.

- Channel-specific notifications: Settings for individual channels.

- Direct message notifications: Alerts for personal messages.

- Thread notifications: Updates on ongoing conversations.

- Keyword notifications: Alerts when specific words are mentioned.

By understanding how these notifications work, you can fine-tune them for maximum efficiency.

Accessing Notification Settings on Mobile and Desktop

Desktop (Windows/macOS/Web)

To manage Slack notifications on a desktop, follow these steps:

1. Click on your **profile picture** in the upper-right corner of Slack.

2. Select **Preferences** from the dropdown menu.

3. Click on **Notifications** in the left sidebar.

4. Customize notification settings according to your preferences.

Mobile (iOS/Android)

To adjust notifications on your Slack mobile app:

1. Tap the **You** tab (profile icon) in the bottom right.

2. Select **Notifications** from the menu.

3. Adjust your notification preferences as needed.

Now, let's explore the different notification customization options.

Customizing Notification Preferences

Slack offers several levels of notification control, allowing users to manage alerts based on their work style.

1. Notification Timing: Setting Work Hours vs. Personal Time

By default, Slack sends notifications anytime a new message arrives. However, for better work-life balance, you can define notification hours.

- On desktop, go to Preferences → Notifications → Do Not Disturb and set quiet hours.

- On mobile, tap You → Notifications → Do Not Disturb and schedule your off-work hours.

Once Do Not Disturb (DND) is active, Slack will mute notifications until the scheduled time ends. You can also manually enable DND by typing /dnd until 8 AM in any channel.

2. Choosing Between Banner Notifications vs. Silent Alerts

Slack allows users to select different types of notifications based on urgency.

- **Banner Notifications** (desktop): These appear as pop-up alerts in the corner of the screen.

- **Push Notifications** (mobile): These appear on your lock screen or notification center.

- **Silent Notifications**: Messages arrive in Slack without triggering a sound or vibration.

To change this:

- On **desktop**, go to **Preferences → Notifications → Sound & Appearance** to adjust pop-ups and sounds.

- On **mobile**, go to **You → Notifications** and select either **All messages, Mentions only, or Nothing**.

3. Managing Notification Sounds and Alerts

Slack allows users to control sound alerts and vibrations for incoming messages.

- **On desktop**, navigate to **Preferences → Notifications → Sound & Appearance** to select sound types or disable them.

- **On mobile**, go to **You → Notifications → Sound & Vibration** and choose whether to enable sound alerts.

To disable sound notifications entirely, select **Mute all sounds** on both mobile and desktop.

Customizing Notifications Per Device

Sometimes, users want to receive notifications on only one device at a time. Slack offers device-specific settings to manage this.

1. Receiving Notifications on One Device Only

By default, Slack sends notifications to the last active device. However, you can manually set your preferred device:

- On **desktop**, go to **Preferences → Notifications → Send notifications to…** and choose either **Mobile only, Desktop only, or Both**.

- On **mobile**, go to **You → Notifications → Pause notifications on other devices** to prevent duplicate alerts.

2. Automatically Switching Notifications from Desktop to Mobile

Slack automatically shifts notifications to mobile if a user is inactive on their desktop. To customize this:

- On **desktop**, go to **Preferences → Notifications → When I'm not active on desktop…**

- Choose a delay time (e.g., **Immediately, After 1 minute, After 5 minutes**).

This ensures that you receive important updates even when you step away from your computer.

Channel-Specific Notification Settings

For better focus, Slack allows users to customize notifications on a per-channel basis.

1. Muting or Prioritizing Channels

Some channels may require more attention than others. To manage this:

- Open the channel you want to modify.
- Click on the **channel name** (desktop) or tap the **channel menu** (mobile).
- Select **Notification preferences**.
- Choose **All messages, Mentions only, or Nothing**.
- Optionally, mute the channel to prevent any notifications.

2. Enabling Keyword Alerts for Important Topics

If you want to be notified whenever a specific keyword is mentioned, Slack allows keyword alerts:

- On **desktop**, go to **Preferences → Notifications → My keywords**.
- Enter words or phrases that should trigger a notification.
- On **mobile**, navigate to **You → Notifications → My keywords** and add relevant terms.

Whenever someone mentions these keywords in any channel, you will receive an alert.

Thread and Mention Notifications

Slack provides special notification settings for @mentions and threads to avoid unnecessary distractions.

1. Managing Mentions (@you, @here, @channel)

Slack offers different levels of mention notifications:

- **@you**: Notifies only the mentioned user.
- **@here**: Notifies all online members in a channel.
- **@channel**: Notifies everyone in the channel, regardless of their status.

To prevent excessive notifications:

- Go to **Preferences → Notifications → Mention settings** and disable unwanted alerts.

2. Following or Muting Threads

If you reply to a thread, Slack will send updates for every new reply. To manage this:

- Click **More options (•••)** on the thread.

- Select **Turn off notifications for this thread** to mute updates.

- Alternatively, select **Follow thread** to receive updates even if you haven't replied.

Notification Management Best Practices

Here are some tips for balancing productivity and responsiveness in Slack:

☑ **Limit notifications to priority channels** to reduce distractions.
☑ **Use Do Not Disturb mode** outside of work hours.
☑ **Enable keyword alerts** for essential topics instead of full-channel notifications.
☑ **Mute unimportant channels** to keep focus.
☑ **Set notification delays** to switch alerts from desktop to mobile when inactive.

By implementing these strategies, you can ensure Slack notifications enhance your workflow rather than disrupt it.

Conclusion

Managing Slack notifications effectively allows you to stay informed without becoming overwhelmed. By customizing settings on both mobile and desktop, prioritizing critical alerts, and using tools like keyword notifications and Do Not Disturb, you can create an optimal Slack experience tailored to your work style.

With these techniques, you can ensure that Slack serves as a tool for enhanced collaboration rather than a source of distraction. Now, let's explore how Slack's built-in productivity tools can further improve your efficiency in the next section.

4.2 Organizing Work with Slack Tools

4.2.1 Using Slack Reminders and To-Do Lists

In today's fast-paced, digital-first workplace, staying organized is one of the most crucial habits for maintaining productivity and reducing stress. Slack isn't just a chat tool—it's a comprehensive collaboration platform packed with features to help you structure your tasks, stay on top of priorities, and make sure nothing falls through the cracks. One of the most underrated but powerful features Slack offers is its **reminders** and its ability to act as a lightweight **to-do list manager**.

In this section, we'll dive deep into how to effectively use Slack reminders and how to turn your workspace into a digital assistant that keeps you and your team aligned, focused, and productive.

What Are Slack Reminders?

Slack reminders are built-in scheduling tools that allow you to get notifications for specific tasks at a time you choose. You can use reminders for:

- Personal task tracking
- Team-wide notifications
- Meeting preparation
- Daily check-ins
- Following up on messages
- Scheduling recurring routines

Unlike standalone task management apps, Slack reminders live inside your conversations. This makes them contextual and action-oriented—you can set a reminder *in the middle of a discussion*, without leaving the app or breaking your flow.

Setting Reminders with Slash Commands

The easiest way to set reminders in Slack is by using the /remind slash command. This is a quick-access command you can type directly into any message box.

Basic Syntax

/remind [who] [what] [when]

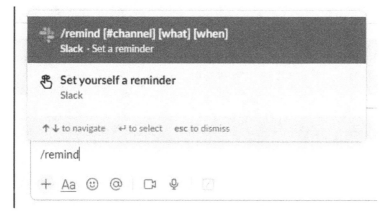

Examples:

- /remind me to submit the report at 4pm

- /remind @john to update the marketing plan tomorrow at 10am

- /remind #design-team to review the prototypes every Monday at 9am

Slack will interpret the time using natural language and send a notification to the right person or channel at the scheduled time.

Tips for Effective Use:

- Use **clear action words** in your reminders (e.g., *"follow up," "submit," "check-in"*)

- Set **reminders for team agreements** during meetings or planning sessions

- Combine reminders with **Slack threads** for better context

---

Using Message Reminders

Sometimes you receive a message and think, "I'll deal with this later." Instead of letting it get buried, you can use the "Remind me about this" feature.

How to Use:

1. Hover over a message.

2. Click the three-dot "More actions" button.

3. Select **"Remind me about this."**

4. Choose a reminder time (e.g., in 20 minutes, tomorrow, next week).

Slack will send you a direct message at your chosen time with a link back to the original conversation—great for keeping track of items in busy channels.

Use Cases:

- Remind yourself to reply to a question

- Follow up after a deadline

- Check back on a discussion thread

Managing Your Reminders

Once you've set a few reminders, you may want to review, edit, or delete them.

To View All Reminders:

Type /remind list in any message box. Slack will return a full list of upcoming and recurring reminders, categorized as:

- Upcoming

- Recurring

- Past Due

To Delete a Reminder:

Click the **"Delete"** button next to the reminder in the list.

To Mark a Reminder as Complete:

Click **"Mark as Done."** Slack will log the task as completed, helping you feel a sense of accomplishment.

Creating To-Do Lists in Slack

While Slack isn't a full-fledged project management tool, you can turn it into a simple, flexible to-do list manager using:

- Pinned messages

- Saved items

- Dedicated personal channels

- Third-party app integrations

Method 1: Personal To-Do List Channel

You can create a private channel or use Slackbot DMs to maintain a personal task list.

Example Workflow:

1. Create a private channel named #my-tasks

2. Add tasks as separate messages (with checkboxes for visual progress):
   ☐ Finish Q2 budget presentation
   ☑ Review candidate CVs

3. Pin important tasks to keep them top of mind.

4. Use /remind in this channel to get notified about specific items.

Method 2: Save Messages for Later

Slack lets you **save messages** to revisit later.

Use this when:

- Someone assigns you a task in a chat.

- A document or link needs action.

- You want to mark important updates without replying instantly.

How to Save: Click the bookmark icon on any message. Access all saved items from your sidebar under "Saved items."

This can be your quick-reference to-do queue.

Method 3: Task Checklists in Messages

Slack supports basic message formatting, including bullet points and checkboxes.

Example To-Do List in a Message:

Here's what I need to complete today:

- [ ] Finish slide deck

- [x] Email client brief

- [ ] Review support tickets

You can update these in real time or repost the message with updates.

Boosting Team Accountability with Shared Reminders

Reminders don't have to be personal. You can build team discipline and accountability by setting **channel-wide reminders**.

Ideas:

- /remind #marketing-team Standup at 10am every weekday

- /remind #sales Submit weekly update every Friday 4pm

- /remind @everyone Turn off devices before the meeting

Use these for regular check-ins, project milestones, or even water-cooler chats.

Advanced Options: Recurring Reminders and Time Zones

Slack's reminder engine supports **recurring schedules** and works across **different time zones**, which is great for distributed teams.

Examples:

- /remind me to stretch every 2 hours
- /remind @alex to check reports every Tuesday at 8am
- Slack automatically adjusts reminder time based on the recipient's time zone.

Be mindful of global schedules when assigning team-wide reminders!

Limitations of Slack Reminders

While Slack reminders are great for lightweight task tracking, they're not a full replacement for tools like Asana, Todoist, or Notion.

Limitations:

- No task categories, labels, or priorities
- Can't assign tasks to multiple users in detail
- Lacks visual task boards or calendar views

But for quick wins, informal planning, and integrating with your daily conversations, reminders in Slack are incredibly effective.

Combining Slack with Task Management Apps

If your team needs more sophisticated to-do tracking, consider integrating Slack with:

- **Trello** – Convert Slack messages to Trello cards
- **Asana** – Get task updates and reminders inside Slack
- **ClickUp** – Create and assign tasks directly from Slack
- **Todoist** – Add to-do items from Slack messages
- **Notion** – Sync notes and tasks with team conversations

With these integrations, you get the best of both worlds—organized planning and instant communication.

Best Practices for Using Reminders and To-Do Lists in Slack

To make the most out of Slack's task tools:

- **Keep reminders actionable and specific**
  Avoid vague notes—be clear about what needs to be done and when.

- **Build a reminder routine**
  Set daily or weekly reminders for recurring responsibilities.

- **Pair with channels or threads**
  Contextual reminders are more effective than isolated ones.

- **Review your /remind list weekly**
  Stay aware of your open loops.

- **Teach your team** to use reminders, too
  Collective habit = collective efficiency.

Conclusion: Make Slack Your Productivity Hub

Slack isn't just a tool for messages—it's your **command center for action**. By embedding reminders and to-do lists into your communication flow, you stay ahead of your responsibilities, reduce cognitive overload, and spend less time jumping between apps.

You don't need fancy project management software to be effective. Sometimes, a well-placed reminder is all it takes to keep your day on track.

Let Slack work *for* you—not just *with* you.

4.2.2 Scheduling Messages for Later Delivery

In a fast-paced work environment, timing is everything. Whether you're communicating with teammates across different time zones, working late at night, or preparing announcements for the following day, Slack's message scheduling feature helps you stay considerate and strategic. It allows you to send your messages at exactly the right moment, without having to be online or risk disturbing others during off-hours.

This section will dive deep into how you can schedule messages in Slack, the practical use cases, best practices, and how this seemingly simple tool can significantly improve your team communication and personal productivity.

Why Scheduling Messages Matters

Before diving into the "how," let's explore the "why." Here are some common scenarios where message scheduling becomes a game-changer:

- 🌍 **Time Zone Considerations**: You're collaborating with colleagues overseas and don't want to ping them in the middle of the night.

- 🕐 **Off-Hour Work Sessions**: You're working after hours but don't want to interrupt others or give the impression they need to reply immediately.

- 📝 **Planned Announcements**: You want a reminder or a channel announcement to appear at the start of the day or during a team meeting.

- 💭 **Brain Dumping Now, Communicating Later**: You've got an idea you don't want to forget—but it's not the right moment to share it.

- 🪶 **Strategic Messaging**: You want to time your message to land right when people are most likely to read it.

How to Schedule Messages in Slack

Scheduling a message in Slack is **intuitive and built-in** to the messaging interface. Here's how to do it on both desktop and mobile:

On Desktop:

1. **Write your message** in the message field as usual.

2. Click the **downward arrow** (🕐) next to the send button.

3. Select one of the **predefined time slots**, like:

   o   *Tomorrow at 9:00 AM*

   o   *Next Monday at 8:00 AM*

4. Or click **"Custom time"** to choose an exact date and time.

5. Hit **Schedule Message**.

Your message will be queued and sent automatically at the scheduled time.

On Mobile:

1. Type your message in the message field.

2. Tap and hold the **send icon**.

3. Select **"Schedule message"**.

4. Choose a time or tap **Custom time**.

5. Confirm to schedule.

Where Do Scheduled Messages Go?

Once scheduled, your message is **saved privately** and won't be visible in the channel or DM until the chosen time.

To view, edit, or delete scheduled messages:

1. Click on **"Scheduled"** in the left sidebar under **Later** (or search "scheduled").

2. Hover over any message to **reschedule, edit, or delete** it.

Best Use Cases for Scheduled Messaging

1. Global Collaboration Made Simple

When your team is spread across the globe, it's courteous—and effective—to send messages when your teammates are actually online. A well-timed message increases visibility and responsiveness. Slack's scheduling feature helps you be a more **empathetic communicator**.

2. Meeting Reminders and Pre-Meeting Materials

You can schedule a reminder to appear right before a meeting, complete with links to documents, agendas, or Zoom calls. It prevents forgetfulness and cuts down on "Where's the link?" messages.

3. Managing Your Own Time More Effectively

Work when you're at your best. Night owl or early bird? Draft messages whenever you're most productive and **schedule them to send during core work hours**, allowing you to disconnect guilt-free.

4. Setting Up a Morning Communication Routine

Imagine scheduling all your morning check-ins, stand-up updates, or motivational quotes at the **start of each week**, then letting Slack deliver them daily. It's like having an assistant who never forgets.

Advanced Tips and Tricks

Combine with Slack Reminders

If you're scheduling a message that asks for input or an action, pair it with a reminder to follow up. For example:

Schedule a message asking for a status update at 10 AM.
Then set a Slack reminder at 4 PM to check replies.

This keeps your workflow proactive and ensures nothing slips through.

Batch Your Communications

Try setting aside 15–30 minutes each morning or evening to **batch-schedule** messages for the day or week ahead. This can reduce context switching and make your communication more deliberate.

Respect "Do Not Disturb" Hours

Even scheduled messages will **not trigger notifications** during a teammate's DND hours unless they've overridden settings. That means you can send messages anytime, knowing Slack won't interrupt your colleagues unless it's urgent.

🗓 Use with Project Milestones

For project managers, message scheduling is perfect for:

- Progress check-ins
- Deadline reminders
- Countdown messages
- Deliverable nudges

It's like building a communication timeline alongside your project timeline.

Common Mistakes to Avoid

✕ Forgetting to Customize the Time

Relying on predefined time slots might not suit all scenarios. Customize the time to match your audience's schedule or your own work cadence.

✕ Overusing Scheduling

While scheduling is powerful, **don't use it to avoid real-time conversations** when appropriate. Slack is still a real-time collaboration tool, so balance is key.

✕ Not Checking Time Zones

Slack doesn't automatically adjust scheduled messages for different users' time zones. What looks like 9 AM to you may be midnight for someone else. Plan accordingly, especially in multi-region teams.

Security and Privacy of Scheduled Messages

Scheduled messages are saved privately and only visible to you until sent. If you decide to edit or cancel them, you can do so with no trace left in the channel.

Slack does not allow scheduling messages on someone else's behalf, so your scheduled communication will always reflect your own account's identity.

Team-Wide Adoption and Etiquette

Encouraging your entire team to adopt message scheduling can:

- Reduce stress from off-hour pings

- Create more thoughtful communication

- Help with async workflows in remote/hybrid teams

You might even want to include **Slack message timing etiquette** in your team's onboarding guide or documentation.

Pro Tip: For managers and team leads, consider setting the tone by **scheduling all non-urgent communication**, and letting your team know it's OK to reply during their normal hours.

Future Possibilities: Scheduled Recurring Messages

As of now, Slack doesn't support **recurring scheduled messages natively**, but there are **workarounds**:

- Use **Workflow Builder** to create recurring messages.

- Integrate tools like **Zapier**, **Make (formerly Integromat)**, or **Slack bots** that support recurring tasks.

These options can automate daily reports, motivational posts, or even standup templates.

Conclusion: Why This Feature Is So Powerful

Scheduling messages in Slack isn't just about convenience—it's about **intentional communication**. It gives you control over timing, tone, and delivery without disrupting others or relying on memory. In distributed, digital-first workplaces, mastering scheduled messaging is one of the **smartest ways to work asynchronously** without sacrificing clarity or connection.

It may seem like a small feature, but used wisely, it becomes a **cornerstone of personal and team productivity**—allowing you to collaborate smarter, not harder.

So go ahead—**work now, send later, and let Slack do the timing for you.**

4.2.3 Creating and Using Bookmarks

In a fast-paced, message-driven platform like Slack, staying organized can be the difference between thriving and feeling overwhelmed. Among the many tools Slack offers for improving productivity and keeping track of important resources, **Bookmarks** stand out as one of the most underutilized yet highly powerful features.

In this section, we'll dive deep into how bookmarks work in Slack, why they are different from traditional message pinning or starring, and how you can leverage them to create a structured, easy-to-navigate digital workspace for both personal and team productivity.

What Are Slack Bookmarks?

Bookmarks in Slack allow users to pin **important links, files, or content directly to the top of a channel or DM thread**, creating a persistent list of quick-access resources. Unlike pinned messages, which appear in a hidden "pinned items" menu, bookmarks are visible at the top of the channel interface — much like tabs in a browser — making them immediately accessible to everyone in the conversation.

Bookmarks can include:

- Messages

- Files

- Google Docs/Sheets/Slides

- External URLs

- Custom workflows or tools

- Channel-specific documentation or FAQs

These bookmarks create a layer of structure and reference within Slack channels, which are often real-time and transient by nature.

Why Use Bookmarks Instead of Pinned Messages?

You might wonder: "Slack already has pinning—why should I use bookmarks?"

Here's a clear comparison to explain the difference:

Feature	Pinned Messages	Bookmarks
Visibility	Hidden behind a menu	Always visible at the top of the channel
Access	Click to open list, then click the message	One-click access from the header
Best For	Message highlights and discussions	Resources, documentation, quick links
User-Friendly	Slight learning curve	Extremely intuitive

Bookmarks are better suited for long-term resources that need to be accessed regularly. For example, a project brief, a shared spreadsheet, a status report template, or an onboarding checklist would be ideal to bookmark.

How to Create a Bookmark in Slack

Creating a bookmark in Slack is incredibly simple. Here's a step-by-step guide:

☑ **To Add a Bookmark:**

1. **Open the Slack channel or direct message** where you want to add a bookmark.

2. In the top right corner, click the **"+ Add a bookmark"** button in the bookmarks bar.

3. Choose what you want to add:

    o Paste a link (e.g., Google Doc, external URL)

    o Select an existing message (click "More actions" on a message and choose "Add as bookmark")

    o Upload a file and bookmark it afterward

4. Add a **title or label** for the bookmark — this is what will appear in the bookmark bar.

5. Click **"Add"**, and it will instantly show up in the channel header.

> 💬 **Pro Tip:**

The label you assign to the bookmark matters — use clear and concise titles like " 📌 Project Plan", " ✅ Onboarding Checklist", or " 📊 Weekly KPIs".

Managing and Reordering Bookmarks

After adding bookmarks, you can edit and rearrange them to keep your list organized and current.

> ✏️ **To Edit or Delete a Bookmark:**

- Click on the **three dots (⋮)** next to the bookmark title.
- Choose **Edit**, **Reorder**, or **Remove** as needed.

> 🔀 **To Reorder Bookmarks:**

- Simply drag and drop the bookmarks from the bookmark bar into the preferred order.

This flexibility allows you to keep the most important resources at the forefront as priorities shift.

Use Cases: How Teams Use Slack Bookmarks Effectively

Let's take a look at how various teams and use cases can benefit from Slack bookmarks:

> 📁 **Project Management Teams**

- Bookmark the **project brief, Gantt chart, standup notes**, and **status tracker**
- Create a living dashboard for everything a team needs to reference

> 🔒 **Engineering Teams**

- Link to the **product spec, PRD, bug tracker**, and **deployment checklist**

- Add bookmarks to CI/CD dashboards or GitHub repositories

📈 Marketing Teams

- Bookmark campaign calendars, brand guidelines, ad performance reports, and creative asset folders

📇 HR and People Ops

- Keep onboarding documents, HR policies, benefits FAQ, and team directories bookmarked for quick reference

🎓 Training & Onboarding

- Guide new team members with a curated list of resources, making onboarding smoother and more self-directed

👨‍⚖️ Legal & Compliance

- Add bookmarks to internal policies, contract templates, and key regulations

---

Bookmarking vs. Creating a Slack Wiki

Some teams go a step further and use bookmarks to **create a lightweight internal wiki**.

For example, by:

- Pinning a **Welcome message** to a new member
- Linking to a **company handbook** or a **training path**
- Creating a **FAQ doc** with common support or policy questions
- Adding **workflow instructions** for recurring processes

This turns Slack into more than a communication tool—it becomes a knowledge base with minimal setup.

Tips for Creating a Useful Bookmarking System

If you want to take your Slack bookmarking game to the next level, here are some tips and best practices:

❄ 1. Group Related Bookmarks Together

Use naming conventions and ordering to cluster similar resources:

- Example: Put all onboarding-related bookmarks first (e.g., "Welcome Guide", "Team Directory", "HR FAQ")

📝 2. Be Descriptive but Concise

Avoid vague labels like "Document" or "Info". Instead, go for:

- "Q2 Roadmap"
- "Budget Approval Workflow"
- "Customer Journey Map"

📅 3. Refresh Bookmarks Regularly

Periodically check to remove outdated bookmarks or broken links. Assign one team member to manage bookmarks in large channels.

👀 4. Make Use of Emoji Icons

Emojis can make bookmarks more scannable and visually appealing:

- ☑ = checklist
- 📊 = report
- 📁 = folder
- 📝 = notes
- 📅 = calendar

🔗 5. Combine with Workflows and Shortcuts

You can bookmark Slack workflows or custom slash commands for recurring tasks like:

- "Submit PTO request"
- "Weekly check-in form"
- "Bug report intake"

This makes your bookmarks actionable, not just static references.

Common Mistakes to Avoid

Like any organizational tool, bookmarks are only as good as how they're used. Here are some pitfalls to watch for:

- ✖ **Too many bookmarks**: Don't overwhelm users — limit to 5–8 essential items.

- ✖ **Unclear labels**: Make sure the purpose of each bookmark is instantly obvious.

- ✖ **Adding one-off links**: Only bookmark persistent, reusable resources, not temporary docs.

- ✖ **Not updating links**: Check that Google Docs or shared URLs still work and reflect current info.

Bookmarks for Personal Productivity

Even if you're not managing a team, bookmarks can enhance your personal productivity within Slack.

Here's how:

- Bookmark your own to-do list in a private channel
- Link to a recurring meeting doc for easy reference
- Add a bookmark for daily priorities or reminders

You can also create a **personal Slack workspace** just for yourself and use bookmarks as tabs for different areas of your work and life.

Conclusion: Bookmarks as Your Slack Dashboard

When used effectively, bookmarks transform Slack from a message feed into a **centralized, structured command center**.

They are:

- Easy to set up

- Always accessible

- Team-friendly

- Fully customizable

Whether you're working solo or collaborating with a large team, mastering bookmarks ensures that key resources are never more than a click away. In an environment filled with noise and constant updates, that kind of clarity is priceless.

Start small — add just one or two bookmarks to your most-used channels. As your needs evolve, so will your ability to create a Slack workspace that not only keeps pace but leads the way.

4.3 Enhancing Productivity with Slack Workflows

4.3.1 Using Shortcuts and Slash Commands

Slack was built with one clear mission: to streamline communication and help teams work smarter—not harder. But effective communication isn't just about chatting; it's also about *navigating and executing actions quickly*. That's where **shortcuts** and **slash commands** come in. These tools are among Slack's most powerful features for enhancing productivity—yet many users don't fully tap into them.

In this section, we'll explore what shortcuts and slash commands are, how to use them, and most importantly, how to integrate them into your everyday Slack usage to unlock speed and efficiency.

What Are Shortcuts and Slash Commands?

At a glance:

- **Shortcuts** are point-and-click actions that help you quickly access powerful features inside Slack—like starting a call, creating a poll, or launching an app.

- **Slash Commands** are typed commands that begin with a / and let you trigger actions or integrate tools right from the message box.

While shortcuts are more visual and accessible for new users, slash commands are favored by power users for their speed and efficiency.

The Shortcut Menu: A Visual Productivity Hub

To access Slack shortcuts:

- Click the **lightning bolt icon** ⚡ to the left of your message input box.

- A menu will appear showing **available actions**, including ones from your installed apps.

Common Built-In Shortcuts

Here are a few that are useful right out of the box:

- **Set a Reminder**: Quickly schedule a task for later.

- **Start a Call or Huddle**: Launch a voice or video session.

- **Create an Event (with Google Calendar)**: Open a calendar event creation modal.

- **Send Feedback or Bug Reports**: Submit forms to HR or IT (if set up).

- **Create a New Post or Note**: Draft longer text content without flooding a channel.

These shortcuts are designed to eliminate friction. You no longer need to switch between tabs or apps to complete simple tasks.

App-Based Shortcuts

Once you connect tools like Trello, Asana, Zoom, or Google Drive, more shortcuts will appear, such as:

- **Create a Trello Card**

- **Attach a Google Drive File**

- **Schedule a Zoom Meeting**

- **Start a Workflow**

You can also **search** the menu to find specific shortcuts, or **pin commonly used ones** at the top.

Slash Commands: Power Up with Your Keyboard

Slack slash commands provide a command-line-like experience inside your workspace.

How They Work

You simply type a command into the message box, like so:

/remind me to call the client at 3pm

Once you hit enter, Slack executes the command instead of sending it as a message.

Popular Built-In Slash Commands

Here are some essentials:

- /remind – Set reminders for yourself or others.

- /away – Set your status to "away."

- /dnd – Turn on *Do Not Disturb* for a custom time.

- /invite – Invite someone to a channel.

- /leave – Leave a channel instantly.

- /collapse – Collapse all inline images and videos in a channel.

- /expand – Re-expand the images.

- /msg or /dm – Send a direct message without leaving your current channel.

App Slash Commands

When you integrate apps, many bring their own slash commands. For example:

- /zoom – Instantly start a Zoom meeting.

- /trello add – Create a new Trello card.

- /asana create – Add a new task to Asana.

- /jira create – Create a new Jira ticket.

These save **dozens of clicks** and eliminate the need to context-switch.

Creating Your Own Shortcuts with Workflow Builder

If you find yourself repeating the same steps daily, consider automating them with **Slack Workflow Builder**, which can be triggered via custom shortcuts.

For example:

- A **daily stand-up prompt** sent to a channel at 9 AM.

- A **bug report form** submitted to the dev team.

- A **new hire checklist** launched via a shortcut when someone joins.

After building a workflow, you can assign a **shortcut trigger** for team members to use via the lightning bolt menu or even a custom slash command.

Productivity Use Cases

Let's look at real-world examples where shortcuts and slash commands drastically improve workflow:

Use Case 1: Daily Reminders

- Set a reminder using /remind:
- /remind #team-daily "Post your stand-up update" every weekday at 9am

Use Case 2: Quick File Attachments

- Instead of opening Google Drive, use the shortcut to attach directly:
    - ⚡ Click the shortcut → "Attach Google Drive File" → Select → Share.

Use Case 3: Scheduling a Meeting

- Instead of opening your calendar, use:
- /zoom

or launch "Start Zoom Meeting" via the shortcut menu.

Use Case 4: Onboarding

- Create a workflow shortcut for onboarding new employees:
    - ⚡ Click "Start New Hire Checklist"
    - It automatically posts welcome messages, sends forms, and assigns tasks.

Tips for Getting the Most Out of Shortcuts and Commands

1. **Memorize a Few Key Slash Commands**: You don't need to know them all. Start with /remind, /dnd, and one app command.

2. **Pin Favorite Shortcuts**: In the shortcut menu, pin the ones you use most.

3. **Use Keyboard Navigation**: Hit Ctrl + K (or Cmd + K on Mac) to jump between channels *and* search for commands.

4. **Train Your Team**: Create a short guide or run a training to help others adopt productivity commands.

5. **Audit Your Apps**: Unused app shortcuts clutter the menu—remove or reorganize integrations periodically.

6. **Automate Repetitive Actions**: Anything you do weekly or daily can probably be built into a workflow.

Common Pitfalls to Avoid

- **Typing slash commands in the wrong field**: Make sure you're in the message box.

- **Over-customizing shortcuts**: Don't overwhelm your team with too many.

- **Forgetting access rights**: Some shortcuts only work if you've authenticated or integrated the relevant app.

- **Ignoring Workflow Builder**: It's not just for developers—anyone can use it with a few clicks!

The Big Picture: Making Slack Your Command Center

Using shortcuts and slash commands is about more than saving clicks—it's about **working smarter**, not harder. They allow you to turn Slack from a passive communication tool into an **active command center** for managing your day.

Whether you're:

- Sending out tasks,

- Tracking meetings,

- Integrating tools,

- Or just keeping your notifications under control,

...shortcuts and slash commands make it all faster, smoother, and more enjoyable.

What's Next?

In the next section, we'll take things further by exploring **Workflow Builder**, where you can chain together commands, automate steps, and truly build a digital assistant inside Slack.

But before we move on—take a moment to try out:

- /remind me to review this section tomorrow

- Open the ⚡ shortcut menu and explore your top 3 tools

Because learning is one thing—**doing** is how you make it stick.

4.3.2 Setting Up Automated Workflows

Introduction: The Power of Automation in Slack

In a fast-paced work environment, manual tasks can quickly become a bottleneck. Copying and pasting messages, sending repetitive reminders, following up on approvals—these are everyday tasks that eat away at your productivity. Enter Slack workflows—a powerful, built-in automation tool that helps you streamline tasks, reduce repetitive work, and create efficient routines for yourself and your team.

This section will walk you through everything you need to know to set up, manage, and optimize Slack workflows using the Workflow Builder. You'll learn how to create automation flows for common use cases, understand the available building blocks, explore advanced tips, and ultimately make Slack work *for you*.

What is Workflow Builder in Slack?

Slack's **Workflow Builder** is a no-code tool that allows users to automate tasks directly inside their Slack workspace. Whether it's collecting information, routing requests, or sending custom messages, you can build workflows with **triggers**, **steps**, and **forms**—all without needing to write a single line of code.

Key features of Workflow Builder include:

- Custom triggers (like a specific keyword or joining a channel)
- Multi-step workflows with logic and branching
- Integration with apps like Google Sheets, Jira, or Zapier
- The ability to collect input using customizable forms
- Notifications and message posting in specific channels

Benefits of Using Automated Workflows

Before diving into the "how," let's highlight **why** workflows are worth your time:

- **Save Time**: Automate recurring tasks, such as daily check-ins or project status updates.
- **Consistency**: Ensure standardized communication and task handling.
- **Data Collection**: Use forms to gather structured input from your team.
- **Integration**: Connect with external tools to expand your automation capabilities.
- **Focus**: Reduce distractions and free up time for deep work by letting workflows handle repetitive actions.

Anatomy of a Slack Workflow

A Slack workflow is composed of three main components:

1. **Trigger**: The event that starts the workflow (e.g., a user joining a channel, a message sent, a form submission, a scheduled time).
2. **Steps**: The actions taken after the trigger. These could include sending messages, asking for input, or pushing data to external apps.
3. **Outputs**: What the workflow produces—typically a message, alert, or stored data.

Think of a workflow as a digital assistant that listens for something to happen and then follows instructions to handle it, step by step.

Getting Started: How to Open Workflow Builder

To access the Workflow Builder:

1. Click your workspace name at the top-left corner.

2. Select **Tools > Workflow Builder**.

3. A new window will open, showing any existing workflows and giving you the option to create new ones.

Note: Depending on your Slack plan (Free, Pro, Business+, Enterprise), you may have access to different features and integrations.

Step-by-Step Guide: Creating Your First Workflow

Let's walk through the creation of a simple workflow: **"Daily Standup Check-In"**

Step 1: Define the Trigger

- Click **Create Workflow**.

- Name your workflow: "Daily Standup Check-In".

- Select a trigger:

- o Choose **Scheduled Date & Time**.
- o Set it to repeat **Monday to Friday at 9:00 AM**.

Step 2: Add a Form Step

- Choose **Add Step > Form**.
- Title the form: "Daily Standup Questions".
- Add fields:
  - o "What did you work on yesterday?"
  - o "What will you work on today?"
  - o "Any blockers or help needed?"
- Select the channel or individual to receive this form (e.g., #daily-standup).

Step 3: Post Responses to a Channel

- Add another step: **Send a Message**.
- Configure it to post a summary of form responses to a Slack channel.
- You can format the message using placeholders like:
- *Standup Update from ${user}*
- - Yesterday: ${field_1}
- - Today: ${field_2}
- - Blockers: ${field_3}

Step 4: Publish

- Click **Publish**.
- Your workflow will now run automatically every weekday morning.

Popular Workflow Use Cases

Here are some powerful examples of automated workflows you can build:

1. Onboarding New Employees

- Trigger: New member joins the #welcome channel.
- Steps:
    o Send a welcome message.
    o Present an onboarding form.
    o Notify the HR team.

2. IT Helpdesk Ticketing

- Trigger: User types /helpdesk in any channel.
- Steps:
    o Present a form asking for issue details.
    o Forward submission to the IT team channel.
    o Optionally, send confirmation to the user.

3. Meeting Preparation

- Trigger: Scheduled time (e.g., every Thursday at 2 PM).
- Steps:
    o Send a checklist for meeting agenda.
    o Collect inputs from team members.
    o Post a compiled agenda.

4. Celebrating Team Wins

- Trigger: Custom emoji reaction (e.g., :tada:).
- Steps:
    o Automatically repost the message to a #kudos channel.
    o Tag relevant team members.
    o Optionally log it to a Google Sheet.

Advanced Tips for Power Users

1. Conditional Logic with External Apps

Use tools like Zapier, Make (Integromat), or Workato to add if/then logic, branching, and conditions.

Example: If a form says "Urgent," trigger a PagerDuty alert. If "Not Urgent," log it in Notion.

2. Chain Multiple Workflows Together

Sometimes you want one workflow to trigger another. Use webhooks and external automation platforms to build chained processes.

3. Collect and Analyze Workflow Data

Use form submissions to populate Google Sheets or Airtable and track trends over time.

4. Permissions and Governance

Only Workspace Owners and Admins can manage all workflows. Regular users can create workflows in public channels they're part of, but make sure to document and govern which workflows are active to avoid redundancy.

Common Pitfalls and How to Avoid Them

Pitfall	Solution
Too many automated messages cluttering a channel	Use DMs or dedicated automation channels
Users ignore workflow forms or alerts	Keep messages concise and engaging
Duplicate workflows or triggers	Regularly audit workflows with your admin team
Incomplete data from form submissions	Make fields required and provide examples
Workflow fails to trigger	Double-check permissions, channel access, and trigger logic

Slack Workflow Builder Limitations

While powerful, Slack's native Workflow Builder does have limitations:

- No built-in branching logic (unless using external tools)

- Limited conditional formatting

- No direct file uploads via forms

- Integration support is more limited compared to dedicated automation tools

For more complex workflows, Slack recommends integrating with services like Zapier or building custom apps using the **Slack API** and **Slack Bolt SDK**.

Future of Slack Automation

Slack is continuing to invest in automation tools. With Salesforce's acquisition of Slack, we're seeing:

- AI-powered suggestions for workflows

- Expanded app integrations

- Tighter links between Slack and Salesforce workflows

As these features roll out, staying updated through Slack's release notes or developer blog will help you stay ahead.

Conclusion: Let Workflows Work for You

Slack Workflows are more than just a nice-to-have—they're essential for reducing friction, simplifying team communication, and eliminating repetitive tasks. Once you've created your first few workflows and seen how much time and mental energy you save, you'll wonder how you ever worked without them.

Whether you're automating a daily check-in, setting up an onboarding sequence, or routing feedback to the right person, Slack workflows help make your work smarter—not harder.

Take the time to explore, experiment, and iterate on your workflows. And remember: even the simplest automation can have a **massive impact** when used consistently.

4.3.3 Avoiding Information Overload in Slack

Introduction

Slack is a powerhouse for team collaboration—but without careful use, it can also become overwhelming. Channels multiplying like rabbits, messages piling up, endless @mentions... it's no surprise that some users feel burned out. In this section, we'll explore how to avoid information overload in Slack while still staying informed and productive.

Whether you're a team leader or an individual contributor, managing the firehose of information in Slack is a critical skill. This section will walk you through practical strategies, settings, and habits that will help you take control of your Slack experience—so Slack becomes your productivity partner, not your biggest distraction.

1. Understanding Information Overload in Slack

Before you can prevent overload, it's important to recognize how it happens. Here are a few common causes:

- **Too many channels**: When you're part of dozens of channels, it becomes hard to know where to focus.

- **Constant pings and notifications**: Notifications that interrupt your work every few minutes break your flow.

- **Lack of channel structure or naming conventions**: Without organization, channels become a chaotic mix of conversations.

- **Poor message practices**: Walls of text, unclear messages, or too many @mentions can cause unnecessary mental fatigue.

- **No prioritization**: If everything seems urgent, nothing truly is.

Slack is designed to be flexible, but that flexibility can backfire if not used intentionally. So, how do you regain control?

2. Audit and Organize Your Channels

One of the best ways to reduce information overload is to evaluate and declutter your Slack environment.

Leave Inactive or Irrelevant Channels

If a channel no longer applies to your role or you haven't participated in months, leave it. You can always rejoin if necessary.

Group Channels by Priority

Use Slack's starred section to pin your most important channels at the top. For example:

- Star: #team-updates, #urgent-support, #manager-meetings
- Don't star: #random, #funny-memes, #old-projects

This helps you focus on what matters first.

Use Channel Naming Conventions

If you're a workspace admin or team lead, advocate for a consistent naming strategy. Examples:

- #proj-website-redesign for projects
- #team-sales for team discussions
- #help-it for support questions

This makes Slack easier to navigate and allows users to filter channels more intelligently.

3. Master Notification Settings

Notification management is your frontline defense against Slack fatigue.

Customize Notification Preferences by Channel

You don't need alerts from every channel. Right-click on a channel > "Change notifications" and choose:

- All new messages (use rarely)

- Mentions & keywords only (recommended for most channels)

- Nothing (for low-priority channels)

Set Keyword Alerts for Critical Topics

You can configure Slack to notify you when specific words are mentioned. Go to Preferences > Notifications > My Keywords. Example keywords:

- "launch"

- "client escalation"

- "yourname" (besides just @yourname)

Use "Do Not Disturb" Mode Regularly

During focus work or off-hours, activate Do Not Disturb to silence alerts. You can also schedule DND times (e.g., 10 PM to 8 AM) to protect your personal time.

---

4. Use Threads and Reactions for Cleaner Conversations

Unstructured replies can quickly clutter a channel. Encourage your team to use **threads** for discussions.

Keep the Main Channel Clean

When someone posts an announcement, respond in the thread—not the main conversation.

Good:
"Big update: We've launched the beta! Let me know thoughts."
[10 comments inside a thread]

Bad:
"Big update: We've launched the beta!"
(20 replies directly in channel = chaos)

Use Emoji Reactions for Quick Acknowledgment

Instead of typing "Got it," "OK," or "Thanks," react with a , , or . It reduces message volume and keeps conversations flowing.

5. Schedule Messages Instead of Sending Immediately

If you think of something late at night or during someone's deep work hours, schedule your message.

Slack lets you send later by clicking the down arrow next to the "Send" button > "Schedule for later".

This keeps teams async-friendly and avoids unnecessary interruptions.

6. Use Slack Workflow Builder to Filter Information

Slack's Workflow Builder can help reduce noise by routing information in a smart way.

Create Intake Forms for Repetitive Requests

Example: Instead of people asking "Can someone reset my password?" in #it-help randomly, build a workflow that:

- Pops up a form with required details
- Sends the request to a private #it-requests channel
- Notifies only on-call IT staff

Less noise, more structure.

Automate Message Routing

You can create workflows that move critical updates from low-visibility channels into high-priority ones. For example:

- When a task in Trello is marked "Blocked," Slack auto-posts to #project-blockers
- When a form is submitted, auto-post to #team-leads only

7. Set Personal Slack Habits for Focus

Sometimes the best way to reduce overload isn't through settings—it's through discipline.

Block Time for Slack Checking

Don't check Slack constantly. Instead, block 3–4 times a day for focused Slack review (e.g., morning, post-lunch, end-of-day). Outside of that, keep notifications off or minimized.

Use the "Mark Unread" Feature for Follow-Up

If you see a message you want to return to later, click the three dots → Mark Unread. You can treat it like an email inbox and return when ready.

Keep Your Sidebar Organized

Use custom sections in your sidebar like:

- Urgent

- Projects

- Inbox

- Low Priority

Drag channels into each section and collapse the ones you don't need to see immediately.

8. Encourage a Healthy Slack Culture in Your Team

Personal discipline helps, but team culture matters more. Encourage team-wide practices that reduce overload:

- Avoid tagging @channel or @here unless necessary

- Post concise, structured messages

- Agree on core hours for discussions

- Document decisions in a wiki or pinned messages

- Use integrations (like Notion, Asana, or Google Docs) for long-form discussion instead of Slack threads

9. Tools and Integrations That Can Help

Several Slack integrations can also help reduce clutter:

- **Halp** – turns messages into help desk tickets

- **Donut** – automates team engagement outside noisy channels

- **Simple Poll** – makes decisions without long debates

- **Google Calendar for Slack** – reminds people of meetings so they don't ask "what time again?"

Use the **Slack App Directory** to discover tools that fit your team's communication patterns.

Conclusion: Slack Should Serve You—Not Stress You Out

Slack is meant to make work easier, but without boundaries, it can lead to mental exhaustion. By combining the right settings, tools, workflows, and habits, you can take control of your Slack experience.

Information overload isn't about having too much information—it's about lacking a system to filter, prioritize, and act on that information. When Slack is managed well, it becomes an engine for clarity, not chaos.

Take time to audit your workspace, refine your habits, and encourage your team to build a smarter Slack culture. You'll be amazed how much more productive, calm, and connected you can feel—without needing to mute everything.

CHAPTER V
Advanced Slack Techniques for Teams

5.1 Managing Team Collaboration

5.1.1 Best Practices for Team Communication

Effective team communication is the backbone of any successful organization. In the digital age, where distributed teams, remote collaboration, and rapid information exchange are the norm, tools like Slack have emerged as essential enablers. However, simply using Slack is not enough—what matters is how you use it. In this section, we'll explore the best practices for team communication on Slack to foster clarity, collaboration, accountability, and team engagement.

1. Establish Clear Communication Guidelines

Slack is versatile, but without clear usage guidelines, it can quickly become chaotic. Every team should define a basic set of "Slack etiquette" rules to ensure consistency in communication.

Key tips:

- **Define when to use threads vs. new messages:** Encourage team members to use threads for follow-ups on specific messages to avoid cluttering the main channel.

- **Use direct messages (DMs) appropriately:** Reserve DMs for private or sensitive conversations. Avoid using them to bypass transparency.

- **Set expectations for response times:** Make it clear when instant responses are expected (e.g., emergencies) and when asynchronous communication is acceptable.

- **Encourage use of statuses:** Team members should update their availability status (e.g., "In a meeting," "Working remotely," "Deep work") to help manage expectations.

2. Structure Channels for Clarity and Focus

Properly organized channels help teams stay aligned and avoid information overload.

Channel organization strategies:

- **Create channels based on function, project, and department:** For example, #marketing-team, #product-feedback, #project-alpha.

- **Use consistent naming conventions:** Prefix channels with tags like team-, proj-, announcements-, or help- to indicate purpose.

- **Pin important messages and files:** Keep key documents, schedules, or onboarding instructions pinned in channels for easy access.

- **Archive unused channels regularly:** Declutter your workspace by retiring old channels that are no longer active.

3. Use Threads to Keep Conversations Organized

One of the most common mistakes in Slack communication is not using threads, leading to disorganized and hard-to-follow conversations.

Thread best practices:

- Always reply in thread unless starting a new topic.

- Tag relevant people in thread replies if their input is needed.

- Summarize long thread conversations in the main channel when appropriate, especially if decisions are made.

Using threads effectively keeps your channel clean and ensures that conversations remain coherent.

4. Leverage Emojis and Reactions for Efficiency

Slack reactions—particularly emojis—are not just for fun. They can speed up communication, provide instant feedback, and keep interactions light-hearted and engaging.

Practical emoji uses:

- ☑ : Task completed

- 👀 : Reviewing a document

- ❓ : Need clarification

- 👍 / 👎 : Agree / Disagree

- 🚧 : Work in progress

- 🔒 : Sensitive content

Reactions reduce the need for unnecessary follow-up messages like "Got it" or "Thanks," keeping communication concise.

5. Designate Communication Channels for Different Purposes

Not all messages require a group discussion. Help your team understand where to post various types of content.

Common types of channels:

- #announcements: For company-wide updates. Only admins/managers should post here.

- #daily-standup: For sharing daily goals, blockers, and updates.

- #watercooler or #random: For social chatter, memes, or team bonding.

- #feedback: For collecting product or team feedback in a structured way.

- #support-it: For raising tech issues with IT or support teams.

When everyone knows where to go for information, time is saved, and productivity increases.

6. Encourage Inclusive and Respectful Communication

Slack can unintentionally create a fast-paced, high-volume environment where quieter voices get lost. To counteract this:

Tips to foster inclusivity:

- **Use inclusive language.** Avoid jargon or slang that not everyone may understand.

- **Give people time to respond.** Don't assume someone isn't contributing just because they haven't answered quickly.

- **Acknowledge everyone's contributions.** Use reactions, shout-outs, or simple thank-yous to make people feel valued.

- **Use audio or video when needed.** Sometimes, text lacks tone. Encourage quick huddles for clarification.

7. Utilize Slack Apps and Integrations to Enhance Communication

Slack offers countless integrations to improve communication and workflow. Some top examples include:

- **Polly:** Create polls or quick surveys to gather input fast.

- **Donut:** Pair up team members randomly to build connections across departments.

- **Google Calendar:** Keep track of meetings and events without leaving Slack.

- **Simple Poll:** Collect team votes with ease during decision-making.

Apps make Slack a true collaboration hub, centralizing your team's digital tools in one place.

8. Set Communication Norms for Distributed and Remote Teams

For remote or hybrid teams, asynchronous communication and digital empathy become more important.

Best practices:

- **Encourage documentation:** Share meeting notes, project updates, and decisions in channels for transparency.

- **Respect time zones:** Schedule messages or use @here instead of @channel if not everyone needs to be disturbed.

- **Balance async and sync:** Use Slack Huddles or short calls when real-time discussion is needed.

9. Establish Communication Roles and Responsibilities

Some teams benefit from assigning communication-related roles. For example:

- **Channel moderators:** Ensure that messages stay on topic and answer new joiners' questions.

- **Announcement owners:** Responsible for updating the team with project or department updates.

- **Information curators:** Pin, bookmark, and organize key documents within channels.

Defining roles helps reduce noise and makes information flow more effectively.

10. Continuously Reflect and Improve Communication Habits

No communication strategy is perfect. Build in time for regular team reflection.

How to improve over time:

- **Run communication retrospectives:** Ask the team what's working and what isn't.

- **Adjust based on feedback:** Reorganize channels, update naming conventions, or change guidelines.

- **Share wins and insights:** Celebrate when Slack is used effectively—like a successful product launch or customer win tracked entirely in Slack.

Improving communication isn't a one-time setup; it's a process of continuous tuning.

Conclusion: Create a Communication Culture, Not Just a Slack Strategy

While Slack provides the platform, it's your team's culture that determines how effective communication will be. Implementing the best practices in this section can transform Slack from a simple messaging tool into a vibrant, aligned, and collaborative digital workspace.

When teams know how to communicate clearly, respectfully, and with intention, they unlock the real power of Slack—not just to message, but to move work forward together.

5.1.2 Creating a Knowledge Hub in Slack

In today's fast-paced digital workplace, teams need centralized access to shared knowledge, documents, and institutional memory to collaborate efficiently and avoid redundancy. Slack offers a dynamic and accessible environment to serve as a "knowledge hub"—a centralized space where vital team information lives and evolves. This section will guide you through understanding what a knowledge hub is, why it matters, and how to build and maintain one using Slack's native features, integrations, and best practices.

What is a Knowledge Hub?

A **knowledge hub** is a centralized, organized repository where teams store, manage, and access important information. It serves as a single source of truth for team processes, workflows, tools, and FAQs. Unlike traditional static knowledge bases, a Slack-powered knowledge hub is dynamic, collaborative, and seamlessly embedded into your team's daily conversations.

In Slack, this can include:

- Pinned messages in channels
- Custom channel naming conventions
- Saved documents and links
- Workflow automations

- Bots and integrations (like Notion, Confluence, Google Drive)

The benefit? Instead of toggling between systems, team members can find what they need directly in Slack.

Why Build a Knowledge Hub in Slack?

Here are several reasons why building a knowledge hub inside Slack can enhance team collaboration:

- **Improved accessibility** – Information lives where the conversation happens.

- **Reduced information silos** – All members can access shared knowledge regardless of their team.

- **Faster onboarding** – New team members can quickly find the information they need.

- **Consistency and accuracy** – Central documentation helps ensure processes are followed uniformly.

- **Real-time updates** – Changes or updates to documents can be instantly shared with the team.

Step-by-Step: How to Create a Knowledge Hub in Slack

1. Identify Core Knowledge Areas

Begin by mapping out the categories of information that your team frequently accesses. Examples include:

- Onboarding documents

- SOPs (Standard Operating Procedures)

- Frequently asked questions

- Team goals and KPIs

- Project timelines

- Technical documentation

- Company policies

These categories will help determine which channels to create and what types of content to pin or store.

2. Structure Your Channels Thoughtfully

Slack's power lies in how you organize your channels. Create dedicated channels for different knowledge topics or workflows. For example:

- #onboarding-info – For all new hire materials
- #team-faqs – A repository for commonly asked questions
- #how-to-guides – Tutorials and SOPs
- #project-templates – Standardized project formats
- #tech-stack – Descriptions and documentation of tools

Pro tip: Use prefixes like info- or docs- to visually group your hub channels.

3. Pin Important Messages and Files

Each Slack channel allows you to "pin" messages so they remain accessible at the top of the channel. Use this for:

- Key documents
- FAQs
- Meeting summaries
- Task guidelines
- Contact points

Example:

"📌 Welcome to #onboarding-info! Please read the pinned messages for your Day 1 checklist, HR documents, and company policies."

Pinned content should be reviewed regularly to ensure it's still relevant and up to date.

4. Leverage Slack's Saved Items and Bookmarks

Every Slack user can **save** messages they find useful by clicking the bookmark icon. Encourage your team to do this for essential links or notes.

You can also **bookmark** links at the top of any channel. These bookmarks can point to:

- Google Docs

- Trello boards

- Internal websites

- Dashboards

- Spreadsheets

Use clear titles like " 🗎 Company Handbook" or " ☑ Onboarding Checklist" for easy navigation.

5. Automate and Enhance with Slack Integrations

Slack's power grows exponentially when combined with external tools. Consider integrating the following:

- Notion or Confluence – Seamlessly link internal wikis

- Google Drive – Store and share documents within Slack

- Dropbox – Share files directly into relevant channels

- Zapier or Slack Workflow Builder – Automate updates to the hub

Example workflow: Automatically post an update in #how-to-guides whenever a new process doc is added to Notion.

6. Use Threads to Organize Related Discussions

Encourage team members to use **threads** when asking or answering questions. For example:

- In #team-faqs, a question like "How do I request vacation time?" should be answered in a thread.

- The original post can be pinned so it's always visible, while the discussion remains nested for clarity.

This prevents clutter and ensures future viewers can read through one topic without scrolling through an entire channel history.

7. Maintain and Update the Knowledge Hub Regularly

A knowledge hub is only valuable if it stays up to date. Assign a "Knowledge Owner" or rotate the responsibility among team members to:

- Review pinned content monthly

- Remove outdated information

- Add new FAQs or documents

- Collect feedback for improvements

8. Create a Knowledge Hub Welcome Message

Every knowledge-related channel should include a welcome message explaining:

- What the channel is for

- How to use it

- Where to start

- Who to ask for help

Example:

👋 Welcome to #how-to-guides!
This channel hosts all our step-by-step guides and SOPs. Check the pinned messages for key docs.
Questions? Ask @Sarah (Knowledge Manager)

Sample Use Case: Onboarding New Hires with Slack as a Knowledge Hub

Let's say you're onboarding a new team member. Here's how Slack can support this:

1. Auto-invite them to #onboarding-info, #team-faqs, and #general

2. Send a welcome DM with links to the Slack knowledge channels

3. Use a workflow to send onboarding tasks as messages each day

4. Provide threads for questions so new hires can see past answers

5. Bookmark links to documents like the employee handbook or benefits guide

The result? A consistent, scalable onboarding process that saves your HR team time and empowers new hires to get up to speed independently.

Common Challenges and Solutions

Challenge	Solution
Content overload	Use clear naming, pinned messages, and bookmarks
Outdated documents	Assign ownership to review content regularly
Confusing organization	Standardize channel naming and create a visual map of hub layout
Low engagement	Announce updates, celebrate contributions, and encourage questions

Best Practices for a Successful Slack Knowledge Hub

- **Be intentional** about structure—don't create too many channels

- **Limit channel noise**—only allow relevant content

- **Promote discoverability**—pin messages, use bookmarks

- **Encourage contributions**—create a culture of knowledge sharing

- **Celebrate improvements**—recognize those who add value

Final Thoughts

A well-crafted knowledge hub in Slack can be a game-changer for your team. It reduces wasted time, supports autonomy, and ensures that knowledge doesn't disappear when someone leaves the company. Instead of forcing your team to search through email chains or scattered cloud folders, give them what they need—right where they already work.

When your team treats Slack not just as a chat tool but as a living, breathing **knowledge platform**, you create a smarter, faster, and more connected workplace.

5.1.3 Using Custom Emojis and Reactions

In the digital workplace, communication is more than just exchanging words—it's also about expression, clarity, and connection. Slack, known for its informal tone and user-friendly interface, thrives on the ability to communicate efficiently and expressively. One often overlooked but powerful tool in this regard is **custom emojis and reactions**.

Custom emojis and emoji reactions may seem like a small feature, but they play a crucial role in team collaboration, especially when used thoughtfully. This section will explore what custom emojis are, why they matter, how they enhance team culture, and best practices for creating and using them effectively.

1. Understanding Custom Emojis in Slack

What Are Custom Emojis?

Custom emojis are user-uploaded icons that can be used just like standard emojis in Slack. These can be static images (like PNGs or JPGs) or animated GIFs. Once added to a workspace, these emojis become available for all members to use in messages and reactions.

Why Use Custom Emojis?

- **Foster Team Identity and Culture**: Custom emojis allow you to reflect your team's culture, inside jokes, brand icons, or even facial expressions of team members.

- **Boost Engagement**: People are more likely to react, respond, or engage when communication feels fun and personalized.

- **Streamline Communication**: Reactions often reduce the need for extra messages. A ☑ or ◌ reaction can confirm a task is complete or show excitement without cluttering the thread.

- **Visual Shortcuts**: Teams often use emoji reactions for workflows—like approving content or tracking feedback—saving time and reducing noise.

2. Adding and Managing Custom Emojis

How to Add a Custom Emoji

To add a custom emoji to your Slack workspace:

1. Click on the emoji icon in the message field.
2. Select "Add Emoji" at the bottom of the emoji menu.
3. Upload your image or GIF (Slack recommends 128x128 pixels, max 64KB).
4. Give your emoji a unique name (used after the colon, e.g., :teamfire:).
5. Click "Save".

Now, your custom emoji is available for everyone in the workspace to use.

Note: Only workspace admins or users with permission can add custom emojis. The number of custom emojis may be limited depending on your Slack plan.

Organizing Your Emoji Library

As your library grows, it's important to keep emojis organized:

- **Naming Conventions**: Use consistent prefixes or names (:team-happy:, :team-done:) to group emojis.

- **Avoid Duplicates**: Check before uploading. Multiple versions of the same emoji (e.g., different thumbs-up icons) can cause confusion.

- **Use Tags or Documentation**: For teams that rely heavily on emojis for workflows, create a shared document listing emoji meanings.

3. Emoji Reactions: More Than Just Fun

Emoji reactions are a simple and powerful feature. Instead of replying with a message, you can just react to a message with an emoji.

Benefits of Emoji Reactions

- **Acknowledge Messages Quickly**: Use a 👍 to acknowledge without replying.

- **Express Emotion or Intent**: 🎉 for celebrations, 😟 for empathy, or 😮 for surprise.

- **Signal Progress or Status**: ✅ for completion, ⏳ for pending tasks, ✖ for cancellation.

- **Encourage Participation**: Reactions make feedback fun and non-intrusive. A message with 15 👏 shows appreciation better than 15 "great job" replies.

Reactions as Workflow Tools

Many teams use emoji reactions to manage tasks and workflows:

- **Approval Processes**: Use ✅ for approved, ✖ for rejected, and ❓ for questions.

- **Polls**: Create informal polls by asking a question and offering emoji reactions as choices.

- **Bug Tracking**: React to a bug report with 🐛, then use ✅ or 🔧 when it's resolved or being fixed.

- **Prioritization**: Use emojis like 🔥 (urgent), 📦 (low priority), or 💡 (idea) to tag messages.

Reaction Summary & Visibility

Slack groups emoji reactions and shows how many people have reacted. Hovering over the emoji shows a list of users who clicked it. This visibility helps teams gauge consensus or engagement at a glance.

4. Creating a Shared Emoji Language

In a team environment, consistency in emoji usage can help align communication.

Build a Common Set of Emojis

Start with a list of 10–20 emojis that everyone understands and uses consistently for common actions. For example:

Emoji	Meaning
	Task complete
	In progress
	Not proceeding
	Bug reported
	High priority
	Important message
	New idea
	Appreciation

Consider publishing this emoji "language" as part of your team onboarding documentation or workspace wiki.

Encourage the Culture

Make custom emoji creation a team event. Let each department or team contribute icons relevant to their work or sense of humor. For example:

- A marketing team might add icons for each campaign.

- A support team could add emojis for each tier of issue severity.

- A design team could use emoji tags to signal different project statuses.

This not only enhances engagement but also promotes ownership of the team's Slack space.

---

5. Fun and Creativity: Emojis That Spark Joy

While productivity is key, don't underestimate the value of fun in team collaboration. Emojis that reflect inside jokes, team photos, or pop culture references (e.g., :thisisfine:) can lighten the mood and build connection.

Popular Fun Emoji Ideas

- Team Faces: Upload cropped headshots of teammates as reaction emojis.

- Celebration Reactions: Create custom GIFs for birthdays, launches, or new hires.

- Company Memes: Turn memorable Slack conversations or team quotes into emoji form.

A fun custom emoji can become part of your team's identity!

6. Emoji Governance and Etiquette

As emojis grow in number and use, it's important to keep things organized.

Set Guidelines for Uploading Emojis

- Ensure emojis are work-appropriate.

- Avoid excessive duplication.

- Use descriptive and searchable names.

Moderate Usage Without Killing the Fun

- Encourage meaningful reactions—don't overreact to every message.

- Avoid clutter by limiting reactions in serious or urgent threads.

- Promote reactions as substitutes, not additions, to comments.

Admin Tools for Emoji Management

Slack workspace owners and admins can:

- Delete outdated or inappropriate emojis.

- Restrict emoji uploads to certain user groups.

- Use third-party apps (like Emoji Packs) to manage large libraries.

7. Real-World Examples of Effective Emoji Use

Startup Team: Fast Feedback Loop

A fast-paced startup uses emoji reactions to approve copy drafts. Writers post content, and editors react with ☑, ❓, or ✘ to indicate approval, questions, or needed edits. No back-and-forth threads—just quick, actionable signals.

Remote Design Team: Collaborative Brainstorming

A distributed design team uses 💡 for new ideas, 🎨 for visual concepts, and 🔍 for items needing review. This lightweight tagging system keeps brainstorms flowing asynchronously.

Customer Support Team: Ticket Triage

Support agents react with 🔔 for urgent tickets, 📦 for low-priority issues, and 🔧 when they're working on it. Managers scan the support channel and instantly know what's in motion.

---

8. Final Thoughts: Power in the Details

Custom emojis and reactions are more than decoration—they are small but mighty tools that foster clarity, save time, and build team culture. In an age where most of our workplace communication is digital, these tiny symbols help us stay human, express ourselves, and work smarter.

When used with intention and consistency, they become a language your team speaks fluently—a language that is fast, visual, and even a little bit fun.

So go ahead—create that dancing parrot, celebrate with 🎉, or close out a task with a confident ☑. Your team will thank you, in emoji form.

5.2 Security and Privacy in Slack

5.2.1 Managing Permissions and Roles

In any collaborative workspace, especially one that acts as a digital headquarters for a team or an entire organization, managing permissions and user roles is not just a best practice—it's a necessity. As Slack continues to evolve into a powerful communication and collaboration platform, understanding how to manage permissions and roles properly is crucial to maintaining both security and operational efficiency.

This section explores everything you need to know about roles, permissions, and administrative controls in Slack. Whether you're a Workspace Owner, Admin, or just curious about how Slack handles access control, this chapter will provide you with a comprehensive understanding of how to safeguard your Slack environment.

What Are Roles in Slack?

Slack assigns roles to help define what different users can and cannot do within a workspace or organization. These roles help maintain security boundaries while empowering users to contribute effectively. Here are the key roles available in Slack:

- **Workspace Owner**

  This is the highest level of authority in a Slack workspace. A workspace can have only one Primary Owner, but can have multiple Owners. Owners can:

  - Manage billing information

  - Delete the workspace

  - Transfer ownership

  - Assign or remove other Owners or Admins

  - Change organization-wide settings

- **Workspace Admin**

  Admins are the hands-on managers of the Slack environment. While they have fewer privileges than Owners, they still have considerable control. Admins can:

- o   Add or remove users

- o   Manage public and private channels

- o   Configure integrations

- o   Set permissions for user groups

- o   Moderate content

- **Members**
  Members are the regular users of Slack. They can:

  - o   Join public channels

  - o   Send messages

  - o   Upload files

  - o   Participate in huddles and calls

  - o   Create new channels (if permitted)

- **Guests**
  Slack offers two types of guest roles:

  - o   **Single-Channel Guests**: Have access to only one specific channel

  - o   **Multi-Channel Guests**: Can access multiple designated channels These roles are useful for freelancers, contractors, or external partners who need limited access.

- **Org-Level Roles (Slack Enterprise Grid)**

  If you're using **Slack Enterprise Grid**, there are additional organizational roles like:

  - o   **Org Owners**

  - o   **Org Admins**

  - o   **Org Primary Owner** These roles operate across multiple interconnected workspaces and are used in large organizations to manage Slack at scale.

Why Permissions Matter

Properly managing permissions is essential for:

- **Security**: Preventing unauthorized access to sensitive information

- **Compliance**: Maintaining audit trails and accountability for access

- **Operational Efficiency**: Ensuring users have just enough access to do their work—no more, no less

- **Minimizing Errors**: Reducing the risk of accidental deletion or leaks

Without clear permission boundaries, Slack can become chaotic, with too many people having too much control. This can lead to unmoderated content, security vulnerabilities, and operational slowdowns.

Customizing Permissions in Slack

Slack allows workspace owners and admins to customize permissions based on their organization's needs. Here are the core areas where permissions can be fine-tuned:

1. Channel Management Permissions

Control who can:

- Create public channels

- Create private channels

- Archive or delete channels

- Rename channels or change their purpose

- Convert channels from public to private (or vice versa, if allowed)

Best Practice: Limit channel creation rights to experienced users or team leads to avoid channel sprawl.

2. Messaging and Posting Permissions

You can define who can:

- Post to announcement channels

- Use @channel, @here, or @everyone

- Pin messages or files

- Edit or delete their own messages

Tip: Overuse of @channel and @here can be disruptive. Restrict their use to team leads or limit them to specific channels.

---

3. Guest Access Management

Guests can be helpful but can also pose security risks if not managed carefully.

- Use **Single-Channel Guests** for freelancers or clients with very limited involvement.

- **Multi-Channel Guests** can be used for consultants who work across departments.

- Ensure that guests do **not** have access to sensitive company-wide channels.

Security Tip: Set expiration dates for guest access to automatically revoke permissions after a set period.

---

4. File Upload and Sharing Permissions

Define:

- Who can upload files

- Whether files can be shared externally

- File size limits

- File retention policies

Slack also integrates with third-party storage tools like Google Drive, OneDrive, and Dropbox, which have their own sharing permissions. Make sure your Slack permissions align with those services.

---

5. Integration and App Permissions

Slack apps and integrations can dramatically increase productivity, but they also represent potential security risks.

- Restrict who can install new apps

- Enable app approval workflows

- Use whitelists or blacklists of approved apps

- Regularly audit installed apps and bot permissions

Pro Tip: Assign an admin to review app usage quarterly to remove unused or risky integrations.

Role-Based Access Control (RBAC) Best Practices

RBAC is a method for restricting system access to authorized users. Here's how you can apply RBAC principles in Slack:

- **Principle of Least Privilege (PoLP)**: Give users the minimum level of access needed to do their job

- **Separation of Duties**: Divide responsibilities so no one role has excessive control

- **Role Grouping**: Create user groups (e.g., marketing, engineering, HR) and assign permissions accordingly

- **Access Reviews**: Regularly review roles and permissions to ensure they're still appropriate

How to Assign Roles in Slack

Roles can be assigned through:

- **Slack Admin Dashboard**: Go to *Settings & administration > Manage members*

- **User Profile Management**: View a member's profile and use the "Edit Role" option

- **Bulk Role Assignment** (Enterprise Grid): Use SCIM provisioning or Slack's Admin APIs for automating user and role management

For developers and IT administrators, Slack also provides <u>Admin APIs</u> for automating role and user provisioning.

Audit Logs and Monitoring Tools

Slack (especially Enterprise Grid) provides tools for monitoring user activity:

- **Audit Logs**: Track who accessed what and when
- **Channel Analytics**: See how channels are used
- **User Reports**: Track usage patterns and suspicious activity
- **Admin Notifications**: Set up alerts for unauthorized actions (e.g., app installations)

Slack can also integrate with security tools like:

- SIEMs (Security Information and Event Management)
- DLP (Data Loss Prevention) tools
- CASBs (Cloud Access Security Brokers)

Case Study: Role Mismanagement Gone Wrong

Let's imagine a fast-growing startup where everyone had admin rights in Slack. It started as a convenience but quickly turned chaotic:

- Dozens of unnecessary channels were created
- Bots were installed without approval
- Files were accidentally deleted
- A departing employee still had full access

After a security audit, the company:

- Implemented role-based access control
- Created admin policies and guidelines
- Reviewed access quarterly

- Set up automatic offboarding procedures

Result: The team became more organized, secure, and confident in their use of Slack.

Tips for Managing Roles in Large Organizations

- Use **User Groups** to apply roles at scale

- Regularly **audit workspace access and roles**

- Implement **offboarding checklists** that include Slack role removal

- Educate users on **responsible permissions usage**

- Establish a **Slack Governance Team** (especially in large enterprises)

- Use **Slack's Enterprise APIs** to automate security and compliance tasks

---

Conclusion: Empower with Control

Managing permissions and roles in Slack is all about striking the right balance: giving users the tools they need to work effectively without compromising your organization's security or integrity.

As your team grows or your Slack usage becomes more sophisticated, revisit your roles and permissions strategy regularly. It's not a one-and-done process. A secure Slack is a productive Slack—and one that fosters trust across every level of your organization.

5.2.2 Handling Sensitive Information in Slack

In today's dynamic digital workspace, the convenience and collaborative power of tools like Slack are unmatched. However, with such power comes a heightened responsibility: managing and protecting sensitive information. Slack, though secure by design, becomes as secure as its users make it. This section is your guide to understanding how to properly handle sensitive information in Slack, minimizing risk while maintaining productivity.

Understanding What "Sensitive Information" Means

Before diving into best practices, it's important to define what qualifies as sensitive information. While this can vary by industry and company policy, some common examples include:

- Personally Identifiable Information (PII): Names, addresses, Social Security numbers, passport numbers, or any information that can be used to identify an individual.

- Financial Data: Bank account numbers, credit card information, budget spreadsheets, or payroll details.

- Login Credentials: Usernames, passwords, API keys, access tokens.

- Confidential Business Information: Contracts, product roadmaps, client lists, sales data, and intellectual property.

- Health Information: Protected Health Information (PHI) under HIPAA for healthcare-related organizations.

- Legal Documents: NDA agreements, lawsuits, and compliance-related files.

Handling such information within Slack requires discipline, awareness, and the right technical measures.

The Risks of Mishandling Sensitive Information in Slack

Many users underestimate the risks of sharing sensitive content in Slack. While Slack encrypts messages in transit and at rest, several vulnerabilities arise from user behavior or improper configurations:

- **Accidental Sharing in Public Channels:** A common risk is accidentally posting confidential data in a public or large team channel where access is not restricted.

- **Persistent Message History:** Messages and files remain stored unless deleted or limited by retention policies.

- **Third-party App Integrations:** Unvetted apps may access content or metadata that could compromise sensitive information.

- **Mobile and Desktop Device Risks:** Lost or compromised devices with logged-in Slack sessions pose a serious data exposure risk.

- **Forwarding or Copying Messages:** Slack makes it easy to share messages across channels or to external collaborators, increasing the risk of unwanted access.

Understanding these risks is the first step toward building a secure communication environment.

Best Practices for Handling Sensitive Information in Slack

1. Avoid Sharing Sensitive Data in Slack Unless Necessary

Slack is a powerful collaboration tool, but it should not be used as a storage or transport mechanism for all types of data. Where possible:

- Use **secure file sharing platforms** (e.g., Google Drive, OneDrive with permissions) and share view-only links instead.

- Avoid sharing **passwords, credit card numbers, or authentication credentials** directly in Slack. Use password managers for secure sharing.

- If you must share sensitive information, **limit its visibility** by sharing it in a private, restricted channel and deleting the message immediately after.

2. Use Private Channels and DMs for Confidential Conversations

- Create **private channels** for discussions involving HR, legal, finance, and other departments dealing with confidential content.

- Use **invitation-only access** to these channels, regularly reviewing membership lists.

- Ensure that **Direct Messages (DMs)** are used appropriately, and move to more secure tools when a higher level of confidentiality is required.

3. Set Custom Data Retention Policies

Slack allows admins to set **message and file retention policies** that determine how long content is stored:

- For channels that may involve sensitive content, consider **shorter retention periods** (e.g., 7–30 days).

- Enable **message deletion** features to allow team members to delete posts if a mistake is made.

- Encourage users to **delete messages** that accidentally contain sensitive information.

Retention settings can be configured differently across channels, giving flexibility to admins.

4. Leverage Slack Enterprise Security Features (if available)

If you're using Slack Enterprise Grid, you gain access to advanced controls:

- **Enterprise Key Management (EKM):** Allows encryption keys to be managed by your organization rather than Slack, giving you greater control over data access.

- **Audit Logs:** Useful for monitoring sensitive events or data flow within your organization.

- **Data Loss Prevention (DLP) Integration:** Can prevent the sharing of sensitive content before it's posted.

Even if you're not on Enterprise Grid, **monitoring app usage and access logs** should be standard procedure.

Data Classification and Slack Usage Policy

To ensure consistent handling of sensitive data across your organization:

Develop a Slack Usage Policy

Your organization should draft and enforce a Slack-specific communication policy that includes:

- What types of information **can and cannot** be shared in Slack.

- Which channels are designated for **secure conversations**.

- Rules around **file sharing, external communications**, and **integration usage**.

- Procedures for **reporting a data breach** or a privacy concern within Slack.

Train your staff to follow this policy and update it regularly.

Tagging and Classifying Messages

Some organizations use tags or codes (e.g., "#Confidential", "#InternalUseOnly") to mark messages that contain sensitive content, helping recipients treat them accordingly. This can be done manually or automated with custom Slack bots or integrations.

Controlling App and Integration Access

Third-party integrations greatly extend Slack's functionality—but they can also become a point of vulnerability.

Steps to Take:

- **Review installed apps** regularly and remove ones that are unused or unvetted.

- Allow only apps that have been **approved by IT or security teams**.

- Use **granular permissions** when granting apps access to channels or data.

- Monitor the **scopes and API tokens** used by integrations, and rotate them when needed.

This proactive management prevents unauthorized data access via apps.

Protecting Slack on User Devices

Slack can be accessed from desktops, mobile phones, tablets, and browsers—which increases convenience but also the attack surface.

Best Practices for Device Security:

- Enforce **device passcodes or biometric locks** on all mobile devices.

- Require **two-factor authentication (2FA)** for Slack logins.

- Enable **Single Sign-On (SSO)** where available.

- Require team members to **log out of unused devices**, especially if shared or lost.

- Use **Mobile Device Management (MDM)** tools for remote wiping if needed.

Educating employees on personal device hygiene goes a long way toward securing Slack access.

Handling External Collaborators and Slack Connect

Slack Connect allows users from different companies to work together in shared channels. It's incredibly powerful—but it also adds complexity to security management.

Safely Collaborating with External Teams:

- Use Slack Connect **only with verified partners or vendors**.

- Set up **separate Slack Connect channels** for each external party—avoid mixing collaborators.

- Ensure **strict permission controls** on what external members can access.

- Review member lists **frequently**, and remove users no longer involved in a project.

- **Label** external channels clearly, e.g., "#ext-clientABC-project".

Slack Connect should be used responsibly, with clear rules and oversight from admins.

Responding to Mistakes and Data Breaches in Slack

Despite best efforts, mistakes happen. Having a response plan is critical:

If Sensitive Data Is Shared by Mistake:

1. **Delete the message or file immediately.**

2. **Notify the Slack admin** or security officer.

3. **Identify who may have seen the content** and follow internal incident response policies.

4. **Log the event** and determine if further legal or compliance steps are required.

Slack Enterprise accounts can integrate with **SIEM and DLP tools** to alert admins to data leakage in real time.

Educating Your Team on Slack Security

Even with all policies and settings in place, human error remains the biggest risk. That's why education is key.

Training Ideas:

- Conduct quarterly **Slack Security Awareness Workshops**.

- Use **real-world scenarios** to demonstrate best practices and common mistakes.

- Share **internal "Do's and Don'ts" guides**.

- Encourage team leads to **model secure behavior** in Slack interactions.

Slack is only as secure as its users. Make sure every user is part of the defense.

Conclusion: Balancing Collaboration and Control

Slack empowers modern teams to collaborate with speed and ease—but managing sensitive information requires thoughtful planning, tools, and behavior. The right combination of Slack features, administrative controls, and human awareness creates a powerful and secure environment.

Key takeaways:

- Avoid oversharing; when in doubt, don't post it.

- Use Slack features like private channels, retention policies, and 2FA to build a safe workspace.

- Train your team, review settings regularly, and respond swiftly to any incidents.

By prioritizing security and privacy alongside productivity, your organization can fully embrace Slack without compromising sensitive data.

5.2.3 Setting Up Two-Factor Authentication

Security is one of the most critical components of any digital workspace, and Slack is no exception. As teams rely on Slack to communicate, share sensitive documents, and collaborate in real-time, it becomes crucial to protect that information from unauthorized access. One of the most effective ways to strengthen the security of your Slack account—

and by extension, your entire organization—is by setting up **Two-Factor Authentication (2FA).**

In this section, we will walk through what 2FA is, why it matters, how to enable it in Slack, best practices for implementation, troubleshooting tips, and how organizations can enforce it across their team. By the end, you'll understand how to make your Slack workspace more secure and resilient against potential threats.

What is Two-Factor Authentication?

Two-Factor Authentication is a security method that requires users to verify their identity using **two different factors** before they can access an account. The first factor is usually something you **know**—like a password. The second factor is something you **have**—such as a smartphone or security token.

The idea is simple: even if someone manages to steal your password, they won't be able to access your account without the second authentication step. This significantly reduces the risk of account breaches due to phishing, weak passwords, or credential leaks.

In Slack, 2FA is implemented via **Time-based One-Time Passwords (TOTP)**. This typically involves using an authenticator app like:

- Google Authenticator
- Authy
- Microsoft Authenticator
- Duo Mobile
- 1Password or LastPass Authenticator

Why Is Two-Factor Authentication Important in Slack?

Slack is not just a chat tool—it's a **central hub for collaboration**. Users exchange project details, attach sensitive files, grant access to integrated tools (e.g., Google Drive, Asana, Trello), and discuss confidential business information.

Here's why 2FA is essential for Slack:

- **Prevents unauthorized access:** Even if your password is compromised, 2FA prevents unauthorized users from logging in.

- **Protects sensitive business data:** Your workspace likely holds internal documentation, strategic plans, financial data, or customer information.

- **Reduces the impact of phishing attacks:** If someone falls for a phishing scam, 2FA provides a second layer of defense.

- **Compliance and regulation:** Many industries require stronger security protocols to meet standards like GDPR, HIPAA, or ISO 27001.

- **Peace of mind for IT admins:** Knowing all accounts are protected by 2FA makes security management less stressful.

How to Enable Two-Factor Authentication in Slack (User Guide)

Step 1: Log In to Your Slack Account Start by logging into Slack using your normal username and password.

Step 2: Go to Your Account Settings

1. Click your profile picture in the top right corner.

2. Select **"Profile"**, then click **"More"** > **"Account Settings"**.

3. This opens your Slack account in a web browser.

Step 3: Navigate to Two-Factor Authentication Settings

In the "Settings" tab, scroll to the section labeled "Two-Factor Authentication" and click "Expand".

Step 4: Click "Set Up Two-Factor Authentication"

You will be prompted to enter your Slack password again for security verification.

Step 5: Choose an Authentication Method

You will be given a QR code. Open your preferred authenticator app and scan the QR code. If you can't scan the code, there is an option to manually enter a setup key.

Step 6: Enter the Verification Code

After scanning the QR code, your app will generate a 6-digit code. Enter that code into Slack to confirm the connection.

Step 7: Save Your Backup Codes

Slack will provide you with **backup codes** in case you lose access to your mobile device. Save these in a secure location (not in your Slack messages!).

Step 8: 2FA is Now Enabled

Slack will now require a verification code from your authenticator app every time you log in.

How to Disable Two-Factor Authentication (If Needed)

Though not recommended unless necessary, you can disable 2FA by going back into the same settings area and selecting "Remove Two-Factor Authentication." You'll be prompted to enter your password and a verification code before removal.

Best Practices for Using Two-Factor Authentication in Slack

To make the most of 2FA, follow these best practices:

1. Use a Trusted Authenticator App

Avoid SMS-based 2FA where possible, as SMS can be intercepted. Instead, use TOTP apps like Google Authenticator or Authy.

2. Store Backup Codes Securely

Keep your backup codes offline, perhaps in a secure notes app or password manager. Never store them in Slack or email.

3. Educate Your Team

Host a quick training session or send instructions to team members on how and why to use 2FA. It's simple, but some users might feel intimidated.

4. Use Device Management Tools

Encourage your IT team to use mobile device management (MDM) software to secure employee devices.

5. Rotate Backup Codes

If you think your backup codes may have been compromised, regenerate and store new ones.

6. Use a Hardware Key (Advanced)

Slack also supports hardware-based security keys such as **YubiKey** for users who want a physical authentication method.

How Admins Can Enforce 2FA for the Entire Workspace

Workspace Owners and Admins can require everyone in the organization to use 2FA. This is highly recommended for any company, especially those with remote employees, sensitive data, or external collaborators.

Steps to Enforce 2FA:

1. Go to Slack Admin Settings

Navigate to your workspace's admin page at: https://[yourworkspace].slack.com/admin/settings

2. Click on "Authentication"

Under **Authentication**, find the section titled **"Two-Factor Authentication"**.

3. Require 2FA for All Members

Toggle the setting to **"Require Two-Factor Authentication for All Members."**

4. Notify Users

Slack will notify users who haven't enabled 2FA. They'll have a limited grace period to enable it before being locked out.

5. Monitor Compliance

Admins can view who has enabled 2FA from the **Manage Members** section and follow up as needed.

Troubleshooting Common 2FA Issues

While 2FA is secure, it can occasionally lead to friction for users. Here are common issues and how to address them:

Lost or Broken Phone

- Use your backup codes to log in.

- If you didn't save your backup codes, ask your Admin to reset your 2FA from the admin console.

Clock Sync Issues

If the authenticator app's time is out of sync, the code might not work. Re-sync your phone's time or restart the app.

Authenticator App Not Working

Try a different TOTP app, or reinstall the current one. Some users find better results with alternatives like Authy or Duo.

Can't Scan the QR Code

Choose the option to enter the key manually into your app.

Case Study: How 2FA Saved a Company from a Breach

In 2022, a mid-sized marketing agency experienced a phishing attack that compromised an employee's Slack password. Because 2FA was enabled, the attacker was blocked from gaining access. Had it not been for that extra layer, the attacker could have accessed private channels containing client data, campaign strategies, and financial reports.

This real-world example shows how 2FA acts as a safety net, even when human error occurs.

Conclusion: Make Two-Factor Authentication Non-Negotiable

Two-Factor Authentication is a **non-negotiable feature** in today's digital workspaces. While Slack provides a user-friendly and efficient communication tool, it is only as secure as the precautions you take. Setting up and enforcing 2FA is one of the **simplest yet most powerful ways** to safeguard your Slack environment.

Whether you're a solo entrepreneur or part of a multinational team, enabling 2FA can be the difference between a protected digital workspace and a devastating breach. Don't wait until it's too late—set it up today, and encourage your entire team to do the same.

Remember: Great collaboration begins with great security. And great security starts with Two-Factor Authentication.

5.3 Using Slack for Cross-Company Collaboration

5.3.1 Understanding Slack Connect

As organizations grow and the nature of work becomes increasingly decentralized and interdependent, effective collaboration between companies is no longer a luxury—it's a necessity. Whether you're working with vendors, clients, freelancers, consultants, or strategic partners, seamless and secure communication across organizational boundaries is essential. Traditionally, cross-company communication has relied heavily on endless email chains, clunky file attachments, and the slow back-and-forth of scheduling calls. This is where Slack Connect comes in.

Slack Connect transforms the way organizations interact by bringing external communication into the same workspace where internal collaboration already thrives. Rather than jumping between different platforms or relying on outdated communication methods, Slack Connect allows you to collaborate with people outside your company just as easily as you do with your own team.

In this section, we'll explore what Slack Connect is, how it works, its benefits, and best practices for using it effectively and securely.

What is Slack Connect?

Slack Connect is a feature that allows users to communicate across organizations using shared channels. It enables two or more companies to collaborate in real time within a single Slack channel, without having to leave their own workspaces. Each participant remains in their organization's Slack environment, but they are able to communicate in a shared space that behaves much like an internal channel.

In short, Slack Connect lets different companies work together as if they were part of the same team—without sacrificing data security or organizational boundaries.

Key Features of Slack Connect

1. **Shared Channels Across Workspaces**: Create a channel that includes members from two or more companies, giving everyone a shared space to chat, share files, and collaborate.

2. **Direct Messaging with External Users**: Send direct messages to people outside your organization without requiring email exchanges or new workspace invitations.

3. **Maintained Identity and Security**: Each user accesses the shared channel through their own organization's Slack, ensuring secure identity management and role-based access controls.

4. **Admin Controls and Auditing**: Workspace administrators have full visibility and control over external connections, with the ability to manage, approve, and monitor Slack Connect activity.

5. **Integration with Existing Tools**: Slack Connect supports third-party app integrations, so teams can continue using their favorite tools—like Zoom, Asana, or Salesforce—within shared channels.

Why Use Slack Connect?

Slack Connect offers a wide range of benefits over traditional communication methods. Below are the most compelling reasons to consider adopting it:

1. Faster Communication

Slack Connect eliminates the delays of email threads. Conversations happen in real-time, which can reduce turnaround times on decisions, clarify expectations quickly, and speed up project timelines.

2. Improved Transparency

Everyone in the shared channel has access to the same context and information. No more "forgot to CC someone" situations. Visibility across teams ensures everyone is aligned and informed.

3. Enhanced Collaboration

With Slack Connect, you can brainstorm ideas, share documents, coordinate meetings, and provide feedback—all in one place. Teams across organizations can collaborate just like internal teams.

4. Reduced Email Dependence

Email is inefficient for fast-paced projects. Slack Connect helps you cut down on inbox clutter, prioritize real-time communication, and reduce the risk of messages getting lost in the shuffle.

5. Stronger Relationships with Partners

Whether you're working with long-term collaborators or new clients, Slack Connect helps build rapport through more frequent and informal communication.

How to Set Up Slack Connect

Slack Connect requires both administrative setup and user-level invitations. Here's a step-by-step guide to getting started:

Step 1: Confirm Admin Permissions

Workspace admins must **enable Slack Connect** and approve external domain connections. Admins can restrict Slack Connect to approved domains or users for additional control.

Step 2: Create a Slack Channel

Start by creating a new channel or selecting an existing one that you want to share externally.

Step 3: Send an Invitation

Use the channel settings to invite people from the external organization. You'll need their email address associated with Slack. Once the invitation is sent, the other party's admin will need to approve it.

Step 4: Await Admin Approval

Both organizations must approve the connection before the shared channel becomes active. This ensures mutual consent and secure configuration.

Step 5: Collaborate!

Once the connection is established, you're ready to begin working together. External users will be marked with an icon, and all members will be able to view messages, share files, and integrate apps as usual.

Best Practices for Using Slack Connect

While Slack Connect can dramatically improve external communication, its effectiveness depends on how it's used. Below are best practices to keep your shared channels productive and secure:

1. Establish Clear Channel Guidelines

Set expectations from the beginning. Define the purpose of the shared channel, who should be invited, how often updates will be provided, and what kind of messages are appropriate.

2. Name Channels Clearly

Use naming conventions that reflect the relationship, such as #client-abc-marketing or #vendor-xyz-logistics. This helps with organization and clarity across your workspace.

3. Limit Access to Essential Participants

Avoid adding too many people to the shared channel. Focus on those who are actively involved in the collaboration to keep conversations focused and efficient.

4. Use Threads for Discussions

To prevent clutter, use message threads for ongoing discussions within a topic. This keeps conversations organized and makes it easier to find important information later.

5. Respect Boundaries

Remember that external users are not part of your internal culture. Avoid jargon, acronyms, or casual references that may confuse others. Maintain professionalism and clarity.

6. Monitor Security and Compliance

Ensure sensitive information is not overshared. Use Slack's admin tools to monitor activity, and remind users of your organization's data protection policies.

7. Periodically Review Shared Channels

Review access and channel activity regularly. If the project ends or the collaboration is complete, archive the channel or remove access accordingly.

Real-World Use Cases of Slack Connect

1. Client Communication

Marketing agencies can use Slack Connect to collaborate with clients on campaign development, feedback loops, and media planning. This allows faster revisions and client engagement.

2. Vendor and Supplier Management

Operations teams can share updates with logistics partners, troubleshoot supply chain issues in real time, and coordinate deliveries across geographies.

3. Joint Ventures or Partnerships

Two tech companies working on an integrated product can use Slack Connect to coordinate dev teams, sync timelines, and manage deliverables.

4. Consulting and Freelancing

Freelancers or consultants working with multiple clients can manage dedicated shared channels for each client, improving transparency and reducing miscommunication.

Security Considerations in Slack Connect

Security is one of the biggest concerns when opening your workspace to external entities. Thankfully, Slack has built robust features to mitigate risks:

- **Granular Admin Controls**: Admins can restrict which users can initiate Slack Connect invitations.

- **Domain Whitelisting**: Only approved domains can be added to shared channels.

- **Audit Logs**: Track all activity, file sharing, and channel creation to ensure compliance.

- **Data Loss Prevention (DLP)** Integrations: Pair Slack with security tools to prevent sensitive data from being shared externally.

- **End-to-End Identity Management**: Each user's identity is controlled by their home organization, minimizing the risk of impersonation or unauthorized access.

The Future of Cross-Company Work with Slack

Slack Connect is a significant leap toward the **future of seamless business collaboration**. It eliminates artificial barriers between companies while preserving the privacy and control that modern businesses require. As more organizations adopt remote or hybrid work models, Slack Connect offers the tools needed to stay agile, informed, and collaborative.

Slack is also continuing to invest in features like **Slack Connect DMs** (direct messages across organizations) and **multiparty shared channels**, making the platform more powerful for cross-functional, cross-company workflows.

Final Thoughts

In today's fast-moving work environment, **working together across company lines is becoming standard practice**. Slack Connect isn't just a feature—it's a philosophy: removing friction in communication, increasing transparency, and accelerating results.

By understanding and implementing Slack Connect effectively, your organization can elevate its external relationships from transactional to collaborative—and ultimately gain a competitive edge.

5.3.2 Collaborating with External Partners

In the modern workplace, collaboration rarely stays within the walls of your company. As businesses become more interconnected, working with clients, vendors, consultants, agencies, freelancers, and strategic partners has become a regular part of day-to-day operations. Slack offers a powerful and flexible solution to facilitate cross-company communication in real-time without the need for endless email threads or switching between tools. This section will guide you through how to collaborate effectively with external partners using Slack, focusing on best practices, privacy and permission management, communication etiquette, and use-case examples.

Understanding Cross-Company Collaboration in Slack

Slack was originally designed for internal team communication, but as its user base grew, so did the demand for external collaboration. This led to the development of **Slack Connect**, a feature that allows multiple organizations to work together in shared channels while keeping their own internal communications secure and distinct.

Through Slack Connect, companies can:

- Create **shared channels** that include members from different organizations.

- Maintain **separate user permissions** for external members.

- Communicate in real-time without relying on third-party collaboration tools.

- Keep conversations secure, monitored, and fully auditable by administrators.

Slack Connect is available to all paid Slack plans, and organizations need to set up connections through admin permissions and approved invitations.

Benefits of Using Slack to Collaborate with External Partners

Let's take a look at some of the key benefits of using Slack for cross-company collaboration:

- **Speed and Responsiveness**: Slack eliminates the long delays often associated with email. With real-time messaging, responses are quicker, which accelerates decision-making.

- **Centralized Communication**: All project-related discussions, files, and updates can live in one shared channel, eliminating silos and miscommunication.

- **Transparency and Accountability**: Threaded discussions and message history allow all team members to stay on the same page and refer back to decisions.

- **Security and Control**: Slack provides enterprise-grade security, including guest access controls and message retention settings that can be customized for each partner.

- **Easy File Sharing**: Files, designs, contracts, and spreadsheets can be instantly shared, commented on, and edited in context.

Setting Up Slack Connect for External Collaboration

Before you can start collaborating with external partners, both organizations must **enable and approve Slack Connect**. Here's how to get started:

Step 1: Enable Slack Connect in Your Workspace

Admins must configure settings to allow Slack Connect invitations:

1. Go to **Admin Settings → Settings & Permissions**.

2. Under **Slack Connect**, enable "Allow members to invite external organizations."

3. Set approval requirements (e.g., all requests must be approved by admins).

Step 2: Create or Convert a Channel

You can either:

- **Create a new channel** specifically for external collaboration, or

- **Convert an existing internal channel** into a Slack Connect channel.

It's recommended to create a **new channel** to maintain separation from internal conversations.

Step 3: Send an Invitation

In the selected channel:

1. Click the **channel name**, then select **Add people → Invite external people**.

2. Enter the email address of the external contact.

3. Slack will notify their workspace admin for approval.

4. Once approved by both sides, the shared channel will become active.

Step 4: Confirm and Customize Channel Settings

- Set **channel purpose and guidelines**.

- Add **channel naming conventions**, e.g., #client-project-name.

- Assign **channel leads** who will help manage the collaboration and serve as communication facilitators.

Best Practices for Working with External Partners in Slack

To ensure smooth and effective collaboration, it's important to establish clear expectations and follow best practices:

1. Establish Communication Guidelines Early

Share a short welcome message or pinned post that outlines:

- The channel's purpose
- Who to contact for what
- Expected response times
- Preferred communication styles (e.g., threads vs. DMs)

2. Use Threads for Clarity

Encourage everyone to use **message threads** for replies instead of cluttering the main channel. This helps maintain focus and keeps topics organized.

3. Avoid Jargon and Internal Shortcuts

When speaking to external partners, avoid acronyms or internal terms that may be unclear. Always provide context when discussing topics.

4. Share Files and Documents Transparently

Use Slack's file-sharing system or link integrations like Google Drive or Dropbox. Make sure access permissions are properly configured.

5. Tag Responsibly

Use @mentions sparingly and purposefully. Overuse can lead to notification fatigue or feel intrusive to your partners.

6. Maintain a Professional Tone

Slack can feel casual, but when dealing with external stakeholders, maintain a tone that reflects your brand professionalism. Emojis are fine—but use them appropriately.

7. Use Channel Naming Standards

Develop channel naming standards that make it clear this is an external collaboration, such as:

- #partner-abc-team

- #client-onboarding-acme

- #vendor-weekly-sync

This reduces confusion and keeps your channel list tidy.

Security and Access Considerations

Security is especially important when working across organizations. Here are some settings and tips to manage external access properly:

1. Guest Accounts vs. Slack Connect

- **Guest Accounts**: Give access to only one channel and are limited to your organization's workspace.

- **Slack Connect**: Allows for more integrated and real-time collaboration across company boundaries.

Use Slack Connect when collaborating long-term; guest accounts are better for one-off or very limited interactions.

2. Control Access Through Roles

Ensure your Slack admins are monitoring:

- Who is invited

- What permissions they have

- Whether they have access to sensitive files or channels

Set **expiration dates** or review cycles for external access.

3. Retention Policies and Compliance

Slack allows you to define **retention settings per channel**, including external ones. You can:

- Automatically delete messages after a certain period

- Archive channels when projects conclude

- Export logs for compliance or legal requirements

Make sure both sides agree on policies for message retention and data handling.

Real-World Use Cases for Cross-Company Collaboration

Let's explore how various teams and industries use Slack to collaborate with external partners:

1. Marketing Agencies and Clients

A marketing agency creates a Slack Connect channel with their client to:

- Share campaign updates
- Collect content approvals
- Discuss real-time ad performance

2. Software Development Firms and Freelancers

A dev team shares a channel with a group of contracted engineers to:

- Share access to GitHub commits
- Coordinate sprint tasks
- Conduct code reviews in real time

3. Startups and Investors

Startups create private channels with investors to:

- Share progress updates
- Provide financial dashboards
- Schedule pitch sessions

4. Vendor and Procurement Teams

A retail business has a shared Slack channel with their main supplier:

- Weekly stock updates
- Issue tracking

- Contract discussions

Common Challenges and How to Overcome Them

Despite its power, Slack collaboration across companies can come with challenges:

Challenge 1: Lack of Communication Boundaries

Solution: Set expectations early and use DMs only for urgent, private matters.

Challenge 2: Overlapping Tools or Systems

Solution: Clarify which platforms to use for which purposes (e.g., use Slack for communication, Google Docs for document editing).

Challenge 3: Notification Overload

Solution: Educate team members on setting personalized notifications and using the Do Not Disturb feature.

Challenge 4: Security Concerns

Solution: Regularly audit access, enforce MFA (multi-factor authentication), and define clear data-sharing protocols.

Key Takeaways

- Slack Connect enables powerful and secure cross-company collaboration.

- Establish clear roles, responsibilities, and communication guidelines from the start.

- Leverage threads, integrations, and naming conventions to keep everything organized.

- Prioritize security through controlled access and workspace policies.

- Treat external Slack channels like a shared office space—keep it clean, purposeful, and professional.

By mastering Slack's external collaboration features, your team can operate more flexibly, respond faster, and deliver results with greater cohesion. Whether you're working with a long-time client or a new strategic partner, Slack helps build stronger, more transparent working relationships that move at the speed of modern business.

5.3.3 Managing Multi-Workspace Accounts

As your organization grows or if you're working with multiple clients, vendors, or departments, you may find yourself involved in more than one Slack workspace. While Slack is incredibly effective for communication within a single workspace, navigating multiple workspaces efficiently requires a strategic approach. In this section, we'll explore why and how to manage multiple Slack workspaces effectively, the tools Slack provides to make this easier, and best practices to ensure you stay organized, productive, and connected.

Understanding Multi-Workspace Use Cases

Before diving into the "how," it's important to understand **why** users often need access to multiple Slack workspaces. Some common use cases include:

- **Freelancers and Consultants**: Working with different clients across separate Slack workspaces.

- **Agencies**: Supporting multiple brands or customers, each with their own workspace.

- **Large Enterprises**: Different departments or subsidiaries may maintain distinct workspaces.

- **Cross-Company Collaboration**: Working with external partners using Slack Connect.

These scenarios can lead to information being fragmented across channels, accounts, and systems unless well-managed. That's where Slack's multi-workspace features come in.

Adding and Switching Between Workspaces

Slack makes it simple to join multiple workspaces using a single email address. Here's how to do it:

Joining a New Workspace

1. Click your workspace name at the top-left of the app.

2. Select **"Add workspaces"**.

3. Enter the email associated with the new workspace or follow an invite link.

4. Once added, the new workspace appears in your sidebar or Slack app switcher.

Switching Between Workspaces

You can switch between workspaces via:

- **Desktop App**: Use the sidebar workspace icons on the left or press Cmd + Shift + Tab (Mac) or Ctrl + Shift + Tab (Windows) to cycle through.

- **Mobile App**: Tap the workspace icon or swipe left/right.

- **Web App**: Each workspace runs in its own browser tab.

Tip: Keep frequently used workspaces open in dedicated browser tabs or desktop windows to minimize switching friction.

Notification Management Across Workspaces

One of the biggest challenges with multiple Slack workspaces is managing notifications without becoming overwhelmed. Slack offers robust notification customization to help:

Per-Workspace Settings

You can customize each workspace's notifications separately:

- Set overall notification level (All messages, Mentions, or Nothing).

- Customize channel-specific alerts.

- Turn off mobile notifications during work hours or DND mode.

Unified Notifications (Mobile Only)

On mobile, Slack consolidates notifications from all workspaces into a single push feed. This is convenient for on-the-go workers but may require fine-tuning if you're getting too many alerts.

Best Practices

- Prioritize your primary workspace with real-time notifications.

- Set others to "Mentions Only" or "Do Not Disturb" during focus hours.

- Use notification schedules to match your working style.

Organizing Channels and Workspaces

Without a system, your Slack usage across multiple workspaces can get messy fast. Here's how to stay organized:

Use Consistent Naming Conventions

If you manage multiple teams or projects, try to keep consistent naming patterns across workspaces (e.g., #marketing, #team-standup, #clients). This reduces mental overhead when switching contexts.

Color-Coding Workspaces

On the desktop, you can assign **custom themes** to each workspace:

- Click your profile picture → Preferences → Themes

- Choose a different color scheme per workspace

- Helps you visually distinguish between workspaces at a glance

Pin Important Channels

Within each workspace, pin your most important channels so they appear at the top of the sidebar. This helps you jump quickly to the discussions that matter most.

Productivity Tips for Multi-Workspace Users

Leverage Slack Keyboard Shortcuts

Mastering shortcuts will save you valuable time:

- Cmd/Ctrl + K: Jump to a different channel or workspace

- Cmd/Ctrl + 1–9: Quickly switch to the first 9 channels or DMs in the sidebar

- Cmd/Ctrl + Shift + K: Open the Direct Message list across all workspaces

Use Status Messages Wisely

Set different statuses per workspace to reflect availability, timezone differences, or task focus (e.g., "Heads-down writing ✍ " in one, "In client call ☎ " in another).

Sync Calendar with Slack

Use integrations like **Google Calendar** to automatically update your status in all workspaces, preventing interruptions during meetings or focused time.

Cross-Workspace Communication Strategies

While each Slack workspace is siloed by design, here are a few strategies to create some cohesion across them:

Bookmarking and Note-Taking

- Use tools like **Notion, Evernote, or Google Keep** to centralize notes from various Slack conversations.

- Copy important links or message threads into a single "command center" document for easy access.

Email Integration

Some users prefer getting email digests or summaries from non-primary workspaces. Use Slack's email integration to forward key channel updates to your inbox or connect via apps like **Zapier**.

Shared Calendar or Dashboard

Create a central dashboard (e.g., using Trello, Asana, or ClickUp) that brings in information from various workspaces and lets you track conversations and deadlines across teams.

Using Slack Enterprise Grid

If you're part of a large organization using **Slack Enterprise Grid**, you may already have access to multiple interconnected workspaces under one domain.

What is Slack Enterprise Grid?

Slack Enterprise Grid allows businesses to create **multiple connected workspaces** with shared access control, search, and user management.

Benefits

- Seamless user identity across workspaces

- Organization-wide search capabilities

- Centralized security and compliance settings

When to Use Grid vs. Separate Workspaces

- Use **Grid** if your company wants to maintain Slack internally with centralized control.

- Use **Separate Workspaces** when collaborating with clients or external partners.

Note: Enterprise Grid requires an upgraded plan and IT involvement.

Maintaining Focus and Reducing Overload

Managing multiple workspaces can lead to **context switching fatigue**. Here's how to stay sane and focused:

Use Daily Check-in Routines

Create a Slack check-in schedule:

- Morning: Review all workspace updates.

- Midday: Respond to critical items.

- Afternoon: Focus on primary workspace.

Use Third-Party Tools

Apps like **Meee, Reclaim.ai**, or **Clockwise** can help you schedule Slack time blocks and minimize distractions.

Audit Your Workspaces Monthly

Remove yourself from inactive workspaces or channels. This reduces mental clutter and ensures you're focusing on where you add the most value.

Security Considerations for Multi-Workspace Users

With multiple workspaces, it's easy to blur lines between internal and external communication. Be sure to:

- Use **strong, unique passwords** and enable **2FA** for each workspace.

- Never **cross-post confidential information** between workspaces.

- Be mindful of **file sharing** permissions, especially with third-party collaborators.

Final Thoughts

Managing multiple Slack workspaces may feel daunting at first, but with the right systems and strategies in place, it can become a seamless part of your daily workflow. The key is to:

- Stay organized and intentional.

- Customize notifications to your work rhythm.

- Prioritize security and clarity in communication.

As remote and hybrid work becomes more common, mastering multi-workspace Slack usage will not only make you more productive — it will make you an essential collaborator across teams, companies, and even time zones.

CHAPTER VI
Slack for Remote and Hybrid Work

6.1 Creating a Remote-Friendly Slack Culture

6.1.1 Best Practices for Remote Team Communication

In a world increasingly shifting toward remote and hybrid work models, effective team communication becomes a cornerstone of success. Slack, as a versatile digital communication hub, is particularly well-suited to serve remote teams—if used strategically. Simply installing Slack and inviting team members is not enough. To truly leverage the platform's power, organizations must embed best practices that foster clarity, transparency, inclusion, and productivity.

This section provides a comprehensive guide to best practices for remote team communication using Slack, including how to structure conversations, establish communication norms, encourage engagement, prevent miscommunication, and maintain team cohesion from a distance.

1. Establish Clear Communication Norms

One of the biggest challenges in remote communication is ambiguity. Without the benefit of physical cues like tone of voice and body language, remote teams are at risk of miscommunication. That's why setting up clear communication norms in Slack is essential.

Set channel guidelines: Define what types of messages go into which channels. For example:

- #announcements: only official company-wide updates

- #project-design: all discussions related to the design team

- #random: casual, off-topic conversation

Define response expectations: Make it clear whether Slack is meant for real-time chatting or asynchronous communication. Not everyone will be online at the same time, especially across time zones. For example:

- "Replies within 24 hours are acceptable for most messages."

- "Use @here or @channel only for urgent matters."

Encourage descriptive messages: Encourage team members to write with clarity. Avoid vague phrases like "Can you check this?"—instead, say "Can you review the Q2 sales report in Google Drive by 3 PM today?"

2. Use Threads and Reactions Thoughtfully

Slack threads help maintain order in conversations. Instead of flooding a channel with scattered replies, threads allow discussions to stay neatly grouped under the original message.

Benefits of using threads:

- Keeps conversations contextual

- Makes it easier to catch up on a topic

- Reduces channel clutter

Encourage your team to:

- Start a thread for each new topic

- Respond to questions in the thread, not in the main feed

- Tag people in the thread when necessary to notify them

Reactions are communication too: Emoji reactions can serve as a lightweight way to acknowledge messages without sending another text. Use 👍 to agree, ✅ to mark completion, or 👀 to indicate that something is being reviewed.

3. Promote Asynchronous Communication

In remote teams, especially global ones, synchronous communication (real-time chatting) is not always feasible. Slack shines as a platform for asynchronous updates.

Create recurring asynchronous rituals:

- Daily stand-ups: Ask team members to post their tasks, blockers, and updates in a dedicated thread each morning.

- Weekly retrospectives: Create a thread where teammates can post what went well, what didn't, and what can improve.

Use scheduled messages: Slack's scheduled message feature lets users compose messages and choose when they're sent. This is ideal for sending messages at appropriate hours for different time zones.

Be mindful of urgency: Encourage people to avoid expecting immediate replies unless it's truly urgent. Emphasize the importance of work-life balance in remote settings.

4. Design Channels for Transparency and Collaboration

Effective channel organization makes Slack easier to navigate and supports transparency across teams.

Use naming conventions: For example:

- #proj-website-redesign

- #team-marketing

- #dept-hr-updates

Create shared channels across departments: Instead of siloed communication, Slack channels should reflect cross-functional collaboration. For example, a shared channel between the design and marketing teams can help both stay aligned on visual campaigns.

Make project documentation accessible: Pin important links, files, and documents at the top of each channel. Use bookmarks or the "pinned items" feature to ensure that new members can quickly find key resources.

5. Balance Formal and Informal Communication

One overlooked challenge of remote work is the erosion of informal conversations that typically happen in hallways or at lunch. Slack can help restore some of that lost connection.

Create social channels:

- #random or #watercooler for memes and casual talk

- #wins for celebrating accomplishments

- #reading-club, #pets, #wellness for shared interests

Celebrate milestones together: Use Slack to celebrate birthdays, work anniversaries, or team achievements. A quick congratulatory message or GIF can help people feel seen and appreciated.

Host virtual coffee chats: Set up a #coffee-pairs channel and use Slack integrations like Donut to randomly pair team members for casual conversations. This promotes bonding across departments.

6. Use Slack Huddles and Clips to Supplement Text

While text is great for documentation and clarity, sometimes face-to-face or voice communication is more effective.

Huddles:
Slack Huddles are lightweight voice and video calls that can be started instantly in any conversation. Use them when:

- Discussions get too complex for threads

- Brainstorming or whiteboarding is needed

- A quick sync is faster than typing

Clips:
Slack Clips allow users to record and send short videos or voice messages. This is especially helpful for:

- Providing detailed instructions

- Offering visual updates on projects

- Giving personalized feedback

These features help replicate the spontaneity of office chats and add a human element to remote communication.

7. Integrate Slack with Your Work Tools

Remote teams often use a wide array of tools—project management, file sharing, video conferencing, and more. Slack can serve as the central hub by integrating those tools.

Examples of helpful integrations:

- **Google Drive or OneDrive** for file sharing and collaboration

- **Asana, Trello, or ClickUp** for project management updates

- **Zoom or Google Meet** for scheduled calls and meetings

- **Calendar integrations** for daily schedule reminders

These integrations reduce the need to switch between platforms and keep everyone informed in real-time.

8. Encourage Inclusive Communication

Remote teams are often diverse across geography, culture, and language. Communication practices should reflect that.

Be mindful of tone: Without vocal cues, messages can be easily misinterpreted. Encourage positive, respectful, and clear writing. Use emojis and punctuation to provide helpful context.

Avoid jargon and acronyms: Unless everyone understands them, avoid internal abbreviations or industry jargon that may alienate some team members.

Make space for quieter voices: Encourage inclusive participation by directly inviting quieter members to share their views—especially in decision-making threads or feedback sessions.

9. Monitor and Evolve Your Communication Culture

Creating a remote-friendly Slack culture is not a one-time task—it requires continual refinement.

Gather feedback: Conduct periodic surveys to understand how the team feels about Slack communication—what works, what doesn't, and what could be improved.

Review channel usage: Are channels serving their purpose? Are there inactive or overlapping channels? Clean up or merge where needed to keep Slack streamlined.

Promote internal Slack champions: Appoint team members to act as Slack coaches or champions who help others learn features, model good behavior, and keep the culture vibrant.

Conclusion

Slack is more than just a messaging app—it's the digital heartbeat of a remote or hybrid organization. By applying best practices in communication, threading, asynchronous updates, tool integration, and inclusive culture-building, teams can overcome the barriers of distance and time.

Creating a remote-friendly Slack culture requires intention, consistency, and care. But with the right approach, Slack becomes not just a platform for work—but a place where remote teams connect, grow, and thrive.

6.1.2 Using Slack to Build Team Engagement

In a world where physical distance often separates team members, fostering meaningful engagement becomes not just a nice-to-have, but an essential pillar of high-performing remote and hybrid teams. Slack—when used intentionally—can be more than just a messaging platform; it can become the digital heartbeat of your company culture. From casual interactions to structured team-building, Slack offers numerous tools and opportunities to strengthen bonds, promote collaboration, and keep morale high.

This section will explore practical strategies and tools within Slack that you can use to build authentic, sustained team engagement in remote and hybrid environments.

1. Understanding Engagement in a Remote Context

Before diving into the tools, it's essential to understand what "engagement" means in a remote setting. In traditional office environments, engagement may stem from casual hallway conversations, team lunches, or shared moments during coffee breaks. Remote teams lack these spontaneous moments, making it necessary to create deliberate alternatives.

Slack provides opportunities for:

- **Connection**: Enabling personal and professional conversations.

- **Recognition**: Acknowledging contributions and milestones publicly.

- **Participation**: Encouraging every team member to be part of discussions.

- **Belonging**: Creating a space where team members feel seen, heard, and valued.

2. Creating Purposeful Channels for Engagement

One of the most powerful features in Slack is **channels**, and when used strategically, they can support engagement in multiple dimensions.

2.1 Social and Interest-Based Channels

Create dedicated channels for non-work discussions and shared interests. These channels provide room for team bonding and a mental break from work-related tasks.

Examples include:

- #random: A classic channel for memes, jokes, and general conversation.

- #pets-of-slack: For sharing adorable pet photos and stories.

- #book-club: Where employees can suggest and discuss books.

- #wellness: Sharing tips, workout challenges, and mindfulness prompts.

- #coffee-break: A virtual space to replicate the watercooler vibe.

Encouraging people to join and participate in these channels can lead to stronger relationships and a better understanding of one another's personalities and interests.

2.2 Celebration Channels

Recognizing accomplishments is critical to motivation. Consider creating:

- #shoutouts: A place for peer-to-peer recognition.

- #wins: For sharing team successes, large and small.

- #birthdays-and-anniversaries: For celebrating personal milestones.

These channels promote positivity and encourage employees to uplift each other.

3. Encouraging Recognition and Appreciation

One of the easiest, yet most impactful, ways to engage remote employees is through recognition. Slack makes it easy to publicly praise and thank colleagues.

Use Emoji Reactions

Reacting with emojis like 👏, 🙌, or 💯 to a message acknowledging someone's work can reinforce appreciation.

Custom Emoji Culture

Create custom emojis that reflect your team's personality. For example:

- A special thumbs-up image of your CEO.

- A team mascot reaction gif.

- Inside jokes made into emoji form.

These unique touches reinforce belonging and add fun to communication.

Slack Apps for Recognition

Integrate apps like:

- **HeyTaco!**: Give "tacos" to teammates as a form of kudos.

- **Bonusly**: Offer a points-based reward system.

- **Karma**: Track and highlight helpful behavior.

These tools gamify engagement and make it easier to embed recognition into daily Slack interactions.

4. Hosting Virtual Team Activities via Slack

Slack can also serve as the coordination hub for virtual team-building activities. Whether you're launching a quiz, hosting an online escape room, or simply playing a weekly game, Slack can bring it all together.

Trivia and Games

Use bots or apps such as:

- **Polly**: Run quick polls or trivia games.
- **Donut Games**: Offers simple and fun Slack-native activities.
- **Water Cooler Trivia**: A weekly trivia game sent via Slack.

Encourage playful competition and light-hearted engagement.

Theme Days and Challenges

Host themed days like:

- "Throwback Thursday": Share old photos.
- "Guess the Desk": Have team members post pictures of their desks.
- "Outfit of the Day": For teams who enjoy fashion or costume contests.

Or create wellness or creativity challenges:

- 7-day meditation challenge.
- Daily drawing prompts.
- Step-count competition.

These activities create recurring opportunities to connect outside of work conversations.

5. Facilitating Informal Interactions

Remote environments can feel transactional if all interactions are strictly task-oriented. You can intentionally recreate informal interactions using Slack features.

5.1 Donut Bot: Virtual Coffee Chats

Donut is a popular Slack integration that randomly pairs team members for casual 1-on-1 chats. You can configure it to run weekly or monthly, encouraging informal conversations that build connection across departments or regions.

Encourage questions like:

- What's your favorite movie of all time?

- If you could have dinner with any historical figure, who would it be?

These conversations help team members connect on a human level.

5.2 Icebreakers and Prompts

Use a recurring post (manually or via bot) to post daily or weekly conversation starters in a social channel.

Examples:

- "What's one food you could eat every day?"

- "What's your dream vacation?"

- "Share a photo of your view right now."

This not only gets people talking but helps reveal shared experiences and interests.

6. Promoting Transparency and Inclusion

Remote engagement isn't just about fun—it's also about **building trust and inclusion**. Use Slack to promote transparency across teams and leadership levels.

Leadership AMA (Ask Me Anything)

Encourage leaders to host scheduled AMAs in a dedicated channel like #ask-leadership. Let team members post anonymous questions using integrated tools like Slido or Polly.

This helps employees feel heard and connected to the bigger picture.

Company Updates and Open Forums

Instead of top-down memos, try:

- Weekly posts in #company-news or #weekly-update.

- Hosting regular "open office hours" where employees can drop in questions to leadership.

This openness builds trust and aligns the team around shared goals.

7. Supporting Mental Health and Wellbeing

An engaged team is a healthy team. Slack can also serve as a tool for emotional support and mental wellness.

Wellness Check-In Bots

Bots like Moodbit or Officevibe let employees report how they're feeling anonymously. These insights can help managers act proactively when morale is slipping.

Mindfulness and Encouragement

Share daily or weekly mindfulness tips, inspirational quotes, or breathing exercises in a channel like #mental-health or #wellbeing.

Encourage employees to:

- Share their self-care tips.

- Join group meditation or yoga sessions.

- Take real breaks during the day.

8. Creating a Culture of Engagement, Not Just Activities

Remember: engagement is not just about scheduling fun events. It's about building a culture where people feel seen, valued, and connected. Using Slack as your platform for culture means:

- Encouraging everyone to use their voice.

- Celebrating small wins, not just big goals.

- Being intentional about inclusion—especially for quiet voices.

As a team leader or engagement champion, your role is to model active participation, highlight great examples of engagement, and empower others to lead initiatives themselves.

9. Measuring Engagement in Slack

Finally, it's helpful to track whether your efforts are actually making a difference.

Look for metrics like:

- Channel participation rates.

- Number of peer recognitions or emoji reactions.

- Responses to engagement surveys or polls.

- Donut meeting completion rates.

Some tools like Slack Analytics, Officevibe, or Culture Amp can help you gather insights and refine your approach.

Conclusion: Build Engagement One Interaction at a Time

Team engagement doesn't happen overnight—and it certainly doesn't happen by accident. By leveraging Slack's tools and building a thoughtful engagement strategy, you can create a vibrant culture where people feel connected, appreciated, and excited to contribute—no matter where they are in the world.

Remember, engagement is about the daily micro-moments: the supportive emoji, the quick "how are you doing?" message, the spontaneous meme, or the shoutout after a hard-fought deadline. Slack gives you the canvas—now it's up to you to paint it with purpose, fun, and empathy.

6.1.3 Setting Boundaries Between Work and Life

In the age of remote and hybrid work, the boundary between our professional and personal lives has become increasingly blurred. Tools like Slack offer us incredible flexibility and connectivity, but without careful management, that convenience can turn into a source of stress, burnout, and imbalance.

This section will help you understand how to use Slack intentionally, enabling you to maintain a healthy boundary between work and life—even when both take place under the same roof.

The Challenge of Always Being Available

Slack is designed to encourage real-time communication. That's part of what makes it such a powerful collaboration tool. But when your notifications keep coming long after your workday has ended, or when your teammates message you late at night because they assume you're still online, it becomes easy to feel like you're never truly "off the clock."

In remote or hybrid environments, where water cooler talk is replaced by emoji reactions and quick DMs, people often feel pressure to appear responsive and available at all hours. This constant connection may feel like dedication, but it can lead to:

- Digital exhaustion
- Decreased productivity
- Poor sleep and mental health
- Reduced job satisfaction

To combat this, creating clear and respectful boundaries within Slack is essential—for yourself and for your team.

Why Setting Boundaries Matters

When you protect your personal time, you're doing more than just avoiding burnout—you're promoting a culture that values balance, clarity, and well-being. Here's why it matters:

- **Improved focus during work hours**: When you're not burned out, you're sharper and more productive.

- **Greater team respect**: When boundaries are modeled and respected, the whole team benefits.

- **Sustainable performance**: Balance supports long-term success, not just short-term output.

Now let's explore some practical strategies to set—and maintain—those healthy boundaries in Slack.

Strategies for Creating Work-Life Boundaries in Slack

1. Define Your Working Hours Clearly

Slack allows you to set a **custom status** or **working hours**, so colleagues know when you're online. Set clear expectations by doing the following:

- **Set your availability in your status.**
  Example: " 🌙 Offline after 6PM | Back at 9AM"

- **Use your profile to communicate working time.**
  Include a line in your Slack bio or display name like:
  "Working hours: 9AM–6PM (Mon–Fri)"

- **Use shared calendar integrations** (like Google Calendar) so your availability appears in Slack when someone tries to message you.

This helps others understand when they can expect responses and when they should avoid pinging you.

2. Use Slack's "Do Not Disturb" Mode

Slack has a built-in **Do Not Disturb (DND)** feature that mutes notifications during specific hours. Here's how to set it up:

- **On Desktop**: Click your profile picture → Pause notifications → Set a schedule.

- **On Mobile**: Tap the You tab → Notifications → Do Not Disturb → Set a schedule.

Use this to automatically pause notifications after your work hours. Slack will also show a small notification to anyone who messages you during DND, so they know you're not ignoring them—they're just outside your hours.

3. Schedule Messages Instead of Sending Them Immediately

Just because you're working late or in a different time zone doesn't mean others should be interrupted. Use **Slack's "Schedule Send"** feature to compose messages during your off-hours but deliver them during normal hours.

For example:

- Draft a message at 10PM, but schedule it to send at 9AM the next day.

- Use this for announcements, updates, or follow-ups that don't require urgent attention.

This small gesture demonstrates respect for your teammates' time and encourages asynchronous communication.

4. Separate Work and Personal Spaces

If you use Slack on your phone or laptop for both work and personal purposes, set clear boundaries between the two:

- **Use Slack's multiple workspaces feature**, keeping work and non-work conversations in separate places.

- **Avoid using work Slack on your personal phone**, or at least disable push notifications outside work hours.

- **Designate a "work zone" at home**, even if it's just a specific chair or desk, and only check Slack while in that space.

Creating physical and mental "zones" helps your brain shift gears between work and rest.

5. Set Expectations with Your Team

Healthy boundaries don't work unless they're supported by your team culture. Consider these tips:

- **Talk openly about boundaries.**
  During onboarding or team meetings, encourage everyone to define their working hours and DND preferences.

- **Lead by example.**
  If you're a manager, avoid sending messages at odd hours. When it's unavoidable, schedule them instead.

- **Establish team-wide agreements.**
  Consider creating a simple Slack etiquette guide that includes:

  - Response time expectations

  - After-hours communication policies

  - Guidelines for using @mentions and channel alerts

6. Use Personal Reminders and Automations

Slack's **/remind** command can help you set reminders to log off or take breaks:

- /remind me to stop working at 6PM every weekday

- /remind me to stretch every 2 hours

For deeper automation, integrate Slack with **apps like Zapier, Google Calendar, or Todoist**, so you can automatically mark yourself as unavailable during calendar events or non-working hours.

7. Reflect Regularly and Adjust

Remote life changes. So do our routines. Once every month or so, reflect on how your Slack usage is affecting your personal life:

- Are you checking messages after hours too often?

- Are notifications causing stress?

- Are you unintentionally making others feel obligated to respond late?

If so, revisit your boundaries and re-communicate them with your team. Consider taking a brief Slack break or logging out entirely during vacations or mental health days.

Redefining "Responsiveness" in Remote Teams

One of the reasons people feel guilty about not responding instantly on Slack is the false belief that **responsiveness equals productivity**. But in remote work, **quality communication** often matters more than speed.

Encourage asynchronous collaboration by:

- Using **threads** to keep topics organized

- Posting **summaries or updates** rather than open-ended questions

- Encouraging teammates to respond when they're able—not immediately

Slack works best when it helps you *focus*, not when it distracts you every time a message appears.

Case Study: Team Harmony Through Slack Boundaries

At a mid-sized tech startup, the engineering team started experiencing burnout due to Slack overuse. After reviewing Slack analytics, they noticed most messages were sent after 6PM, with engineers often replying within minutes.

The team decided to:

- Set DND for all team members from 6PM–8AM

- Ban @channel mentions outside of emergencies

- Begin using the "schedule send" feature for all late-night updates

Within two months, the team reported:

- Higher work satisfaction

- Less anxiety about "missing" messages

- No drop in performance or collaboration

Conclusion: Protecting Your Energy While Staying Connected

Slack is a fantastic tool for collaboration—but it should serve you, not enslave you.

By intentionally setting and maintaining boundaries between work and life, you gain:

- More focused, high-quality work time

- Greater rest and personal fulfillment

- A more respectful, sustainable remote culture

Whether you're leading a team or contributing as an individual, you have the power to shape how Slack works for you. Take control of your notifications, your time, and your space—and you'll discover that balance and productivity can, in fact, go hand in hand.

6.2 Managing Projects in Slack

6.2.1 Using Slack with Project Management Tools

In the evolving landscape of remote and hybrid work, project management has become more digital, more dynamic, and more distributed than ever before. Traditional, email-heavy project coordination methods no longer meet the needs of fast-moving teams. Slack, with its robust communication features and deep integration ecosystem, offers a powerful platform to centralize your project management efforts and keep everyone aligned—regardless of location.

This section will guide you through how to leverage Slack alongside popular project management tools to streamline workflows, ensure transparency, and keep teams focused on outcomes. You'll learn about best practices, integration options, automation opportunities, and real-world examples of how organizations are using Slack to coordinate projects effectively.

Why Integrate Project Management Tools with Slack?

Before diving into the how, it's important to understand the why. Slack is not a dedicated project management tool—but it **complements and enhances** them in valuable ways.

Here's what you gain by integrating Slack with tools like Trello, Asana, ClickUp, Jira, Notion, or Monday.com:

- **Centralized Communication**: No more scattered emails and updates. Everything related to a project—from task assignments to status updates—can flow through Slack.

- **Real-Time Notifications**: Get instant updates when tasks are created, completed, or commented on.

- **Improved Transparency**: Teams can easily track progress, blockers, and discussions without toggling between multiple apps.

- **Increased Accountability**: When actions and deadlines are visible to everyone in a shared Slack channel, accountability improves.

- **Automation & Efficiency**: Routine workflows (e.g., assigning tasks, tracking time, sending reminders) can be automated via Slack integrations and bots.

Choosing the Right Project Management Tool for Slack Integration

Slack integrates with a wide range of project management platforms. Choosing the right one depends on your team's size, working style, and project complexity. Here's a quick overview of some popular tools and how they work with Slack:

1. Trello

Trello is known for its simplicity and card-based system, which works well for visual thinkers.

- **Slack Integration Highlights:**
  - Create Trello cards directly from Slack messages.
  - Get updates in Slack when cards are moved or updated.
  - Assign members and set due dates via Slack commands.

- **Use Case Example**: A content marketing team uses a Trello board to manage blog posts. When a new idea is posted in Slack, a card can be instantly created in Trello with /trello add.

2. Asana

Asana is ideal for task management, timelines, and complex workflows.

- **Slack Integration Highlights:**
  - Turn Slack messages into Asana tasks.
  - Get Slack notifications for project changes.
  - Link projects to channels for centralized updates.

- **Use Case Example**: A product team tracks a launch campaign in Asana. All relevant updates are piped into a dedicated Slack channel, so no one misses key deadlines.

3. Jira

Jira is best for software development and bug tracking.

- **Slack Integration Highlights:**
  - Create, assign, and update issues from Slack.
  - Get alerts when tickets are moved or commented on.
  - Use slash commands for quick actions.

- **Use Case Example**: A software team monitors sprints and bug tickets using Jira. Critical updates automatically post in Slack's #engineering channel for visibility.

4. ClickUp

ClickUp is an all-in-one tool combining docs, goals, and task management.

- **Slack Integration Highlights:**
  - Create tasks from Slack messages.
  - Add comments to existing ClickUp tasks directly from Slack.
  - Receive real-time updates in channels.

5. Monday.com

Monday.com provides a highly customizable work operating system.

- **Slack Integration Highlights:**
  - Automatically post updates to Slack when task status changes.
  - Get reminders for upcoming deadlines.
  - Create new items from Slack.

Setting Up Slack Integrations with Project Tools

Most integrations can be set up in just a few clicks:

1. **Go to Slack's App Directory** (https://slack.com/apps) and search for your tool (e.g., Trello, Asana).

2. **Install the app** and grant necessary permissions.

3. **Connect your account** (e.g., log into your Asana account via the Slack prompt).

4. **Configure notifications**—choose which projects, boards, or tasks should send updates to which channels.

5. **Use slash commands** or message actions to start using the integration.

Best Practices for Managing Projects in Slack

To truly unlock the power of Slack for project management, consider these tips:

1. Use Dedicated Project Channels

Create a channel for each major project (e.g., #project-website-redesign). This becomes a centralized hub where conversations, updates, and integrations live.

- Pin important documents, Trello boards, or Notion pages.

- Invite only relevant stakeholders to reduce noise.

2. Use Message Actions to Create Tasks

Instead of copying and pasting, turn any Slack message into a task directly. Most integrations support message actions like "Create Task" or "Add to Board."

3. Automate Repetitive Workflows

Use tools like Zapier, Slack Workflow Builder, or Make.com to automate routine actions:

- When a Trello card is due, send a Slack DM.

- When a Jira issue is marked "Done," send a message to the #team-updates channel.

- Create weekly reminders for sprint reviews or standups.

4. Keep Updates Short and Consistent

Encourage your team to share brief, regular updates in Slack using a common format. For example:

- Done: Homepage wireframe

- In Progress: Hero image animations

- Blocked: Waiting on client feedback

5. Limit Notification Overload

Too many automated updates can drown important messages. Choose the most relevant events to post in Slack. You can always adjust your integration settings later.

Using Slack Huddles & Threads for Project Discussions

Slack isn't just for task updates—it's a real-time collaboration space. You can enhance project flow by using:

- **Huddles**: For quick team syncs or brainstorming without setting up a Zoom call.

- **Threads**: Keep discussions organized. Always reply in threads when discussing a specific task or update.

- **Polls & Emoji Voting**: Use /poll or reactions for lightweight decision-making.

Real-World Workflow Example

Let's say your remote product team is launching a new app feature:

- You create a Slack channel #feature-launch-alpha.

- You integrate Trello and link the board to the channel.

- As tasks move across the Trello board, the Slack channel reflects those updates.

- Daily standups happen in Slack using an automated reminder and a format template.

- Questions are asked and answered in threads to avoid clutter.

- A weekly huddle is scheduled every Monday morning for live updates.

This kind of setup allows your team to move fast, stay informed, and feel connected—even across time zones.

Conclusion: Slack as a Project Command Center

Slack isn't just for chatting—it's the digital command center for your projects. By connecting it with project management tools and adopting intentional workflows, your team can reduce miscommunication, eliminate delays, and work more transparently.

In remote and hybrid environments where teams span cities or continents, Slack offers the **connective tissue** that keeps everyone aligned. Whether you're managing a product launch, a marketing campaign, or a development sprint, Slack can serve as the single source of truth where communication and project execution come together.

With the right integrations, structure, and habits, your projects won't just be managed—they'll **flow**.

6.2.2 Creating Dedicated Project Channels

In a remote or hybrid work environment, seamless project coordination becomes a vital factor in determining team success. Traditional methods like endless email threads or scattered messaging platforms often create confusion, silo information, and delay progress. Slack revolutionizes project management by allowing teams to create dedicated project channels—virtual spaces where conversations, files, deadlines, and decisions are centralized and transparent.

This section will guide you through why dedicated project channels are essential, how to create them effectively, and best practices to maximize their impact.

Why Dedicated Project Channels Matter

A dedicated project channel acts as the digital "war room" for your project. Instead of information being buried in private DMs or lost in disconnected emails, every team member has access to a single source of truth. Here's why they matter:

- **Focus:** Project-specific channels prevent off-topic discussions, helping members stay focused on objectives and tasks.

- **Transparency:** Everyone involved in the project—regardless of location—can see progress, ask questions, and provide input.

- **Efficiency:** With pinned messages, file uploads, and app integrations, Slack channels can function like lightweight project management hubs.

- **Accountability:** Having a visible timeline and responsibilities reduces the likelihood of miscommunication and ensures clear ownership of tasks.

How to Create a Project Channel in Slack

Creating a dedicated channel for a project is simple. But for maximum effectiveness, it requires thoughtful setup. Let's break this down:

Step 1: Choose the Right Channel Type

Slack offers two types of channels:

- **Public Channels:** Visible to everyone in the workspace. Best when you want open collaboration or your project affects multiple departments.

- **Private Channels:** Visible only to invited members. Ideal for sensitive projects or when dealing with confidential information.

Tip: Start with a private channel during the early planning phase. You can later convert it to public (though not vice versa).

Step 2: Establish a Clear Naming Convention

Consistent naming helps users quickly identify the channel's purpose. For example:

- #proj-marketing-launch-q3

- #proj-website-redesign-2025

- #proj-customer-survey

Use a prefix like #proj- to separate project channels from department or social channels.

Step 3: Write a Purposeful Channel Description

When creating the channel, write a **clear and concise description** of its intent. For example:

"Channel for the Q3 marketing campaign. Includes planning, timelines, asset tracking, and launch updates."

This helps new members understand what the channel is about and reduces off-topic discussions.

Step 4: Add Relevant Members Immediately

Invite all stakeholders, team members, and contributors to the channel right away. Make sure they know **why** they've been added and what's expected of them.

For cross-functional teams, don't forget to include:

- Project manager or team lead

- Designers or content creators

- Developers or technical team

- Marketing/communications team

- Operations or finance representatives (if applicable)

Structuring the Channel for Success

A cluttered channel can quickly become a noisy place. Set up the channel thoughtfully from the beginning to streamline collaboration.

Pin Important Messages

Use the pin feature to highlight critical posts:

- Project timeline or roadmap

- Meeting schedules

- Links to shared documents

- Decision logs

Pinned messages appear in the channel details sidebar, making them easy to find for all members.

Set Guidelines in a Welcome Message

Post a welcome message with basic instructions. Example:

👋 Welcome to #proj-marketing-launch-q3
This channel is for updates, questions, and resources related to the Q3 marketing campaign.
✅ Check the pinned messages for the timeline and key assets
ℹ️ Weekly check-ins are scheduled every Monday at 10am
📥 Tag @john.smith for copywriting questions
Let's make this a smooth and successful campaign!

This sets the tone and provides clarity from the start.

Use Threads to Keep Conversations Organized

Instead of responding to a message directly in the channel, reply in a **thread**. Threads prevent conversations from getting lost or overwhelming the main view.

Encourage your team to:

- Use threads for task discussions

- Mention relevant people in thread replies

- Keep each thread focused on a single topic

Integrating Project Management Tools

To take your project channels to the next level, integrate Slack with your favorite project management tools. Some popular integrations include:

- **Trello:** Create and update cards from within Slack

- **Asana:** Assign tasks, mark completions, and receive updates

- **Jira:** Link tickets, view issue statuses, and automate workflows

- **Google Drive/Dropbox:** Share and preview documents easily

- **Miro/Figma:** Collaborate on whiteboards and designs directly

With these integrations, your Slack channel becomes a command center—not just a chatroom.

Maintaining Channel Hygiene Over Time

As the project progresses, channels can become cluttered or difficult to follow. Implement simple practices to keep things tidy:

Regularly Update Pinned Messages

As tasks are completed or timelines change, refresh pinned content.

Summarize Weekly Progress

Post a weekly summary with:

- Completed milestones

- Upcoming tasks

- Open questions

Archive When Complete

Once the project wraps up, archive the channel to keep your Slack workspace organized. You'll still be able to search it later if needed.

Best Practices for Project Channels

Let's summarize some golden rules for managing effective project channels:

1. **Limit Membership to Active Contributors:** Avoid adding passive observers unless necessary.

2. **Encourage Accountability:** Ask team members to post task updates or blockers directly in the channel.

3. **Avoid Side Conversations in DMs:** Keep project discussions in the channel to ensure visibility.

4. **Use Emojis and Reactions:** These are great for quick responses, approvals, and keeping things fun.

5. **Tag Strategically:** Avoid over-tagging everyone. Use @here and @channel sparingly to avoid alert fatigue.

Example: A Real-World Use Case

Let's imagine a fictional company, **BrightWorks**, launching a new mobile app.

They create the channel #proj-mobileapp-launch.

Here's how they structure it:

- Channel topic: "Tracking all progress and collaboration for Mobile App Launch – Q2"

- Pinned messages: roadmap, timeline, shared folders, Zoom link for weekly calls

- Weekly Monday post:

🚀 **Week 3 Progress Report**
☑ UI/UX review completed
🛠 Development 70% complete
📅 Launch beta testing next Friday

- Tools integrated: Trello, Google Drive, Figma

This one channel becomes a living, breathing space where collaboration happens efficiently and asynchronously, across time zones and departments.

Conclusion: Empowering Project Success with Slack

Creating dedicated project channels in Slack isn't just a feature—it's a strategic approach to modern collaboration. By centralizing communication, enhancing transparency, and connecting tools, teams can stay aligned and agile throughout the project lifecycle.

Whether you're running a two-week sprint or managing a six-month rollout, Slack gives you the environment to communicate clearly, share progress, and make smarter decisions—together.

As remote and hybrid work continues to evolve, mastering project channels will help you lead more effectively and deliver results with clarity and confidence.

6.2.3 Tracking Progress and Deliverables in Slack

Slack has revolutionized the way we communicate and collaborate, especially for remote and hybrid teams. One of its most powerful features is its ability to integrate various tools and keep team members aligned, no matter where they are working from. Managing projects and tracking progress within Slack is not only efficient but also keeps everyone on the same page, reduces the need for constant meetings, and helps managers maintain control over project deliverables. In this section, we will explore how Slack can be utilized to track progress, manage deliverables, and ensure that your team is always on target.

1. Setting Up Your Project Management Workspace in Slack

Before diving into the specifics of tracking progress and deliverables, it's essential to establish a well-organized Slack workspace. Slack channels are the primary tool for organizing conversations, and they can be configured to suit different aspects of project management. Start by creating dedicated project channels for your team. These channels can be organized by project, department, or function.

For example, you can create a channel called #project-marketing-campaign for a specific project. This channel can house all discussions, updates, files, and even project milestones related to the marketing campaign. You could also create sub-channels like #project-marketing-campaign-creative or #project-marketing-campaign-analytics to focus on particular aspects of the project.

Once your channels are set up, you can invite team members based on their roles and responsibilities. Slack offers flexibility by allowing you to create both private and public channels. Public channels allow anyone in the workspace to join, whereas private channels restrict access to invited members only. When it comes to tracking progress and deliverables, it's essential to ensure that all relevant stakeholders have access to the appropriate channels.

2. Integrating Project Management Tools with Slack

While Slack provides a wealth of features to communicate and organize work, it works even better when integrated with external project management tools like Trello, Asana, Monday.com, or ClickUp. These integrations enable you to bring your project management into Slack, allowing you to track deliverables without leaving the platform.

Using Asana with Slack

Asana is one of the most widely used project management tools, and its integration with Slack offers a powerful solution for tracking project progress. Once you integrate Asana with Slack, you can receive notifications in specific channels whenever tasks are completed, comments are added, or deadlines are approaching. You can also create tasks directly from Slack, keeping the process seamless.

For example, if you're working on a project with several deliverables, you can create tasks for each deliverable and assign them to the responsible team members. As tasks are completed, Slack will notify everyone in the designated project channel, so you can keep track of the project's progress in real-time.

Using Trello with Slack

Trello is another popular tool that allows you to visually organize tasks on boards. When integrated with Slack, you can set up notifications for changes in Trello boards, such as when cards are moved, due dates are changed, or tasks are completed. This provides an immediate overview of your project's progress without having to check multiple platforms.

A great use case for Trello in Slack is the ability to add comments and attach files directly in Trello from within Slack. This can save time and streamline communication, ensuring that relevant information stays in one place.

3. Setting Up Milestones and Deadlines in Slack

One of the key ways to track progress and deliverables is through the use of milestones and deadlines. In Slack, you can use tools like reminders, calendar integrations, and checklists to ensure that the team remains on track.

Using Slack Reminders to Track Deadlines

Slack's built-in reminder feature is an invaluable tool for tracking deadlines. You can set reminders for yourself or for the team at any time. For example, when you assign a task to someone, you can set a reminder for when it is due. To do this, simply use the /remind command in the appropriate channel. For instance, if you are working on a deliverable with a due date of Friday, you could use the following command: /remind @channel "Submit the final report" on Friday at 3pm. This reminder will alert everyone in the channel at the designated time, ensuring that nothing is missed.

Using Slack Calendar Integration

Slack integrates well with tools like Google Calendar or Outlook, making it easy to manage deadlines directly within the platform. When you link your calendar to Slack, you can get daily updates on upcoming events and due dates. Calendar events can be added to channels or direct messages, so team members are reminded of important deadlines or meetings.

To make sure everyone is on the same page, you can set up a recurring weekly sync to review project progress. By integrating Slack with Google Calendar, for example, your team can automatically receive reminders and updates about project milestones.

Creating Checklists with Slack

You can also create simple checklists within Slack to track tasks and deliverables. There are many Slack apps like Trello, Google Keep, or Simple Poll that help you create checklists and task lists within your channels. These checklists can be used to visualize what's been done and what still needs attention. By turning this into a recurring task, you can effectively ensure that your team is staying on top of deliverables.

4. Using Slack's Analytics and Reporting Features

To better track project progress and team performance, Slack provides several analytics and reporting tools that can be invaluable for managers. Slack's built-in analytics provide insights into the number of messages sent, active users, and channel engagement. These metrics can give you a sense of how engaged your team is and whether any communication bottlenecks are affecting your project.

For instance, if you notice that a specific channel has fewer interactions, you may want to investigate if team members are struggling to keep up with updates or if the project needs more frequent check-ins. Analytics can also help identify which deliverables are causing delays, allowing you to reallocate resources if necessary.

Additionally, Slack's third-party integrations, such as those with Asana and Trello, offer more in-depth project reporting. You can pull reports from these tools directly into your Slack channels, providing you with live status updates on task completion, upcoming deadlines, and project metrics.

5. Encouraging Transparency and Accountability

Transparency is a crucial aspect of tracking progress in Slack. When all communication, updates, and deliverables are stored in an accessible space, everyone can track progress easily. It's essential to cultivate a culture of accountability within your team. Slack's features enable everyone to see what tasks are in progress, who is responsible for them, and what deadlines are approaching.

Using @Mentions for Accountability

One of the most effective ways to hold people accountable within Slack is by using @mentions. By tagging specific team members or entire teams in messages, you draw their attention to important tasks, updates, or feedback. For example, if a task is behind schedule, you can mention the person responsible and ask for an update on the project's status.

Public Channels for Transparency

While private channels are great for specific sub-teams or confidential discussions, public channels allow everyone in the organization to see project updates and progress. This transparency can motivate team members to stay on track, as they will know that their progress is visible to everyone. It also allows for cross-team collaboration, as other teams can see how their work intersects with yours.

6. Regular Check-Ins and Progress Reviews

Finally, to track progress effectively, it's essential to schedule regular check-ins with your team. These check-ins can be informal, such as a quick daily stand-up in Slack, or more formal, like weekly or monthly project review meetings.

Daily Stand-Ups

Using Slack to facilitate daily stand-up meetings is an excellent way to keep track of progress and ensure everyone is aligned on project deliverables. You can ask each team member to provide a quick update on what they accomplished yesterday, what they plan to do today, and whether there are any roadblocks. You can create a recurring reminder for these stand-ups, so the team knows to check in daily at a specific time.

Weekly Progress Reviews

In addition to daily check-ins, weekly progress reviews in Slack are vital for tracking larger deliverables. At the end of the week, you can set up a review where team members post updates on their tasks. You can use Slack's integrations with project management tools to pull reports directly into the channel, so everyone has a clear picture of where the project stands.

Conclusion: Streamlining Project Tracking with Slack

Slack is an incredibly powerful tool for managing projects, tracking progress, and ensuring that deliverables are met on time. By leveraging Slack's integrations with project management tools, customizing channels, setting up reminders, and fostering transparency, your team can stay on top of tasks and project milestones without unnecessary meetings or confusion. Slack provides all the features needed to track deliverables effectively, from task management to real-time updates and comprehensive reporting.

The ability to track project progress in Slack allows teams to move faster, stay aligned, and be more productive. By ensuring that all communication and updates are contained within Slack, you empower your team to work smarter, not harder. With the right setup and processes in place, Slack can be your ultimate tool for project management in remote and hybrid work environments.

6.3 Hosting Virtual Events and Meetings in Slack

In today's digital workplace, virtual events and meetings have become essential for teams working remotely or in hybrid environments. Slack provides a variety of tools and features that can help facilitate these events and meetings, making them more interactive, engaging, and efficient. One of the most valuable features in this regard is the ability to run **polls and surveys** directly within Slack. This simple yet powerful functionality enables teams to gather feedback, make decisions, and keep everyone engaged without leaving the Slack platform. In this section, we will explore how to effectively run polls and surveys within Slack, using both built-in features and third-party integrations.

6.3.1 Running Polls and Surveys

Why Use Polls and Surveys in Slack?

Polls and surveys are an essential tool for gathering opinions, making decisions, and ensuring that team members are aligned with group goals. In the context of remote and hybrid work, where teams may be scattered across different locations and time zones, polls and surveys are especially beneficial for getting quick feedback and making data-driven decisions in real-time.

Some key benefits of using polls and surveys in Slack include:

- **Instant Feedback**: Unlike traditional methods that may require follow-up meetings or emails, polls and surveys in Slack provide immediate responses, enabling faster decision-making.

- **Engagement**: Polls and surveys encourage participation and foster engagement among team members, which is particularly important in remote or hybrid teams that may not interact face-to-face regularly.

- **Democratic Decision Making**: Polls give everyone a voice, ensuring that decisions are inclusive and representative of the team's collective input.

- **Data Tracking**: Surveys allow teams to track responses and analyze trends over time, which can inform future decisions or highlight areas needing improvement.

Setting Up Polls in Slack:

There are several ways to create polls within Slack, ranging from simple, built-in features to more advanced integrations. Below are the most common methods:

1. Using Slack's Built-In Emoji Reactions for Polls

For a quick, informal poll, you can use Slack's emoji reaction feature. While this method isn't as detailed as a formal survey, it's a quick and easy way to gather feedback on a question or decision.

Steps to Create an Emoji Poll:

1. In the Slack channel, type out your question or prompt.

2. Add a few emoji options that represent the different answers. For example, a thumbs up emoji for "Yes," a thumbs down emoji for "No," and a party popper emoji for "Maybe."

3. Ask team members to respond by reacting to the message with one of the emojis.

4. Slack will automatically count the number of emoji reactions, providing a simple view of the results.

Pros:

- Quick and easy to set up.

- No additional integrations required.

- Great for informal decision-making or gauging interest.

Cons:

- Limited to basic responses (e.g., Yes/No/Maybe).

- Lacks advanced customization (e.g., multiple choice, open-ended answers).

2. Using Slack's Polls and Surveys Feature with Workflow Builder

For teams that require more structured polling, Slack's Workflow Builder can be a valuable tool. Workflow Builder is a feature that enables you to automate tasks in Slack, and it can be used to create custom polls and surveys.

Steps to Create a Poll Using Workflow Builder:

1. Open Slack and navigate to the **Workflow Builder** by clicking on the lightning bolt icon in the message input field.

2. Select **Create a Workflow**.

3. Choose **Create a Custom Poll** from the available templates or start from scratch.

4. Customize the poll by adding the question and answer options. You can also add deadlines, reminders, and custom responses for specific answers.

5. Once the poll is live, Slack will automatically collect responses and allow users to view the results.

6. Optionally, you can set up automated reminders to encourage team members to complete the poll.

Pros:

- More structured than emoji reactions.

- Can collect more detailed responses.

- Customizable to fit your team's needs (e.g., deadlines, reminders, follow-ups).

Cons:

- Requires some setup and familiarity with Slack's Workflow Builder.

- Limited to predefined workflows and templates.

3. Using Third-Party Slack Apps for Polls and Surveys

While Slack's native features are helpful for basic polling, you may want more advanced features, such as anonymous responses, open-ended questions, or more comprehensive survey tools. For these cases, third-party Slack apps can significantly enhance your poll and survey capabilities. Some popular third-party apps for polls and surveys include:

- **Polly**: A powerful and easy-to-use app that allows you to create polls, surveys, and quizzes directly in Slack. Polly can gather anonymous responses, integrate with Google Sheets for analysis, and provide real-time feedback.

- **Simple Poll**: A lightweight polling app that enables users to create polls with multiple choice options in seconds. It's particularly useful for quick team votes.

- **SurveyMonkey**: If you're looking for a robust survey platform, SurveyMonkey integrates with Slack to help you create more complex surveys with detailed analytics.

Setting Up a Poll with Polly (Example):

1. Install Polly from the Slack App Directory.

2. In a channel or direct message, type the following command: /polly followed by your question and answer options. For example: /polly "What's your favorite time for the team meeting?" "9:00 AM" "11:00 AM" "1:00 PM" "3:00 PM".

3. Polly will automatically create a poll with the specified options, and team members can vote.

4. After the poll ends, Polly will provide a summary of the responses, and you can even export the data for further analysis.

Pros:

- Advanced options for anonymous responses and detailed surveys.

- Easy-to-use interface for non-technical users.

- Integrates well with other apps and systems.

Cons:

- Requires installation of third-party apps.

- May require a subscription for access to premium features.

Best Practices for Running Polls and Surveys in Slack:

1. **Keep It Simple**: Avoid overwhelming your team with long, complicated surveys. Focus on the most important questions that will lead to actionable insights.

2. **Set Clear Deadlines**: If you are running a time-sensitive poll or survey, set a clear deadline to encourage participation.

3. **Encourage Participation**: Make sure to promote the poll in the channel and remind team members to participate.

4. **Make Results Visible**: Share the results with your team to show that their input is valued. This transparency will help increase future engagement.

5. **Use Anonymous Polls for Sensitive Topics**: If you are gathering feedback on sensitive issues, ensure that the poll is anonymous to encourage honest responses.

Analyzing and Acting on Poll Results

Once you've gathered the responses, it's essential to take the next steps based on the feedback you receive. Slack allows you to easily review the results of polls and surveys, but how you act on the data is crucial.

- **Track Trends**: If you run polls frequently, look for trends over time. For example, if you consistently receive feedback about a recurring issue or need, take proactive steps to address it.

- **Share Insights**: After analyzing the results, share a summary of the findings with your team. This demonstrates that their feedback matters and encourages future participation.

- **Make Decisions**: Use the data gathered to make informed decisions. For example, if a poll indicates that a majority of the team prefers a new meeting time, go ahead and implement the change.

Conclusion

Running polls and surveys in Slack is an effective way to engage your remote or hybrid team and gather valuable feedback. Whether you are using Slack's built-in features, Workflow Builder, or third-party apps, you can easily collect data, track team sentiment, and make decisions that align with the group's preferences. Polls and surveys are not just for decision-making—they can be an important part of creating a collaborative, transparent, and responsive work culture. With the right tools and practices, Slack can become a central hub for team communication, feedback, and growth.

6.3.2 Organizing Company Announcements

In today's rapidly changing business landscape, companies are increasingly relying on digital tools to facilitate communication and collaboration. Slack, a popular team messaging platform, has emerged as a central hub for many organizations, especially in remote and hybrid work environments. One of the powerful features that Slack offers is the ability to host virtual events and meetings, making it an invaluable tool for communication within distributed teams.

Among the most important types of communication for any organization are company-wide announcements. Whether you're sharing company news, new product launches, policy changes, or celebrating key milestones, organizing and broadcasting effective announcements is critical for keeping everyone on the same page. Slack's robust functionality offers several methods to do this, ensuring your message reaches the right audience at the right time.

Why Use Slack for Company Announcements?

Before diving into how to organize company announcements in Slack, it's important to understand why Slack is an excellent platform for this purpose.

1. **Centralized Communication**: Slack is the core communication tool for many organizations. Using it for company announcements ensures that everyone is accessing the information from the same place. Employees are already accustomed to checking their Slack channels, making it an ideal tool to capture attention quickly and effectively.

2. **Real-Time Reach**: Unlike traditional email, Slack delivers instant notifications to users. Announcements sent via Slack are seen in real time, making it an efficient way to deliver time-sensitive information.

3. **Targeted Messaging**: Slack allows you to tailor your message to specific audiences. Whether you want to reach the entire company, a department, or a specific team, you can customize the channels where your announcement will appear.

4. **Engagement and Interaction**: Slack is a two-way communication tool. When making an announcement, employees can easily respond, ask questions, or react to

the message with emojis. This level of interaction fosters engagement and helps clarify any doubts immediately.

Now that we understand the advantages of using Slack for company announcements, let's dive into best practices for organizing them effectively.

Best Practices for Organizing Company Announcements in Slack

1. Choose the Right Channel for Announcements

The first step in organizing a successful company announcement is determining where it will be posted. Slack allows users to create different types of channels—public, private, and shared channels with external partners.

- **General Channel**: The default channel in most Slack workspaces is often called #general. This is usually a good place to share company-wide announcements, as everyone is likely to have access to it. However, ensure that only relevant messages are posted here to avoid overwhelming employees with non-essential updates.

- **Dedicated Announcement Channel**: Many organizations create a dedicated channel for announcements, such as #company-announcements. This makes it easier for employees to filter out distractions and only focus on important information. With a dedicated channel, you can ensure that every announcement is stored in one place for easy access.

- **Private Channels**: In some cases, you may want to limit access to certain announcements to specific teams or groups. For example, a department-specific announcement or an internal update might be better suited for a private channel. However, you should be cautious about fragmenting your communications too much, as it can lead to confusion or missed information for some team members.

- **Slack Connect**: If your company works with external partners, suppliers, or clients, you can use Slack Connect to create shared channels with these external stakeholders. Announcements that impact partners or clients can be shared through these shared spaces, ensuring that they're kept in the loop.

2. Craft Clear and Concise Announcements

When crafting a company announcement, clarity is key. While Slack is a conversational platform, announcements require a slightly different approach to ensure that the information is easily digestible and actionable.

- **Headline**: Start with a clear, attention-grabbing headline. This helps employees quickly understand the purpose of the announcement. A concise and descriptive headline should summarize the key message.

- **Important Details First**: After the headline, provide the most important information at the top. This should include the "who, what, where, when, and why" of the announcement. Be direct and to the point, as employees may not have the time to read a long message.

- **Use Bullet Points**: To make your announcement easy to read, use bullet points to break up key information. This is especially helpful for updates or changes that involve multiple steps, dates, or actions. Bullet points improve readability and ensure that employees don't miss any crucial details.

- **Keep it Short**: Although Slack is a messaging platform, announcements should still respect employees' time. A lengthy message can lead to disengagement. Try to keep your announcement short and sweet, focusing on the essential information. If more details are necessary, include a link to a more detailed document or a specific Slack thread.

- **Include Actionable Steps**: If the announcement requires employees to take action, be sure to specify exactly what they need to do. This can include signing up for a meeting, completing a survey, or reviewing a document. Actionable steps should be clear and easy to follow.

3. Utilize Slack's Formatting Tools for Clarity

Slack offers several formatting options that can enhance the presentation of your announcements:

- **Bold and Italics**: Use bold text for important points or to emphasize key phrases. Italics can be used to highlight additional context or secondary information. Make sure to use these formatting tools sparingly to avoid overwhelming your message with too much emphasis.

- **Headings and Subheadings**: Use headings and subheadings to break up your message into easy-to-read sections. Slack supports basic markdown, so you can use * for bold headings, _ for italics, and ~ for strikethrough text.

- **Links and Attachments**: If you want to provide further information or resources, Slack allows you to easily insert links and attachments. For example, you might link to a full announcement on your company's intranet or attach a PDF with further details. Including these resources helps employees access all the information they need in one place.

- **Emojis**: While emojis are often used for casual communication, they can also add clarity and engagement to announcements. For example, you might use the 🗓 emoji to signify a date or the 📢 emoji to grab attention. But be sure not to overuse emojis, as they can detract from the message's seriousness.

4. Pinning Important Announcements

In Slack, you can pin important messages to the top of a channel for easy access. This is an excellent way to ensure that key announcements remain visible and accessible to everyone, even as the conversation moves forward.

For example, if you've made a company-wide announcement about a policy change, you can pin the message in the #company-announcements channel. This ensures that employees can always refer back to it, no matter how many new messages are posted in the channel afterward.

5. Using Reactions to Encourage Engagement

One of the unique features of Slack is the ability to react to messages with emojis. This feature can be incredibly useful when it comes to company announcements, as it encourages employees to engage with the content.

For example, after making an announcement, you can encourage team members to react with a specific emoji (e.g., 👍 for acknowledgment or 💬 for questions). This can be particularly useful for gauging how employees feel about an announcement or identifying which updates may need further clarification.

6. Scheduling Announcements for Optimal Timing

Timing is critical when it comes to company announcements. While Slack allows real-time communication, it also offers a feature to schedule messages to be sent at a specific time in the future. This can be incredibly helpful for ensuring your announcement is delivered at the most appropriate time for your audience.

For instance, if you're making an announcement about a major update, scheduling the message to go out during working hours ensures maximum visibility. Additionally, scheduling announcements can help avoid sending messages outside of work hours or during holidays, which could lead to confusion or unwanted disruptions.

Conclusion

Organizing company announcements in Slack can dramatically improve how information is communicated across your organization, especially in remote and hybrid work environments. By using the right channels, crafting clear messages, utilizing formatting tools, and encouraging engagement through reactions, you can ensure that your announcements are well-received and acted upon promptly. Furthermore, scheduling messages and pinning important announcements can help ensure that everyone stays up to date, even as the flow of communication continues. With these best practices, Slack can become an essential tool for organizing and delivering company-wide messages efficiently and effectively.

By leveraging Slack's features for company announcements, you can not only improve communication but also foster a culture of transparency, engagement, and productivity within your organization.

6.3.3 Hosting Q&A Sessions and AMAs

In today's remote and hybrid work environments, staying connected with your team is more critical than ever. Slack provides an ideal platform for hosting virtual events, meetings, and engagement activities that allow teams to interact, ask questions, and share ideas. One of the most engaging ways to leverage Slack for communication is by hosting **Q&A sessions** and **Ask Me Anything (AMA)** events. These events are not only great for fostering open communication but also for enhancing team collaboration and building stronger connections between leadership and team members.

In this section, we will guide you through the process of hosting successful Q&A sessions and AMAs in Slack. From planning and organizing to executing and following up, these tips will ensure that your events are interactive, insightful, and impactful.

What Are Q&A Sessions and AMAs?

Before diving into the specifics, it's important to understand what Q&A sessions and AMAs are and why they are effective communication tools in remote and hybrid work environments.

- **Q&A Sessions** are organized events where participants can submit questions to a specific individual or group, who then provide answers during the session. These questions could be about any topic relevant to the organization, team, or project. The goal is to provide clarity, address concerns, and encourage open dialogue.

- **Ask Me Anything (AMA)** is a popular format in which a guest, often a leader or expert, answers any questions submitted by participants. It's an informal, transparent, and open conversation that provides insight into the speaker's role, experiences, and perspectives on various issues.

Both formats are designed to create an interactive space where team members feel comfortable engaging and getting to know each other better, while also gaining valuable insights.

Why Use Slack for Q&A and AMAs?

Hosting Q&A sessions and AMAs in Slack has numerous benefits, especially in remote and hybrid work environments. Some key advantages include:

1. **Asynchronous Participation**: Slack's messaging platform allows team members to participate at their convenience. Unlike live video events that may require everyone to be online at the same time, Slack's thread and message features make it easy for people in different time zones or with varying schedules to participate.

2. **Inclusive and Open Dialogue**: Slack's features such as reactions, threaded replies, and message pinning make it easy for everyone to get involved. Unlike one-way communication methods, Slack fosters two-way interaction and ensures that no one's voice is drowned out.

3. **Easy Access to Information**: All messages, questions, and answers are stored in the Slack channel, providing participants with a searchable record of the event. This makes it easy for individuals who may have missed the session to catch up or for anyone to refer back to important insights.

4. **Customizable Experience**: With Slack, you can use bots, integrations, and Slack apps to enhance the experience, such as using reminders, setting up polls, and more.

Let's now walk through the steps involved in planning and hosting a successful Q&A session or AMA in Slack.

Step 1: Planning the Q&A Session or AMA

The first step in hosting an effective Q&A or AMA is to plan the event. This involves setting clear goals, choosing the right participants, and organizing the event structure. Here are some tips for getting started:

Define the Purpose and Scope

Before organizing the event, determine the purpose of the Q&A session or AMA. Are you looking to address specific team concerns? Do you want to provide a platform for leadership to share insights about a new company direction? Having a clear goal will help you decide the structure and tone of the session.

Choose the Right Host or Speaker

The host or speaker plays a crucial role in shaping the tone and effectiveness of the event. Choose a speaker who is knowledgeable, approachable, and capable of engaging with the audience. This could be a team leader, department head, or even an external guest speaker.

If it's an AMA, the speaker should be someone with a high level of expertise or influence within the organization. Consider leadership figures like the CEO, CTO, or any key decision-makers who are willing to interact with team members in a candid, approachable manner.

Select the Format and Duration

While Q&A sessions often revolve around answering pre-submitted questions, AMAs can be more open-ended. Decide on the format based on your objectives:

- **Pre-Submitted Questions**: If you anticipate a large volume of questions, ask participants to submit them in advance. This allows the host to prioritize the most relevant questions and structure their responses in an organized manner.

- **Live Questions**: Alternatively, allow team members to ask questions in real-time during the event. This works best when the session is less formal and focused on spontaneous conversation.

Decide how long the session will last—typically, AMAs can range from 30 minutes to an hour, while Q&A sessions can extend longer if there are more detailed answers to provide.

Choose the Right Slack Channel

To maintain organization, create a dedicated Slack channel for the event. This ensures that all questions and answers are collected in one place, and participants can easily reference them later.

Step 2: Promoting the Event

To ensure high participation and engagement, you need to promote your Q&A or AMA event within your team or organization. Here are some strategies to build awareness:

Announce the Event in Advance

Create excitement by announcing the event well ahead of time. Use a general Slack channel or your team's primary communication space to inform everyone about the event. Be sure to include the event's purpose, date, time, and how to participate. For example:

🔔 AMA with the CEO 🔔
Have questions about the company's new strategy or future growth plans? Join us for an AMA with our CEO this Friday at 2 PM. Ask anything!
Use the #ask-me-anything channel to submit your questions ahead of time.

Use Reminders and Announcements

Slack allows you to set reminders in channels. Use this feature to send out reminders a day or two before the event. You can also pin a message in the channel to keep the event top of mind. Consider using Slack apps like *Simple Poll* or *Polly* to send out a quick survey or poll to gauge interest or collect initial questions before the event.

Build Anticipation

Encourage participants to submit questions before the event by setting up a thread for question submissions. This ensures a smoother flow of the event and gives your speaker time to prepare. It also gives participants who may not be able to attend the live session a chance to engage.

Step 3: Running the Q&A Session or AMA

On the day of the event, you'll need to make sure everything runs smoothly. The host or speaker should be ready to address questions, and participants should be engaged.

Establish Ground Rules

At the start of the event, set expectations. Explain the event format, how participants can submit their questions, and how you will handle them. For instance:

"Please ask your questions in the thread below. Feel free to upvote the questions you'd like to hear more about. We'll address the most popular ones first."

This will keep the event organized and ensure that everyone knows how to participate.

Engage with the Audience

While the speaker answers questions, encourage participants to interact by reacting to messages, adding comments, or posting follow-up questions. Slack reactions, such as thumbs-up, applause, or question marks, are excellent ways for participants to show their approval or seek clarification.

In addition, the host can ask for feedback or insights from the audience, turning the event into a more collaborative experience.

Moderating the Session

To maintain order, you may want to appoint a moderator who will help manage the flow of questions. The moderator can sift through submitted questions, remove duplicates, or combine similar questions. This keeps things moving and ensures the speaker isn't overwhelmed with too many questions at once.

Step 4: Following Up After the Event

After the Q&A session or AMA, it's important to follow up to keep the momentum going and provide value to the participants. Here's how you can do that:

Share Key Takeaways

Pin important messages or answers in the Slack channel for easy reference. You can also create a summary of the session and share it with the entire team.

Encourage Continued Discussion

If any questions were left unanswered or if there was interest in a topic that wasn't fully explored, encourage continued discussion in the Slack channel. This will help keep the conversation going and encourage more engagement in the future.

Gather Feedback

Send a quick survey to attendees to gather feedback on how the event went. Use this feedback to improve your future events and make them more effective.

Hosting Q&A sessions and AMAs in Slack can dramatically improve communication, transparency, and engagement in remote and hybrid teams. By making these events interactive and accessible, you create an inclusive environment where everyone's voice can be heard. With the tips and strategies outlined in this section, you'll be well-equipped to host successful events that drive meaningful conversations and foster a more connected team.

CHAPTER VII
Troubleshooting and Best Practices

7.1 Common Slack Issues and Fixes

Slack is an incredibly powerful tool for team communication and collaboration. However, like any technology, issues may arise from time to time. Understanding how to troubleshoot common problems can save you valuable time and prevent unnecessary frustration. This section covers common Slack issues, particularly focusing on notifications and messages, and offers practical fixes to help you get back on track.

7.1.1 Troubleshooting Notifications and Messages

Slack notifications are essential for keeping users up-to-date with messages, alerts, and reminders. However, at times, users might find that they are not receiving notifications, or they might be receiving them too frequently. These issues can hinder communication and productivity. Here's how to troubleshoot and resolve common notification and messaging problems in Slack.

1. Understanding Slack's Notification System

Before diving into the troubleshooting process, it's important to understand how Slack's notification system works. Notifications are designed to help you stay informed about important messages, mentions, and activities within your Slack workspaces. These notifications are delivered through different channels, such as:

- **Desktop Notifications**: Pop-up alerts that appear on your screen when new messages or mentions are received.

- **Mobile Notifications**: Push notifications sent to your mobile device to alert you of new activities.

- **Email Notifications**: An email notification is sent when you have unread messages or other significant updates if you have chosen to enable this option.

Notifications in Slack can be customized to suit individual preferences and workflow, but if they aren't functioning as expected, here are some steps to help troubleshoot and fix the problem.

---

2. Fixing Notification Issues in Slack

If you are experiencing problems with Slack notifications, follow these troubleshooting steps:

2.1 Check Your Notification Preferences

Slack provides various options to customize your notifications. You may accidentally disable certain notifications or set preferences that prevent you from receiving them. To review or adjust your notification settings:

1. **Open the Slack app** (desktop or mobile).

2. **Go to Preferences** by clicking on your profile picture in the top right corner, and select **Preferences** from the dropdown.

3. In the **Notifications** section, check the following settings:

    o **Notification Settings**: Make sure you are set to receive notifications for direct messages, mentions, and keywords.

    o **Channel-Specific Notifications**: You can also adjust notifications for specific channels. Ensure that the channels you want to stay updated with are set to the appropriate notification level (All new messages, Mentions, or Nothing).

    o **Do Not Disturb Mode**: If this is activated, you will not receive any notifications. Make sure it is turned off unless you need to temporarily mute alerts.

Slack will allow you to customize whether you want to receive notifications for every message, mentions only, or nothing at all.

2.2 Check the "Do Not Disturb" Mode

"Do Not Disturb" (DND) mode is a useful feature that temporarily silences notifications, but if you forget to turn it off, you may miss important updates. To ensure you are not in DND mode:

1. Click on your profile picture in the top-right corner of the Slack window.

2. If the option says **"Do Not Disturb"** with a time set, click it to either **Disable DND** or adjust the time window to your preference.

You can also set DND for specific periods, such as when you are in meetings or need focused work time. However, remember to check whether it's turned on accidentally.

2.3 Check Mobile and Desktop Notifications

If you're using both mobile and desktop Slack apps, you may encounter discrepancies in notifications. Here's how to check if both apps are receiving notifications correctly:

1. **On the Mobile App**: Go to **Settings > Notifications** and check if notifications are enabled.

    o   Make sure to allow notifications from Slack through your device's **Settings** app (under **Notifications** for iOS or Android).

2. **On the Desktop App**: Go to **Preferences > Notifications** and confirm your settings. Make sure to enable notifications for message types you want to receive.

    o   Also, ensure that **Slack has permissions** in your operating system's notification settings. For instance, on macOS, Slack must be enabled in **System Preferences > Notifications**.

If you've set up both mobile and desktop apps, they should sync notifications properly. However, if one is showing notifications and the other is not, it's worth verifying your notification settings in both places.

2.4 Check for Notification Muting

Sometimes, specific channels or conversations might be muted, meaning you won't receive notifications for any new activity. To check if you've muted any channels or threads:

1. Go to the channel or thread in question.

2. If the channel is muted, the bell icon next to it will have a line through it.

3. To unmute, click on the channel name or thread title, select **Mute Channel**, and toggle the option off.

Muting can be useful in channels that you don't need constant updates from, but be careful not to mute important channels inadvertently.

2.5 Review "Keyword" Notifications

Slack allows you to set up keyword alerts, so you get notified whenever specific words are mentioned in messages. This feature is extremely useful for staying on top of discussions relevant to you. However, if your keywords are too broad, you may receive excessive notifications.

To adjust this:

1. Go to **Preferences > Notifications**.

2. Scroll down to **Keyword Alerts** and review the words or phrases you've added.

3. Remove unnecessary or overly broad keywords to prevent a flood of notifications.

2.6 Troubleshooting Syncing Issues

Syncing issues often prevent messages from appearing promptly on all devices. This is commonly experienced when using Slack on both mobile and desktop devices simultaneously. To address syncing issues:

1. **Restart Slack**: Sometimes simply quitting and reopening the Slack app on your device can fix syncing issues.

2. **Check Your Internet Connection**: Slack requires a stable internet connection. Ensure that your Wi-Fi or cellular data connection is strong. If you're on a mobile device, try switching between Wi-Fi and cellular data.

3. **Clear Cache**: On the desktop app, you can clear Slack's cache to resolve issues related to old or unsynced messages. Go to **Help > Troubleshooting > Clear Cache**.

If issues persist, consider logging out and logging back in to reset your session, which may help resolve syncing issues.

3. Fixing Message Delivery Issues

While notifications may be disrupted, it's also possible that messages themselves are not being delivered. This can occur when Slack experiences a service disruption, or there may be issues with the Slack app or your device.

3.1 Check Slack's Status Page

Slack has a status page that shows whether there are any known outages or disruptions. If messages are not being delivered, it's worth checking Slack's **status page** to see if the issue is on their end. If Slack is experiencing downtime, the issue will likely be resolved when their service is restored.

3.2 Update the Slack App

Outdated versions of the Slack app may have bugs that interfere with message delivery. Always make sure you are using the latest version of Slack:

- **Desktop app**: Slack will prompt you for updates. You can also manually check for updates by selecting **Slack > Check for Updates** on macOS or **Help > Check for Updates** on Windows.

- **Mobile app**: Go to the **App Store (iOS)** or **Google Play Store (Android)** and check for any available updates.

Updating to the latest version can often resolve bugs related to message delivery and notifications.

---

4. Conclusion: Ensuring Optimal Slack Notifications

Ensuring that you receive the right notifications at the right time is essential for maintaining efficient communication in Slack. By reviewing your notification preferences, checking your device settings, and being mindful of issues like muting or syncing, you can avoid common notification-related frustrations.

Remember that Slack provides robust notification settings to give you control over what's important to you. By customizing Slack's notification system according to your personal workflow, you can keep your team informed and responsive without feeling overwhelmed.

In the next section, we'll look at additional fixes for syncing issues and how to manage the overwhelming number of channels that can sometimes cause notification overload.

7.1.2 Fixing Connectivity and Syncing Issues

Slack is a powerful collaboration tool, but like any application, it can sometimes experience connectivity and syncing issues. These problems can be frustrating, particularly when you need to stay connected to your team, collaborate on projects, or receive important updates. Fortunately, many of these issues can be resolved with a few simple steps. In this section, we'll explore the common causes of connectivity and syncing issues in Slack, provide troubleshooting tips, and offer solutions to help you get back to work faster.

Understanding the Issue: What Causes Connectivity and Syncing Problems in Slack?

Before diving into troubleshooting steps, it's important to understand why connectivity and syncing issues occur. There are a variety of reasons why Slack may not sync properly or have trouble maintaining a stable connection to its servers. Some common causes include:

1. **Internet Connection Issues:** A weak or unstable internet connection is one of the most common causes of Slack connectivity problems. If your Wi-Fi or cellular network signal is weak, Slack may struggle to stay connected and sync your messages and files.

2. **Server-side Issues:** Sometimes, the problem isn't on your end at all. Slack's servers may be experiencing high traffic, technical difficulties, or downtime, which can impact your ability to access the app or sync messages.

3. **Outdated App Version:** Running an outdated version of the Slack app can lead to syncing and connectivity issues. This is especially common with desktop and mobile apps, where regular updates are essential for ensuring compatibility with Slack's evolving features.

4. **Cache and Data Corruption:** Over time, the Slack app may accumulate cached data, which can cause syncing issues. This cache can become corrupted or outdated, preventing the app from syncing new messages and updates properly.

5. **Firewall or Proxy Settings:** If you're using a corporate network or firewall, the settings may be blocking Slack's connection. Similarly, if you're using a proxy server to connect to the internet, it can interfere with Slack's ability to sync data in real-time.

6. **Device-Specific Problems:** On mobile devices, syncing issues may be caused by low storage, power-saving settings, or device-specific bugs. On desktop computers, issues may arise from system settings or conflicts with other applications.

Troubleshooting Slack Connectivity and Syncing Issues

Now that we've identified the potential causes of connectivity and syncing issues, let's take a closer look at how to troubleshoot and resolve them effectively.

1. Check Your Internet Connection

Before doing anything else, ensure that your device is properly connected to the internet. If you're on Wi-Fi, check the strength of your signal. Weak signals can cause Slack to have trouble syncing and maintaining a stable connection. Try the following:

- **Switch Networks:** If you're using Wi-Fi, try switching to a different network or moving closer to your router. If possible, connect directly to your router using an Ethernet cable.

- **Switch to Cellular Data:** If you're on a mobile device and Wi-Fi is unreliable, switch to cellular data to see if the problem persists.

- **Run a Speed Test:** Test your internet speed using online tools like Speedtest.net. Slack recommends a stable connection with at least 1 Mbps download and upload speed for optimal performance.

2. Check Slack's Server Status

Sometimes, the issue may be on Slack's end rather than yours. Slack operates in a cloud-based environment, and while rare, issues with their servers can cause syncing problems for users. To check if there are any ongoing issues:

- **Visit Slack's Status Page:** Go to Slack's Status Page to see if there are any reported outages, slowdowns, or maintenance updates affecting the service. If there is an ongoing issue, you'll likely see a notification indicating that Slack is working to resolve it.

- **Follow Slack's Twitter Account:** If Slack is experiencing widespread issues, they often post updates on their Twitter account (@SlackStatus) about the situation.

If the issue is due to Slack's servers, there's little you can do except wait for their team to fix it. Slack usually provides real-time updates on their status page.

3. Update Your Slack App

An outdated version of Slack may not sync properly with Slack's servers or have the latest bug fixes and performance improvements. Keeping your app updated is essential for maintaining seamless connectivity and syncing. Here's how to update Slack:

- **Desktop App (Windows/macOS):**
  - On Windows: Open the Slack desktop app, click on your profile picture in the top right corner, and select "Check for Updates."
  - On macOS: Open the Slack app, click "Slack" in the menu bar, and select "Check for Updates."
  - If an update is available, the app will download and install it automatically.

- **Mobile App (iOS/Android):**
  - Go to your device's app store (App Store for iOS or Google Play for Android).
  - Search for Slack and tap "Update" if an update is available.

After updating, restart Slack and check if your connectivity and syncing issues are resolved.

4. Clear Slack's Cache

Clearing the cache can often resolve issues caused by corrupted or outdated data. The method for clearing the cache depends on the platform you're using:

- **Desktop (Windows/macOS):**
  - In the Slack desktop app, click on your profile picture in the top right corner and select "Preferences."
  - Under the "Advanced" tab, click on "Clear Cache."
  - Restart Slack and check if the syncing issue is resolved.

- **Mobile (iOS/Android):**

> o On mobile devices, Slack doesn't offer a built-in cache-clear option. However, you can try reinstalling the app to clear cached data.

Note: Clearing your cache will not delete your messages or files, but it will refresh the app's stored data, which may help resolve syncing problems.

5. Adjust Firewall or Proxy Settings

If you're working within a corporate environment or using a network with strict security settings, it's possible that a firewall or proxy is blocking Slack's connection. In such cases, try the following:

- **Disable VPN/Proxy:** If you're using a VPN or proxy server, temporarily disable it to see if it resolves the syncing issue.

- **Check Firewall Settings:** Work with your IT department to ensure that Slack's connection is not being blocked by the firewall. Slack's server addresses and ports should be whitelisted to allow smooth communication.

  - o Slack's domain names include: slack.com, slack-files.com, and slackhq.com.

  - o The necessary ports for Slack are TCP ports 443 and 80.

6. Check for Device-Specific Issues

If you've narrowed down the issue to your device, there are a few things you can do:

- **Restart Your Device:** Sometimes, a simple restart can resolve connectivity and syncing issues by resetting the device's network connections.

- **Free Up Storage Space:** On mobile devices, low storage can cause apps, including Slack, to perform poorly. Free up space by deleting unused apps, files, and media.

- **Update Your Device's Operating System:** Ensure that your device's operating system is up-to-date. This is especially important for mobile devices that may have specific compatibility requirements with Slack.

- **Close Background Apps:** If you're on a mobile device, close other apps running in the background that may be consuming network resources.

7. Contact Slack Support

If none of the above steps resolve your issue, it's time to contact Slack's support team for further assistance. Here's how you can get in touch with them:

- **Submit a Help Request:** Go to Slack's <u>Help Center</u> and submit a request for support. Provide as much detail as possible, including the device you're using, the steps you've already tried, and any error messages you've received.

- **Live Chat Support:** For real-time assistance, Slack offers live chat support for users on paid plans (such as Standard, Plus, or Enterprise Grid).

Preventing Future Connectivity and Syncing Issues

To avoid recurring connectivity and syncing problems, consider these best practices:

1. **Regularly Update Slack:** Keep your Slack app updated to ensure it is always running the latest version with all the latest fixes and features.

2. **Monitor Your Internet Connection:** Make sure you have a reliable internet connection, especially if you're working remotely or using mobile data.

3. **Use Slack's Offline Mode Wisely:** If you're experiencing intermittent connectivity, take advantage of Slack's offline mode to continue working and sync later when a connection is restored.

4. **Clear Cache Periodically:** Occasionally clear your app's cache to remove outdated data and maintain optimal performance.

5. **Use Slack's Mobile App for On-the-Go Work:** If you encounter issues on your desktop, try switching to Slack's mobile app as it can sometimes perform better in certain situations.

By following these guidelines, you can minimize the impact of connectivity and syncing issues on your workflow and ensure that Slack remains a reliable tool for collaboration and productivity.

7.1.3 Managing Too Many Channels and Alerts

Slack can be an incredibly powerful tool for team collaboration, but like any platform, it has the potential to overwhelm users if not managed properly. One of the most common challenges Slack users face is managing the sheer number of channels, messages, and notifications. As teams grow and the number of conversations increases, it can be difficult to keep track of everything without getting distracted or overloaded. In this section, we'll explore the issue of managing too many channels and alerts and provide practical solutions to help you stay organized and focused.

The Problem: Overwhelmed by Too Many Channels and Alerts

When you first start using Slack, it's easy to get excited about the endless possibilities for communication. You create channels for every project, department, team, and topic imaginable, and as your team grows, so do the number of channels. Before long, you may find yourself in dozens, if not hundreds, of channels. This can quickly lead to notification overload, making it hard to prioritize important conversations or track the messages that truly matter.

In addition to the sheer volume of channels, Slack's notification system can exacerbate this feeling of being overwhelmed. With so many conversations happening at once, the constant stream of notifications can make it feel like you're constantly playing catch-up. Whether it's the little red notification badge on your app or a constant barrage of desktop and mobile pings, notifications can be more distracting than helpful. And if you don't know how to manage them properly, it can lead to unnecessary stress, missed messages, or burnout.

1. Assessing Your Channel Usage

The first step in managing too many channels is to assess your current usage. Ask yourself:

- **How many channels am I part of?** Are you a member of channels that you rarely use or that no longer serve a purpose? You might have joined channels with great intentions, but over time, they may have become irrelevant or unnecessary.

- **Are the channels organized properly?** Are there too many channels for similar topics? For example, if you have one channel for marketing and one for social media, but they overlap significantly, consider consolidating them into a single channel.

- **Do you need to be part of every channel?** Some channels are informative, while others are meant for specific teams. Being part of every channel may not be necessary, and it could contribute to your notification overload.

By regularly reviewing and cleaning up your channels, you can ensure that you're only involved in conversations that are relevant to your role and responsibilities.

2. Archiving and Leaving Unnecessary Channels

Once you've assessed your channel usage, it's time to take action. Slack allows you to leave or archive channels that no longer serve a purpose. Here's how you can manage that:

- **Leave Channels You Don't Need:** If you no longer need to follow a channel, simply leave it. You can always rejoin later if needed. To leave a channel, click on the channel name at the top, select **"Channel settings"**, and choose **"Leave Channel"**. Doing this will remove you from the notifications and clutter associated with that channel.

- **Archive Old or Inactive Channels:** For channels that are still useful but no longer require active participation, consider archiving them. This way, the channel remains accessible for reference without cluttering your sidebar. To archive a channel, go to **Channel settings**, then choose **"Archive Channel"**. Archiving a channel stops new messages from being posted but keeps the content for future reference.

- **Consolidate Channels:** Instead of having multiple channels for closely related topics, consider consolidating them. For example, if you have channels for various departments (e.g., #marketing, #social-media, #content), see if you can group them under a more general channel, like #marketing-team, and use specific threads for different topics. Slack threads help keep conversations organized within a channel and reduce the need for multiple channels.

By archiving and leaving channels, you can significantly reduce the noise and clutter in your Slack workspace.

3. Organizing Your Sidebar for Better Navigation

Another effective way to manage too many channels is by customizing your sidebar. Slack allows you to reorder your channels, pin important conversations, and even create custom sections to group channels together. Here are a few tips for optimizing your sidebar:

- **Pin Important Channels:** Pinning important channels to the top of your sidebar helps you easily access the ones that matter most. To pin a channel, click on the three dots next to the channel name and select **"Pin to Sidebar"**. This can be particularly helpful for channels that you need to check frequently.

- **Create Custom Sections:** Slack enables you to create custom sections in your sidebar to group channels based on categories. For example, you can create a section for active channels, one for archived channels, and another for project-related channels. To create a custom section, hover over your sidebar and click **"Create New Section"**. Organizing your channels this way makes it easier to prioritize what you need to focus on and reduces visual clutter.

- **Star Channels for Quick Access:** If there are certain channels you check regularly but don't need to pin, consider starring them. Starring channels makes them easy to find, even if they're not at the top of your sidebar. Simply click on the star icon next to the channel name to add it to your starred list.

4. Customizing Your Notification Settings

In addition to managing your channels, customizing your notification settings is crucial for controlling Slack overload. Slack offers a variety of notification options that allow you to fine-tune what you're alerted about. Here are a few strategies for managing Slack notifications effectively:

- **Mute Channels or Conversations:** If there's a channel that's too noisy but you don't want to leave it entirely, consider muting it. Muting a channel will stop all notifications, but you can still check it at your convenience. To mute a channel, click on the channel name, select **"Mute Channel"**, and you'll no longer receive notifications unless you're specifically mentioned.

- **Set Custom Notification Preferences:** Go to **Preferences > Notifications**, and customize your notification settings based on your priorities. You can adjust settings for channels, direct messages, mentions, and keywords. For example, you can set Slack to only notify you of direct messages or mentions, reducing the number of unnecessary pings.

- **Use Do Not Disturb Mode:** Slack's **Do Not Disturb** mode is a game-changer when you need uninterrupted focus time. When enabled, Slack will silence notifications for a set period, allowing you to concentrate on deep work. You can set this manually or schedule it for recurring periods (e.g., during meetings or working hours).

- **Set Up Keyword Alerts:** For important topics or keywords, you can set up personalized keyword alerts. Slack will notify you whenever your chosen keywords are mentioned in any channel or conversation. This feature is great for tracking critical updates without having to monitor every single message.

5. Using Slack's Workflow and Automation Features

If managing too many channels and alerts is becoming a significant challenge, consider leveraging Slack's workflow and automation tools. Slack offers a **Workflow Builder** that allows you to automate certain tasks, such as posting reminders, notifications, and even managing messages.

- **Automating Reminders:** For channels that require regular check-ins, you can set up automated reminders. For instance, you can create a workflow to automatically remind a team every Friday to submit their reports. This reduces the need for constant manual reminders and ensures that important tasks don't fall through the cracks.

- **Automating Notifications:** Slack workflows can be customized to send notifications at specific intervals, which can help prevent notification overload. For example, you could set up a daily summary of key messages in a channel rather than receiving constant notifications throughout the day.

- **Creating Custom Commands:** For teams with frequent repetitive tasks (like reporting), create custom slash commands to automate processes within channels. For example, you could create a command like /weekly-report that prompts team members to input their updates.

6. Using Slack's Mobile App Efficiently

Managing too many channels and alerts isn't just a desktop problem—it can also be overwhelming on mobile. However, Slack's mobile app offers several features that can help you stay in control:

- **Set Mobile-Only Notification Preferences:** You can adjust notifications separately for your desktop and mobile app. This allows you to reduce the number of notifications on your phone while still receiving critical alerts on your computer.

- **Use the Mobile "Threads" Feature:** Instead of being bombarded with individual messages, use the mobile app's **Threads** feature to keep discussions organized.

This allows you to track a conversation in a specific channel without clogging up your main feed.

7. Conclusion

Managing too many channels and alerts in Slack can feel overwhelming, but with a few simple strategies, you can regain control of your workspace. By regularly assessing and cleaning up your channels, organizing your sidebar, customizing your notification settings, and using automation tools, you can make Slack a powerful and efficient tool for your work rather than a source of constant distraction. Remember, the key is to keep Slack organized, focused, and tailored to your needs—so you can work smarter, not harder.

7.2 Best Practices for Slack Power Users

7.2.1 Reducing Distractions and Staying Focused

Slack is a powerful tool that enhances collaboration and communication in teams, but like any communication tool, it can easily become a source of distractions. Constant notifications, messages, and the sheer volume of information flowing through channels can make it difficult to focus and maintain productivity. The key to using Slack effectively without becoming overwhelmed is to take a proactive approach to managing distractions. In this section, we will explore strategies that Slack power users employ to reduce distractions and stay focused.

Understanding the Distraction Problem

Before diving into solutions, it's important to understand why Slack can be so distracting. The platform is designed for real-time communication, which means it is constantly pinging you with notifications when someone mentions you, posts in a channel you follow, or updates a task. While real-time communication can enhance collaboration, it can also lead to cognitive overload if not managed correctly.

Moreover, Slack enables you to interact with various channels, direct messages (DMs), file sharing, and third-party integrations. This continuous flow of information from multiple sources can scatter your attention and make it harder to prioritize your most important tasks. Studies on multitasking and cognitive load show that switching between tasks frequently actually reduces efficiency, leading to burnout over time.

The good news is that there are effective ways to manage Slack's distractions without sacrificing the benefits of staying connected with your team. Below are some strategies that power users rely on to maintain focus.

1. Customize Notification Settings

One of the simplest and most effective ways to reduce distractions is by customizing your notification settings. Slack offers a wide range of options for managing notifications that can significantly cut down on interruptions. Let's explore the key options available:

a. Set Do Not Disturb (DND) Mode

Slack's **Do Not Disturb** mode is a lifesaver for anyone trying to focus on deep work without constant interruptions. When you activate DND, you won't receive notifications, but messages and updates will still be stored in your Slack workspace. You can schedule DND to turn on automatically at specific times of the day (e.g., during your "focus hours") or manually toggle it on when you need to concentrate.

To set DND:

- Click your profile picture in the top-right corner of the Slack app.

- Select **"Pause notifications"** and choose a time duration.

- You can also set custom DND schedules in **Preferences** under **Notifications**.

b. Customize Channel Notifications

Not every Slack channel deserves your full attention all the time. Slack allows you to customize notification settings for each channel individually. For example, you might want to receive notifications for mentions or important messages in high-priority channels but ignore non-urgent updates in others.

To do this:

- Right-click on the channel name and select **"Notification Preferences"**.

- You can choose to receive notifications for **All New Messages**, **Mentions & Direct Messages**, or **Nothing**.

- You can also choose to receive notifications only when you're mentioned or when there's a specific keyword in the conversation.

c. Mute Channels Temporarily

Another way to reduce distractions is by muting channels that aren't immediately relevant to you. Slack allows you to mute channels for a set period or indefinitely. Muted channels won't send notifications, but the messages are still available for you to check at your convenience.

To mute a channel:

- Click on the channel name, then click on the bell icon and choose **"Mute Channel"**.

You can always unmute channels when you're ready to engage with them.

2. Prioritize Communication Using Threads

Slack encourages quick, real-time communication, which can often lead to fragmented conversations spread across multiple channels. One of the best practices for reducing distractions is using **threads** to keep conversations organized.

Threads help by:

- **Keeping related messages together**: This reduces the number of notifications you get for each message and avoids interrupting the main channel conversation.

- **Allowing focused discussions**: Conversations can continue without clogging up the channel with off-topic discussions, helping you focus on the broader objectives of the group.

To start a thread, hover over a message and click the **Reply in thread** button. You'll then be able to reply to that message privately, and others will be notified only if they're mentioned or are following the thread.

Encourage your team to use threads for detailed discussions rather than replying to every message in the main channel. Over time, this reduces clutter and allows for a more structured approach to communication.

3. Time Management Tools and Scheduling Slack Interactions

Sometimes, the best way to manage distractions is to limit how often you interact with Slack throughout the day. While Slack's immediacy can be a blessing in certain situations, it can become a productivity killer if you constantly check in to see what's new. Setting time limits for checking Slack is one way to stay focused.

a. Schedule Slack Check-ins

Set specific times throughout the day to check and respond to Slack messages. For instance, you might choose to check Slack first thing in the morning, at lunch, and toward the end of the day. This method allows you to stay connected without the constant distractions of a flood of new messages.

You can also use **Slack's Workflow Builder** to automate certain tasks (e.g., daily check-ins, automatic reminders for certain channels) to optimize your interaction times.

b. Use Time-Blocking Techniques

Combine Slack with time-blocking techniques, where you allocate specific chunks of time to focused work and Slack interaction. Time-blocking helps you concentrate on a task without distractions, ensuring that Slack doesn't interrupt your workflow. For example:

- Block the first 45 minutes of your day for deep work.

- Check Slack for 10-15 minutes after your deep work session, respond to any mentions or direct messages, then return to your task at hand.

This technique allows you to limit the impact of Slack distractions while still keeping up with team communication.

4. Organize Your Slack Workspace Efficiently

A disorganized workspace can be a major distraction. Channels, messages, and files that are difficult to navigate can waste time and create cognitive overload. Slack's powerful organizational tools can help you reduce this chaos.

a. Create Separate Workspaces for Different Teams or Projects

If your workspace is becoming overwhelming, consider splitting up your Slack activity into different workspaces for different teams or projects. You can create a separate workspace for various departments, such as sales, marketing, and product, so that you can focus on specific areas without constantly switching between channels.

b. Use Starred Channels and Direct Messages

To ensure that the most important conversations are easy to access, use the **Star** feature for critical channels or conversations. Starred channels and direct messages will appear at the top of your sidebar, making them quicker to find. This reduces the need to search for frequently used channels or messages, saving you time and mental effort.

c. Archive Inactive Channels

Old, inactive channels can clutter your workspace and become distracting. Slack allows you to archive channels that are no longer in use. Archiving them removes them from your active workspace but still retains all the information for future reference.

To archive a channel, click on the channel name and select **"Archive this channel"**.

5. Manage Multi-Tasking with Focus Mode

One of the most important aspects of reducing distractions is learning how to avoid multi-tasking. Multi-tasking is often counterproductive and can cause mental fatigue. Slack, with its constant stream of messages, can easily encourage multi-tasking. However, a Slack power user knows that focusing on one task at a time is far more effective.

When you need to concentrate on a specific project, turn on **Focus Mode** by:

- Using **Focus Apps** (such as Focus@Will) to help enhance your concentration with music or soundscapes.

- Setting your Slack status to let people know you're focusing and shouldn't be disturbed.

6. Set Clear Expectations with Your Team

To minimize Slack distractions, it's essential to set expectations around communication. Slack is a fast-paced tool, but not everything needs to be answered immediately. Establish clear guidelines with your team about:

- When to use Slack vs. email or other tools.

- When to respond to messages and what constitutes a priority message.

- Whether urgent matters require direct messaging or can be handled in a thread.

By communicating expectations clearly, you can reduce the urgency that often leads to distractions.

Conclusion: Managing Slack Distractions for a Productive Workflow

Slack is an excellent tool for communication and collaboration, but its potential for distraction is undeniable. By customizing notifications, organizing your workspace, using threads effectively, and limiting multitasking, you can significantly reduce the impact of distractions and stay focused on the work that matters. As a Slack power user, taking these steps will not only improve your personal productivity but will also foster a more organized and efficient team culture.

7.2.2 Creating a Slack Etiquette Guide for Your Team

When teams begin using Slack, the immediate benefits can be seen in the way communication becomes faster, more organized, and less reliant on email. However, as the platform scales and more people join, it can quickly become overwhelming. To ensure that communication remains clear, efficient, and respectful, creating a Slack etiquette guide for your team is essential. This guide is not just a set of rules; it helps to establish best practices that create a culture of effective, harmonious communication on Slack.

In this section, we'll explore how to create a Slack etiquette guide that sets clear expectations for behavior, maintains professionalism, and ensures that the tool is used to its full potential. A solid guide can help team members use Slack with purpose, avoid distractions, and cultivate an environment where Slack works to their advantage.

Why Slack Etiquette Matters

Slack is a versatile tool, but its success largely depends on how users engage with it. Without proper etiquette, Slack can quickly devolve into a chaotic mix of constant notifications, irrelevant channels, miscommunication, and wasted time. By establishing clear guidelines, you can help ensure that Slack remains a productive tool that fosters collaboration and communication while minimizing distractions.

An effective Slack etiquette guide promotes:

- **Professionalism:** Slack is a workplace communication tool. It's important to ensure that the tone and content of messages remain professional.

- **Efficiency:** Well-structured communication ensures team members spend less time sifting through irrelevant messages.

- **Respect:** Proper etiquette ensures that team members' time and attention are respected, creating a more focused work environment.

- **Clear Communication:** A guide helps prevent misunderstandings and ensures that key messages are delivered clearly and effectively.

Steps to Create a Slack Etiquette Guide for Your Team

Creating an etiquette guide is not about creating rigid rules, but instead establishing a set of guidelines that encourage productivity and respectful communication. Here's a step-by-step approach to developing your team's Slack etiquette guide:

1. Define Slack's Purpose for Your Team

Before diving into specifics, it's essential to define the role Slack plays in your team. Is it for quick conversations, project collaboration, announcements, or something else? Setting expectations around Slack's purpose helps prevent misuse and ensures that everyone is on the same page.

For example:

- **Slack for collaboration:** If Slack is used primarily for project collaboration, encourage team members to keep conversations on-topic and related to work.

- **Slack for socializing:** While Slack can support casual conversations, make sure it doesn't dominate or distract from work. Setting boundaries for off-topic conversations helps maintain focus.

Actionable Tip: Consider creating specific channels for certain purposes, such as project discussions, company announcements, casual chats, or even pet pictures, to keep work-related channels focused.

2. Establish Guidelines for Channel Usage

Slack allows teams to create different channels for different purposes, and without proper guidelines, channels can become cluttered and disorganized. Creating well-defined guidelines for channel usage is crucial.

What to do:

- **Create purpose-specific channels:** Encourage team members to only join relevant channels. For instance, having channels for specific teams (e.g., Marketing, Sales, Product) or specific projects can help streamline communication.

- **Channel naming conventions:** Establish clear naming conventions to help easily identify channels. This is especially important as your workspace grows. For example, naming channels like #marketing-ideas or #product-launch makes their purpose immediately clear.

- **Public vs. private channels:** Ensure that private channels are used for sensitive topics and that public channels are open for broader discussions to maintain transparency and inclusion.

Actionable Tip: When creating new channels, add a description to make it clear what the purpose of the channel is and who should be part of it. Encourage people to read the channel descriptions before joining.

3. Encourage Threaded Conversations

One of Slack's most powerful features is the ability to reply in threads, which helps keep channels organized. Without threads, conversations can quickly get lost in the noise of continuous message streams.

What to do:

- **Use threads for replies:** Encourage team members to reply to messages in threads rather than cluttering the main channel. This makes it easy for others to follow and reduces unnecessary scrolling.

- **Avoid one-off messages:** If a message is directly related to a prior post, encourage team members to add their response to a thread instead of starting a new message in the main channel.

Actionable Tip: Set up a quick Slack tip for your team to use when responding to a message: **"Reply in a thread to keep the conversation organized and easy to follow."**

4. Set Expectations for Message Timing and Response Times

One of the challenges with Slack is the real-time nature of messaging, which can result in team members feeling pressured to respond immediately. Setting expectations for response times can alleviate this pressure and ensure that people are not distracted from their tasks.

What to do:

- **Set expectations for response times:** It's important to clarify that not every message requires an immediate response. For example, messages sent outside working hours may not need a response until the next day.

- **Use "Do Not Disturb" mode:** Encourage your team to use Slack's "Do Not Disturb" mode when they need focused work time. Set clear expectations that it's okay to not respond immediately when someone is in "Do Not Disturb."

Actionable Tip: Establish a team-wide policy that during certain hours (e.g., lunch break, or focused work periods), responses may not be immediate, but everyone will respond as soon as possible.

5. Promote Use of Slack's Features for Efficiency

Slack is filled with helpful features designed to make communication smoother and more efficient. Encourage your team to utilize them to enhance their productivity.

What to do:

- **Use @mentions appropriately:** Encourage the use of @mentions to call someone's attention to a message, but avoid overuse. Using @everyone or @channel can be disruptive if used too frequently.

- **Pin important messages:** Pin key messages in channels, so they remain easily accessible to everyone. This is especially helpful for important updates or guidelines.

- **Use reminders and tasks:** Slack allows users to set reminders, which can be a useful way to stay on top of tasks and deadlines. Encourage team members to use reminders to stay organized and ensure important messages don't get lost.

Actionable Tip: Create a Slack channel for announcements only, and pin any important messages or deadlines there, so everyone can easily access them.

6. Address Tone and Language Guidelines

In a remote or hybrid work environment, tone can often be misunderstood. What is intended as a casual message can come across as blunt or even rude. Creating guidelines on how to communicate effectively and professionally in Slack is essential for maintaining a positive team culture.

What to do:

- **Encourage a positive tone:** Remind your team that the tone of written communication can sometimes be misinterpreted. Encourage using emojis, exclamation points, and clear language to express positivity.

- **Be mindful of directness:** While Slack allows quick communication, make sure that messages are polite and constructive. Avoid using overly blunt or curt messages that might come off as rude.

- **Set guidelines for humor and casual chats:** Humor can help build camaraderie, but it's important to set boundaries to ensure that Slack doesn't become too distracting or inappropriate.

Actionable Tip: Remind the team to pause and consider how a message might be perceived before hitting send. Encourage them to keep tone and context in mind.

7. Educate Your Team on Slack Best Practices Regularly

Slack etiquette is not something that should be established once and left alone. As Slack evolves and new features are introduced, it's important to revisit your etiquette guide and refresh your team on best practices.

What to do:

- **Regularly revisit your Slack etiquette guide:** Create a culture where team members are encouraged to review and update Slack guidelines as needed.

- **Provide regular Slack tips:** Send out regular Slack tips to your team, either through an internal newsletter or during team meetings, to keep Slack usage top of mind.

- **Encourage feedback:** Ask your team for feedback on how Slack can be better utilized within the company. This can help identify areas of improvement and adapt your etiquette guide as needed.

Actionable Tip: Have an internal Slack channel dedicated to Slack best practices, where team members can post helpful tips or improvements they've discovered.

Conclusion

Creating a Slack etiquette guide is an essential step in fostering a positive and productive communication environment. By setting clear expectations for how Slack should be used, you not only improve the overall user experience but also ensure that Slack remains an efficient tool for collaboration. Remember, the goal is not to impose restrictions but to create an environment where everyone can communicate effectively without distractions.

With a solid etiquette guide in place, your team can harness the full potential of Slack, leading to better communication, more efficient workflows, and a healthier work culture.

7.2.3 Keeping Slack Organized and Efficient

Introduction

As a power user of Slack, you may find yourself managing multiple channels, messages, and integrations on a daily basis. Over time, Slack can quickly become overwhelming if not properly organized, leading to lost messages, cluttered channels, and confusion about where to find important information. However, by implementing a few key strategies, you can streamline your Slack workspace, maintain focus, and work more efficiently. This section will provide practical steps to help you keep Slack organized and running smoothly.

1. Structuring Channels for Maximum Clarity

The first step to keeping Slack organized is structuring your channels in a way that makes sense for your team's workflow. Slack's flexibility allows you to create numerous channels, but that flexibility can also lead to clutter if not properly managed.

Create Clear Channel Naming Conventions

One of the easiest ways to prevent confusion in your Slack workspace is by creating a consistent naming convention for your channels. A well-structured naming system allows everyone in your workspace to understand the purpose of each channel at a glance. Consider using prefixes that denote the channel's function, such as:

- **#team-[team name]** for team-specific channels (e.g., #team-marketing, #team-dev).

- **#project-[project name]** for project-based channels (e.g., #project-website-redesign).

- **#department-[department name]** for department-specific channels (e.g., #department-hr, #department-sales).

- **#topic-[specific topic]** for discussion channels centered around specific themes (e.g., #topic-new-product-ideas, #topic-remote-work).

By applying a consistent structure to your channel names, you make it easier to identify the right channels for various discussions, improving both the speed and accuracy with which you find information.

Archive Inactive Channels Regularly

Slack gives you the option to archive channels that are no longer in use. Archiving old or inactive channels helps keep your sidebar clean and ensures that only relevant channels remain visible.

Make it a practice to periodically review your channels and archive those that are no longer needed. For example, once a project has been completed, you can archive the associated project channel. Additionally, you can set up a regular review cycle (e.g., monthly or quarterly) to ensure that inactive channels are properly archived.

Use Channel Purpose and Pinning Effectively

Every channel in Slack has a "Purpose" field where you can describe the channel's goal or function. This field is often underutilized but is incredibly valuable for ensuring clarity about what each channel is used for.

Take advantage of this feature by including a clear, concise description in the channel purpose. This will help new members understand what to expect when they join and prevent people from posting off-topic content.

Additionally, pin important messages within channels to ensure that critical information is always easy to find. Pinning documents, key updates, or frequently used links can save time for team members who are looking for key resources.

---

2. Managing Notifications to Stay Focused

One of the major challenges of Slack is managing notifications without feeling overwhelmed. While notifications are designed to alert you to important messages, they can quickly become distracting and lead to productivity loss if not properly managed.

Customize Notification Settings for Each Channel

Slack allows you to customize notification settings for each channel you belong to, giving you the power to filter out non-essential alerts.

For example, in channels with a high volume of messages, you may want to reduce the frequency of notifications or mute the channel entirely. On the other hand, for critical channels, such as those related to your immediate team or important projects, you can choose to receive notifications for all messages.

To customize notifications:

- Click on the channel name, then go to **Notification Preferences**.

- Select **All Messages**, **Mentions & Keywords**, or **Nothing** based on your preference.

- Use **Do Not Disturb** mode to silence all notifications when you need focused work time.

By carefully selecting which notifications you receive, you can eliminate distractions while still staying informed about key updates.

Use Keywords to Filter Important Messages

Slack allows you to set up custom notifications for specific keywords that matter most to your work. This feature can help ensure you never miss important messages related to your projects, even in busy channels.

To set up keyword notifications:

- Go to **Preferences** > **Notifications** > **My Keywords**.

- Add any words that are relevant to your work or interests (e.g., your name, project names, client names).

- Whenever these keywords are mentioned, you'll receive a notification, even if you have muted the channel.

By using keyword notifications, you can stay focused while ensuring that you are alerted to important discussions without being inundated by irrelevant updates.

---

3. Utilizing Slack's Search Function to Find Information Quickly

Slack's search function is one of the most powerful tools for staying organized. As your workspace grows, Slack can quickly become a sea of messages, files, and conversations. The key to staying efficient is mastering Slack's search capabilities.

Use Search Operators to Narrow Results

Slack offers several search operators that help you refine your search and find exactly what you're looking for. Here are a few useful operators:

- **from:[username]**: Search for messages sent by a specific person.
- **in:[channel name]**: Search for messages within a specific channel.
- **has:[file type]**: Search for specific types of files, such as images, documents, or videos.
- **before:[date]** or **after:[date]**: Search for messages sent before or after a certain date.

By combining these search operators, you can quickly locate messages, files, or conversations, making it easier to find critical information.

Use Advanced Filters for Messages

In addition to search operators, you can use Slack's built-in filters to narrow down search results. You can filter by date, file type, and even message type (e.g., pinned messages or unread messages).

If you need to find a specific file, for example, you can use the filter option to show only files, then sort them by the type of document you're looking for (PDFs, Word docs, etc.).

4. Automating Workflows to Stay Efficient

Slack's automation tools, such as Slackbots and Workflow Builder, are designed to help you stay organized without requiring manual intervention for repetitive tasks.

Set Up Workflow Builder for Routine Tasks

Slack's **Workflow Builder** lets you automate a variety of tasks, such as sending daily reminders, collecting information through forms, or posting welcome messages to new team members. Workflow Builder can significantly reduce the time spent on administrative tasks and streamline routine processes.

For example, you can create a workflow that automatically sends a reminder every Monday morning to all team members about the status of their tasks or meetings. This ensures that everyone stays on track without needing manual follow-up.

Use Slackbots to Automate Alerts

Slackbots are another powerful tool that can be customized to suit your needs. You can set up Slackbot to send automated messages or alerts based on specific conditions. For example, you can use Slackbot to notify you if certain keywords are mentioned or if someone asks a question that requires a specific response.

By setting up Slackbots to handle repetitive tasks or alerts, you free up more time to focus on your actual work.

5. Streamlining Workflows with Integrations

Slack's true power lies in its ability to integrate with a wide variety of apps and services. By integrating your favorite tools into Slack, you can consolidate your work into one place, improving both organization and efficiency.

Integrate with Project Management Tools

For teams that use project management software like Trello, Asana, or Jira, integrating these tools into Slack can significantly improve workflow efficiency. You can receive notifications about project updates, create tasks directly from Slack, and collaborate on tasks without ever leaving the platform.

For example, you can integrate Asana with Slack so that when a new task is assigned to you, you'll receive an instant Slack notification. This way, you can stay updated on your projects without needing to manually check multiple platforms.

Integrate with Google Workspace or Microsoft 365

For teams that rely on Google Workspace or Microsoft 365 for documents, emails, and calendar events, integrating these services with Slack can improve collaboration. You can view, edit, and share documents directly within Slack, keeping all relevant information in one place.

Additionally, integration with calendar tools can help streamline scheduling by notifying you of upcoming meetings or deadlines directly in Slack.

Conclusion

By following these best practices, you can maintain an organized and efficient Slack workspace that enhances your productivity and streamlines communication. Whether it's structuring channels for clarity, managing notifications to reduce distractions, leveraging powerful search functions, or automating repetitive tasks, keeping Slack organized is key to becoming a Slack power user.

Investing the time to set up Slack effectively now will pay off in the long run, allowing you and your team to focus on what truly matters—working smarter and achieving your goals. As you continue to use Slack, remember that an organized workspace is not just about tidying up; it's about maximizing efficiency, reducing friction, and creating an environment that fosters collaboration.

7.3 Future of Slack and Emerging Features

7.3.1 What's New in Slack?

Slack, as one of the most widely used team communication platforms, has continuously evolved since its inception. With its robust suite of features aimed at simplifying and improving workplace collaboration, Slack has consistently introduced new tools, integrations, and enhancements designed to keep teams organized, engaged, and productive. Understanding the latest updates and the direction in which Slack is heading can help businesses leverage its full potential and stay ahead of the curve.

In this section, we'll explore some of the exciting new features and updates Slack has rolled out recently, as well as provide insight into some upcoming changes that will shape the way you and your team use Slack moving forward.

1. Slack Connect: Redefining Collaboration Across Companies

One of the most game-changing updates Slack has introduced in recent years is **Slack Connect**, which allows teams to work together more seamlessly across organizations. This feature enables secure, real-time communication between external partners, clients, or collaborators, all within the same Slack workspace.

Before Slack Connect, teams were typically limited to internal communication within their own workspace. Now, you can join channels with external companies and have shared conversations just as easily as you would with your own team. Whether it's a client meeting, a cross-company project, or simply sharing updates with an external vendor, Slack Connect provides a unified space where communication can flow freely and securely.

- **Why it's important**: Slack Connect eliminates the need for jumping between different platforms to communicate with external teams, making it more convenient for users to manage relationships and projects. It also enhances security by maintaining the high standards of encryption and data protection that Slack is known for.

- **What's next**: Future updates to Slack Connect will likely include enhanced features for managing cross-company permissions and deeper integrations with third-party applications, streamlining the way you collaborate outside of your company.

2. Slack Huddles: Simplified Audio & Video Meetings

Another recent feature that has gained significant popularity is **Slack Huddles**. Introduced as a lightweight alternative to more formal video calls, Huddles allow users to initiate quick, informal audio or video conversations with one or more colleagues. This feature was designed with remote work in mind, offering a more spontaneous and less formal way to communicate with teammates.

Slack Huddles are perfect for impromptu brainstorming sessions, quick check-ins, or casual discussions that would otherwise require scheduling a formal meeting. With the ability to screen share, collaborate on documents, and switch to video, Huddles have become an invaluable tool for distributed teams.

- **Why it's important**: Slack Huddles make it easier to connect and collaborate without the friction of setting up a full-fledged video call. It's an ideal solution for remote teams that need quick, efficient communication without the formality of traditional video conferencing tools.

- **What's next**: Slack is continuously working to enhance Huddles by adding features like background noise cancellation, meeting transcriptions, and improved video quality. Expect even more integrations with other Slack tools to make Huddles a one-stop solution for all communication needs.

3. Workflow Builder: Automating Routine Tasks

Slack's **Workflow Builder** has proven to be one of the most powerful tools for automation within the platform. This feature allows teams to automate repetitive tasks and workflows directly within Slack, reducing manual efforts and increasing overall productivity. With no coding required, users can create workflows that streamline processes such as onboarding new team members, collecting feedback, or setting up routine reminders.

By using pre-built templates or creating custom workflows, teams can automate responses to specific triggers, making Slack a more integrated part of the daily work process. Workflow Builder can be used to automatically send reminders, post messages to channels, or even integrate with external tools like Google Forms or Trello.

- **Why it's important**: Automation saves time and ensures consistency in the way tasks are completed. Workflow Builder empowers Slack users to design their own solutions, which means workflows can be tailored specifically to the needs of each team or organization.

- **What's next**: Future improvements to Workflow Builder may include more sophisticated triggers, integration with additional third-party apps, and advanced conditions for customizing workflows. Expect even greater flexibility as Slack looks to make task automation more powerful and user-friendly.

4. Advanced Search Enhancements

Slack has always had a robust search function, but recent updates have significantly improved its search capabilities. The introduction of advanced search filters allows users to search for specific types of content—whether it's messages, files, or even particular channels. With enhanced filters for date ranges, file types, and keyword relevance, Slack users can now find exactly what they need more quickly and with greater accuracy.

Additionally, Slack's search now offers more powerful indexing, making it easier to search through larger workspaces and deeper message histories. This is especially beneficial for organizations with large volumes of messages and files, ensuring that nothing gets lost in the shuffle.

- **Why it's important**: The enhanced search functionality makes Slack a more efficient tool for managing knowledge. Whether you're a team leader looking for a specific conversation or an employee trying to find an important file, these search upgrades make it easier to access critical information in no time.

- **What's next**: Expect even more features related to search, such as more customizable search alerts and better AI-driven search predictions. Slack is also likely to continue integrating search functionality with other platforms like Google Drive, allowing for an even smoother experience when looking for documents or files across multiple tools.

5. AI and Automation Features: Slack's Future with Artificial Intelligence

Slack has begun experimenting with **artificial intelligence (AI)** to enhance its platform's capabilities. In the near future, we can expect Slack to incorporate more AI-powered features that will help improve team productivity and communication.

For example, Slack might introduce AI-driven assistants that can automatically organize conversations, prioritize messages, or recommend relevant channels and files based on the context of your work. Slack could also use AI to provide real-time insights and analytics to help teams understand the flow of communication and identify bottlenecks or areas for improvement.

- **Why it's important**: AI will bring Slack into the next generation of smart collaboration tools. By leveraging machine learning and data analysis, AI can help teams make more informed decisions and automate repetitive tasks, ultimately saving time and improving efficiency.

- **What's next**: Look for more intelligent features that integrate with Slack's existing tools, such as automatic task management, predictive message recommendations, and context-aware notifications. AI may also play a role in enhancing Slack's virtual assistant capabilities, allowing teams to interact with Slack in more dynamic and intuitive ways.

6. Integrations with New Tools

As the digital workplace continues to evolve, Slack is adding support for a broader range of tools and platforms. For instance, Slack now integrates with more advanced project management software like **Monday.com** and **ClickUp**, as well as enhanced integrations with CRM systems like **Salesforce**.

In addition, Slack continues to deepen its integration with the Microsoft Office 365 suite, including Word, Excel, and Teams, to create a more seamless experience for users who rely on these tools in tandem with Slack.

- **Why it's important**: By expanding its integration capabilities, Slack allows users to consolidate their tools into one platform, streamlining workflows and ensuring that all information is accessible from a single workspace. The ability to access all your tools from within Slack eliminates the need to jump between applications, which boosts productivity and reduces friction.

- **What's next**: Expect even more integrations to be rolled out in the coming years. Slack is likely to continue building relationships with other leading software providers, offering even more out-of-the-box integrations to make it a central hub for your work.

Conclusion

As Slack continues to evolve, the platform remains committed to helping teams work smarter, not harder. Whether it's through enhancing collaboration across organizations, improving communication through Huddles, automating routine tasks with Workflow

Builder, or incorporating AI and new integrations, Slack is positioned to become an even more powerful tool in the modern workplace.

By staying up-to-date with these emerging features, you can ensure your team is leveraging the full potential of Slack to work more efficiently, engage more effectively, and stay ahead of the competition. As the future of work becomes increasingly digital and interconnected, Slack will remain a cornerstone in transforming how teams collaborate and communicate in the modern era.

7.3.2 Upcoming AI and Automation Features

As Slack continues to evolve into an even more powerful tool for workplace communication and collaboration, the platform is increasingly incorporating cutting-edge technology, such as artificial intelligence (AI) and automation features. These innovations are designed to enhance productivity, streamline workflows, and enable teams to communicate more effectively. This section will explore the upcoming AI and automation features in Slack, and how they can revolutionize the way you work.

The Rise of AI in Slack

Artificial intelligence is making waves in virtually every industry, and Slack is no exception. The integration of AI capabilities is not just a trend but a significant step forward in improving communication, organization, and decision-making processes within teams. For Slack users, AI-powered features offer enhanced experiences by automating repetitive tasks, optimizing workflows, and providing smarter, more intuitive interactions.

1. AI-Powered Search

Slack's search functionality is one of its most important features, and with the rise of AI, it's about to get even better. Currently, searching for messages, files, and conversations in Slack can be done with basic keyword searches. However, AI integration is set to enhance this experience significantly. In the near future, Slack will implement AI-driven search capabilities that not only look for keywords but also understand the context behind a query. For example, if you search for something like "project update," Slack will be able to identify not just messages with the words "project" and "update," but also the context in which those words were used, making it easier to find relevant information quickly.

Additionally, AI will help predict what you may want to search for next, based on your work patterns and the types of information you've accessed in the past. This predictive search feature will save time and ensure that you're always a few steps ahead in finding the information you need.

2. Smart Message Summarization

Another exciting AI feature coming to Slack is message summarization. Slack's messages can sometimes become long and convoluted, especially in active channels with multiple threads of conversation. With AI-powered summarization tools, Slack will soon be able to provide automatic summaries of lengthy messages and discussions. This feature will allow team members to quickly grasp key points and action items, without having to read through an entire message thread.

The AI algorithm will analyze the context of conversations, identify important information such as deadlines, key decisions, and next steps, and provide a concise summary. This feature is particularly useful for busy team members who may not have time to go through every message but still need to stay informed.

3. Enhanced Workflow Automation with AI

Slack has already made strides in workflow automation with its Workflow Builder, which allows users to automate various tasks such as sending messages, collecting information, and triggering actions in other apps. However, the next generation of Slack's automation tools will be significantly more intelligent. Leveraging AI, Slack will be able to automatically suggest workflow improvements based on user behavior and team needs.

For instance, if you regularly create reminders or send repetitive messages to certain team members, Slack may automatically suggest creating a workflow to streamline those tasks. Furthermore, AI will help identify bottlenecks or inefficiencies in your team's processes and recommend automation solutions to improve productivity. With these smart automation tools, Slack will not just be a messaging platform but a dynamic assistant that helps you streamline your work in real-time.

4. AI-Powered Slack Bots for Personalized Assistance

Slack bots have long been a part of the platform, but they are set to become much more sophisticated with the incorporation of AI. Upcoming AI-powered Slack bots will be able to provide more personalized assistance, learn from user interactions, and offer contextual support based on ongoing projects and conversations.

For example, an AI-powered bot might recognize when a team member is struggling with a particular task and offer suggestions based on prior knowledge and best practices. The bot could also assist with tasks such as meeting scheduling, file organization, and even tracking project progress by analyzing message threads and updates in real time. These bots will act as highly efficient, proactive assistants, anticipating your needs and providing recommendations that can save you time and effort.

5. AI-Powered Analytics for Teams

In addition to individual productivity enhancements, AI will soon provide valuable insights for entire teams. Slack's new AI-powered analytics tools will offer in-depth reports on team collaboration, communication patterns, and workflow efficiency. This feature will help managers and team leaders identify areas of improvement, track team engagement, and make data-driven decisions to optimize their teams' performance.

For example, AI will be able to analyze how often team members communicate with one another, whether certain channels are underutilized, and which workflows are taking the longest to complete. By using this data, teams can improve collaboration strategies, fine-tune their workflows, and ensure that everyone is staying on track.

6. Sentiment Analysis for Team Communication

Sentiment analysis, powered by AI, will be another emerging feature in Slack that can provide valuable insights into team dynamics and communication. This feature will analyze the tone of messages sent in Slack and give team leaders and managers insights into the overall mood and sentiment of their team. For example, if there's a lot of frustration or confusion in a particular channel, Slack could automatically detect this and notify the team leader, suggesting that action may be needed.

Sentiment analysis can also be used to ensure that communication remains positive and constructive. If a conversation takes a negative turn, AI could prompt team members to reconsider their tone or rephrase their message to foster more positive and productive communication.

7. AI-Powered Task Management and Follow-Ups

Managing tasks and ensuring that deadlines are met is an ongoing challenge for many teams. AI is poised to take task management in Slack to the next level. Upcoming features will allow Slack to automatically track tasks that are assigned, due dates, and dependencies. For example, if a team member mentions a task in a message, Slack's AI will recognize the context and automatically create a task in the integrated project management tool (such as Trello or Asana).

Furthermore, AI will help follow up on tasks by sending automated reminders to ensure that team members are on track to meet deadlines. This feature will reduce the chances of important tasks slipping through the cracks, ensuring better project management and greater accountability across the team.

The Role of Automation in Slack's Future

Automation has been a key part of Slack's functionality for a while, but its future with AI-driven capabilities looks even more promising. The combination of AI and automation will allow Slack to not only automate repetitive tasks but also predict what tasks need to be automated and improve workflow efficiency on a large scale.

With AI-powered tools in Slack, the platform will learn from user behavior and automatically suggest improvements for everyday processes. Whether it's automating meeting schedules, task assignments, or providing reminders, Slack will increasingly serve as an intelligent platform that drives work forward.

Conclusion

The integration of AI and automation features into Slack is a game-changer for users and teams. These advancements will not only improve how teams communicate but also enhance productivity by reducing manual tasks and providing valuable insights into team dynamics and workflows. As Slack continues to innovate, users can look forward to a future where AI and automation not only simplify daily tasks but also enhance the overall work experience, making Slack an indispensable tool for any modern workplace.

By embracing these features, teams can stay ahead of the curve and work smarter, not harder. The possibilities are endless, and with Slack leading the way, the future of work has never been more exciting.

7.3.3 How to Keep Up with Slack Updates

Slack, like many other modern tools, is constantly evolving. As a result, keeping up with its new features, updates, and best practices is essential to maximizing its effectiveness.

Staying current with Slack's updates ensures that you're leveraging the latest tools and enhancements to improve team communication and collaboration. This section will guide you through the best ways to stay informed about Slack's updates and help you make the most out of new features as they roll out.

1. Enable Automatic Updates

One of the easiest ways to keep Slack up to date is to ensure that you're always running the latest version. Slack provides automatic updates on most platforms, so if you're using the desktop app, it will generally update itself in the background. However, it's always a good idea to check whether your Slack app is up to date.

For Desktop Users (Mac/Windows):

- **Mac**: Slack updates automatically. To manually check for updates, click on the **Slack** menu in the top-left corner and select **Check for Updates**. If an update is available, it will automatically install.

- **Windows**: Open the app, click on the **Help** menu, and select **Check for Updates**. Slack will inform you if an update is available, and you can install it manually.

For Mobile Users (iOS/Android):

- Both iOS and Android apps typically update automatically when connected to Wi-Fi and plugged into a power source. You can always check for updates by visiting the **App Store** or **Google Play Store**, searching for Slack, and tapping **Update** if needed.

2. Subscribe to the Slack Blog

Slack's official **Slack Blog** is an excellent resource for staying up-to-date with the latest product updates, new feature releases, tips, and insights into how other teams are using Slack. Here, Slack's development team shares in-depth posts, new feature announcements, and other news about the platform.

You can visit the blog at https://slack.com/blog.
There are also RSS feed options available if you prefer to stay updated through an RSS reader.

- **Key Sections to Watch**:

- o **Product Updates**: Slack regularly posts detailed articles about new features and improvements.

- o **Tips & Tricks**: The blog provides helpful articles on making the most of Slack, including advanced tips for power users.

- o **Customer Stories**: Learn how other businesses and teams have implemented Slack into their workflow.

3. Join Slack's Community

Slack has a vibrant and active community of users who share knowledge, troubleshoot issues, and provide feedback on the platform. Slack's **Community Forum** and **Slack User Groups** offer an ideal place to stay in the loop about upcoming updates, hear user experiences, and ask questions about new features.

Slack Community Forum:

This forum is an active space for users to post their experiences, get help, and learn about updates directly from other Slack users. You can visit the forum at https://slackcommunity.com.

Slack User Groups (SUGs):

Slack User Groups are geographically-based communities that hold meetups (in-person and virtual) and discuss Slack's best practices, new features, and how teams around the world are utilizing the platform.

You can find a user group near you or learn more about it on the **Slack Community** page: https://slack.com/community.

4. Stay Connected to Slack's Social Media Channels

Slack has a presence on various social media platforms where they actively share news, updates, and tips on how to use Slack effectively. Following these channels will keep you informed in real-time about the latest changes.

- **Twitter**: Follow @SlackHQ for real-time updates on product changes, new features, and announcements.

- **LinkedIn**: Slack shares more in-depth articles, including case studies and user stories on their official LinkedIn page.

- **Facebook**: Slack's Facebook page regularly shares feature announcements, and you can interact with other users through comments and discussions.

- **YouTube**: Slack's official YouTube channel is home to product demos, user guides, webinars, and tutorial videos, which are excellent resources for discovering new features and updates.

5. Enable Slack's New Features in Beta

Slack occasionally releases new features as part of its **beta program**. These early access features are made available to users who are interested in testing and providing feedback on upcoming functionalities. Participating in beta testing allows you to try new features before they are widely rolled out to the general public.

To join the beta program:

1. Go to the **Slack Help Center**.

2. Look for **Beta Features** or **Early Access** options under settings or notifications.

3. Follow the steps to join the program.

By joining the beta, you can explore Slack's experimental features and give feedback directly to the development team. This also allows you to stay ahead of new tools that can improve your workflow.

6. Utilize Slack's Release Notes

Slack's **Release Notes** are an essential resource for anyone who wants to stay informed about product updates. These release notes provide detailed explanations of new features, bug fixes, performance improvements, and more.

You can access the release notes from the **Slack Help Center** or through the app itself:

- **Slack Help Center**: https://slack.com/help.

- **Release Notes Link**: https://slack.com/release-notes.

Release notes are a fantastic way to familiarize yourself with changes and new features on the platform, especially if you're responsible for managing Slack within your organization.

7. Set Up Notifications for New Updates

If you want to ensure that you are among the first to know about any important changes, consider enabling notifications for product updates. This way, you'll be alerted to any significant changes made to Slack, including new features, integrations, or any system changes.

You can enable these notifications via:

- **Slack's App Preferences**: You can opt in to get notifications about new features and updates.

- **External Notification Systems**: Some third-party tools or Slack bots can be used to keep you up-to-date with the latest features.

8. Explore Slack's Help Center and Learning Resources

Slack provides a comprehensive **Help Center** filled with articles, guides, and tutorials that explain new features and updates in detail. These resources are essential for both new and experienced users who want to make the most of Slack.

Additionally, Slack offers a variety of **free webinars** and **on-demand video tutorials**. These sessions cover everything from beginner tips to advanced best practices, and they often highlight new features.

- **Slack Help Center**: https://slack.com/help.

- **Slack Learning Hub**: https://slack.com/learn.

9. Participate in Feedback Programs

Slack highly values feedback from users, and they regularly invite users to provide input about their experience with new features. If you have suggestions, bug reports, or general feedback about the platform, Slack encourages you to participate in their feedback programs.

By engaging in these programs, you'll have an opportunity to directly influence future Slack features and receive information on upcoming changes. To participate, keep an eye on the **Help Center** for surveys and feedback requests, or contact Slack's support team.

10. Keep a Regular Schedule for Reviewing Slack Updates

Lastly, set aside time in your weekly or monthly routine to review any Slack updates that have been released. This habit will ensure that you remain aware of any new features, changes to existing features, or updates to Slack's integrations.

Creating a habit of exploring new features can drastically improve your team's productivity and the way you use Slack in your daily operations.

Conclusion

Slack is a continuously evolving tool that regularly introduces new features and updates designed to improve the user experience and streamline workflows. By staying informed and adopting new features early, you can ensure that your team remains productive and takes full advantage of the platform's capabilities. Whether through subscribing to blogs, following social media channels, or enabling beta features, there are numerous ways to stay ahead of the curve and make Slack work even better for you and your team.

Conclusion

8.1 Recap: The Key Takeaways from This Book

As we come to the end of this guide on how to work smarter with Slack, it's time to reflect on the key takeaways that will help you make the most of this powerful communication tool. Whether you're using Slack to connect with your team, collaborate on projects, or streamline your day-to-day work processes, Slack can transform how you work, boosting both efficiency and productivity. Let's review the essential points we've covered throughout this book.

1. Understanding Slack and its Core Features

In the first chapters, we laid the foundation by introducing Slack as a dynamic platform that brings together messaging, collaboration, and integrations all in one place. Slack's core features — such as Channels, Direct Messages (DMs), file sharing, and integrations — are designed to enhance team communication. We learned that organizing communications into Channels (for group chats) and DMs (for private conversations) is one of the key principles for maintaining clarity and focus.

Slack's ability to house both synchronous (real-time) and asynchronous (delayed) conversations is essential for modern teams. Channels help keep discussions organized by topic, department, or project, while DMs ensure that private and one-on-one conversations are just a click away. We also discussed the power of Slack's search function, allowing users to access message history, find files, and even track down important conversations from the past, ensuring that nothing gets lost.

2. Setting Up Slack for Success

We explored the importance of setting up your Slack workspace effectively. By understanding how to customize your notification preferences and manage your settings, you can prevent distractions while still staying on top of important updates. Slack's ability to integrate with various tools, such as Google Drive, Dropbox, and Asana, helps centralize your work in one place.

From customizing your profile to adjusting workspace settings, it's essential to configure Slack in a way that fits your needs. This includes setting up team channels based on function or projects and ensuring that everyone in your workspace understands the purpose of each channel. Slack also offers extensive user management options, including adding new team members and managing roles and permissions. A well-organized workspace reduces confusion and increases overall productivity.

3. Mastering Communication with Slack

Effective communication is at the heart of Slack, and in this book, we discussed how to use Slack to master both individual and team communication. Using Slack's wide range of messaging options — from text to images, links, emojis, and gifs — you can communicate more effectively with your colleagues.

We introduced the concept of "threaded conversations," where you can reply to specific messages without cluttering the channel. This functionality allows teams to have detailed discussions around specific points while keeping the main channel focused on broader topics. By using reactions and mentions, Slack makes it easy to acknowledge or respond to specific team members without interrupting the flow of the conversation.

We also delved into Slack's powerful file sharing and collaboration features. Uploading documents, images, and links directly into conversations makes it easier for teams to access critical resources instantly. Additionally, integrating Slack with external tools like Google Drive, Box, or Dropbox ensures that everyone has access to up-to-date files and documents directly within Slack.

4. Leveraging Slack for Team Collaboration

Collaboration in Slack is about more than just messaging. We examined several tools and features within Slack that can supercharge teamwork. The Workflow Builder, for example, automates repetitive tasks and can help streamline processes like onboarding new team members, scheduling meetings, or sending reminders.

Slack also supports real-time collaboration during meetings. Slack's voice and video call features, as well as the innovative Slack Huddles, allow teams to have impromptu conversations or structured meetings without needing to jump into another tool like Zoom or Microsoft Teams. This seamless integration of communication and collaboration ensures that you can focus on the work at hand, not the logistics of setting up meetings.

In addition to communication, Slack offers a suite of project management tools that enhance team coordination. Integrations with task management apps like Asana or Trello, and the ability to set reminders and follow-up tasks, make sure that projects stay on track and everyone is clear on their responsibilities.

5. Enhancing Productivity with Slack

One of the main goals of Slack is to help teams stay productive and reduce the clutter of email inboxes. Through smart use of notifications, you can stay up to date without being overwhelmed by constant interruptions. We discussed how to customize your notification settings based on channels or keywords, ensuring that you are notified only about what truly matters.

Slack allows you to streamline your workday by providing useful tools like reminders and the ability to schedule messages. Whether it's setting reminders for important meetings, daily check-ins, or deadlines, Slack helps you stay on top of your work. The "Do Not Disturb" mode further empowers you to focus on deep work without constant interruptions.

Additionally, we discussed the importance of using Slack's various integrations, such as calendar apps or task managers, to centralize your workflow. The ability to manage projects directly in Slack, without switching between multiple tools, is a productivity booster. Slack's flexibility allows you to set up automated workflows that take care of repetitive tasks, freeing up more time for critical thinking and creativity.

6. Ensuring Security and Privacy

A secure workspace is a productive workspace, and we explored how to ensure the privacy and security of your Slack environment. By setting up strong user permissions and understanding Slack's security settings, teams can manage who has access to what information. Slack's two-factor authentication adds an extra layer of protection to ensure that only authorized users can access sensitive data.

We also discussed how to handle private or confidential information within Slack. Using direct messages for private conversations and protecting sensitive files with password protection are just a couple of ways you can maintain confidentiality. With Slack's comprehensive audit logs and reporting tools, you can ensure that team members adhere to security policies.

7. Overcoming Challenges with Slack

In Chapter 7, we covered some common challenges users face with Slack and how to troubleshoot them. Whether it's connectivity issues, syncing problems, or being overwhelmed by too many channels, there are simple solutions that can help you get back on track. Learning how to manage Slack's numerous features and notifications effectively will enable you to work smarter and avoid burnout.

Additionally, we provided tips for managing Slack's many features and keeping it organized. Learning to navigate Slack with focus and purpose, using Slack etiquette guides, and avoiding unnecessary distractions are all key steps toward becoming a Slack power user.

8. The Future of Slack

We also took a look at the future of Slack and how the platform continues to evolve. The introduction of AI-powered tools and new automation features promises to make Slack even more intuitive and user-friendly. As Slack continues to integrate more AI and machine learning capabilities, teams will be able to work even smarter, automating tasks, finding relevant information more easily, and improving team communication. Keeping up with these new features and updates will help you maximize the potential of Slack in the long term.

Final Thoughts

By now, you should have a clear understanding of how to use Slack not just as a communication tool, but as a comprehensive platform for team collaboration, productivity, and project management. Through careful setup, effective communication practices, and maximizing Slack's features, you can work smarter and streamline your work processes.

This book has provided you with the foundational knowledge to transform the way you work. By consistently applying the principles and strategies outlined here, you can create an efficient, productive, and secure work environment for yourself and your team.

Now that you're equipped with the tools and techniques to master Slack, the next step is to put this knowledge into action. Start applying these practices today and watch how Slack can change the way you work for the better.

8.2 How to Keep Improving Your Slack Experience

Slack is an immensely powerful tool that has revolutionized the way individuals and teams communicate, collaborate, and work together. Whether you're a beginner just starting with Slack or an experienced user looking to refine your skills, there's always room to improve your Slack experience. The key to mastering Slack is not only understanding its features but also continuously finding ways to optimize its use to align with your specific needs and workflow. In this section, we will explore several strategies, tips, and practices to help you elevate your Slack experience and make it even more effective for your personal productivity and team collaboration.

1. Regularly Review and Update Your Notifications

One of the most powerful features of Slack is its notification system. Slack allows you to customize notifications for different channels and direct messages, helping you stay on top of important conversations while minimizing distractions. However, as your team and communication needs evolve, it's essential to periodically review and adjust your notification settings.

Tailor Notifications to Your Workflow

Over time, you may find that certain channels or direct messages no longer require your immediate attention. For instance, notifications from channels where you have minimal involvement can be reduced or turned off entirely, while channels dedicated to high-priority topics might need more immediate notifications.

Slack's "Do Not Disturb" mode can also be a valuable tool for controlling when and how you receive notifications. You can set it to specific hours or manually activate it when you need uninterrupted focus time. Additionally, Slack offers a feature called "keyword notifications," which alerts you whenever a specific word or phrase is mentioned in a conversation. This feature can be particularly useful for keeping track of relevant topics or important updates.

Experiment with Notification Sounds

Notifications in Slack come with various sound options, and it's a small detail that can impact your experience. If you find the default notification sound distracting, consider customizing it or using more subtle sound cues to help maintain your focus without being disrupted by every ping.

2. Leverage Slack Integrations and Bots

Slack is not just a messaging platform—it's also a hub for all your work tools and services. By integrating Slack with the apps and tools you already use, you can create a seamless and more efficient workflow.

Explore Slack's Built-in Integrations

Slack provides a vast array of integrations with popular tools like Google Drive, Asana, Trello, Zoom, and many others. If you haven't already, explore these integrations and start using them to connect Slack with your other work applications. By doing this, you can receive updates, manage tasks, and conduct meetings directly within Slack, saving you time and minimizing the need to switch between different apps.

Set Up Custom Integrations

If you use tools that are not part of Slack's default integrations, you can still enhance your experience by setting up custom integrations using Slack's API. Many third-party services and bots can help automate repetitive tasks and improve your workflow, whether it's for tracking project progress, sending automated reminders, or generating reports.

Slack's "Workflow Builder" is a powerful tool for automation. It allows you to create custom workflows that automate repetitive tasks like sending welcome messages to new team members, requesting feedback, or generating status updates. By investing time into creating and refining these workflows, you can save countless hours and streamline your day-to-day operations.

3. Organize Your Channels and Direct Messages

Slack works best when your channels and conversations are well-organized, and it's important to take the time to structure them thoughtfully.

Create Focused Channels for Specific Topics

A common mistake in Slack is having too many broad channels that lack clear focus, leading to disorganization and information overload. Instead, consider creating more specific channels tailored to certain projects, teams, or topics. For example, if you're working on a marketing campaign, create a dedicated channel like #marketing-campaign-xyz. This will help keep discussions focused, relevant, and easier to navigate.

Archive and Clean Up Inactive Channels

Over time, teams accumulate inactive channels that no longer serve a purpose. Periodically review your channels and archive or delete those that are no longer relevant. This will help reduce clutter and make it easier to find important conversations in the future. You can also "pin" key channels that you need quick access to, ensuring they're always at the top of your sidebar.

Use Slack's Search Feature Effectively

Slack's search function is incredibly powerful but often underutilized. You can filter searches by channels, date ranges, or users to quickly find past messages, files, or discussions. Becoming proficient at using the search bar will help you find the information you need without sifting through endless conversations.

4. Maximize the Use of Slack's Advanced Features

There are numerous advanced features in Slack that, when used correctly, can make your work process much more efficient and organized.

Master the Use of Slack Threads

Slack threads help keep conversations organized and prevent clutter in channels. Instead of replying to a message in the main channel, you can start a thread to keep the discussion focused on a specific topic while keeping the main conversation clear. Make sure to check and respond to threads promptly, as they are often used for more detailed discussions or follow-ups.

Use Slack Shortcuts to Save Time

Slack has several keyboard shortcuts that can speed up your workflow. Familiarize yourself with these shortcuts to avoid clicking through the interface repeatedly. For example, using "Cmd + K" (Mac) or "Ctrl + K" (Windows) allows you to quickly jump to any channel or conversation, while "Cmd + Shift + A" (Mac) or "Ctrl + Shift + A" (Windows) brings up the channel activity feed.

Customize Your Slack Experience

Slack provides various customization options to help tailor the interface to your preferences. You can adjust the theme of the workspace, use dark mode for reduced eye strain, and even modify your sidebar layout. Additionally, you can customize your profile with a unique status, emoji reactions, and a personalized photo, which helps add a personal touch to your communications.

5. Continuously Educate Yourself on Slack Updates

Slack is constantly evolving, adding new features, and improving its functionality. To stay ahead of the curve, it's crucial to regularly educate yourself on new updates.

Keep an Eye on Slack's Release Notes

Slack frequently releases new features and improvements. By subscribing to release notes or reading Slack's blog, you can stay informed about the latest additions to the platform. Whether it's a new integration, a UI change, or an improved feature, keeping up-to-date will ensure you're leveraging the most advanced tools available.

Participate in Slack Communities

There are several communities, both official and unofficial, where Slack users share tips, advice, and new features. By joining these communities, you can learn from other users' experiences, ask questions, and share your own insights. Participating in such communities helps you stay connected with the broader Slack ecosystem and improve your usage of the platform.

6. Encourage Slack Best Practices Across Your Team

To ensure that your entire team is maximizing their Slack experience, it's important to establish clear guidelines and best practices for using the tool.

Establish Slack Etiquette

One of the most effective ways to improve your Slack experience is by creating an etiquette guide for your team. This guide should cover communication norms, such as when to use direct messages versus public channels, how to manage mentions and reactions, and best practices for using threads. Having a set of guidelines will help keep everyone on the same page and ensure that Slack remains a productive tool rather than a source of frustration.

Encourage Slack Usage Across Teams

Encourage your team to use Slack for all internal communication, whether it's for sharing updates, asking quick questions, or collaborating on projects. The more consistent everyone is with using Slack, the more effective it will become as a communication hub.

Conclusion

Improving your Slack experience is an ongoing process, but by applying the strategies outlined in this section, you'll be well on your way to becoming a Slack power user. Whether it's customizing your notifications, leveraging integrations, or keeping your channels organized, each small improvement can have a significant impact on your productivity and collaboration. By staying up-to-date with Slack's new features and maintaining a disciplined approach to its usage, you'll not only enhance your own work experience but also contribute to a more efficient and collaborative team environment.

Remember, Slack is not just a tool—it's a key part of the way you and your team work. So, take the time to refine your usage, experiment with new features, and always be open to learning and improving your Slack skills. As you continue to optimize your Slack experience, you'll find that it becomes an even more valuable asset in your daily workflow, helping you work smarter and achieve more.

8.3 Final Thoughts and Next Steps

As you have now explored the core functionalities of Slack and learned how to leverage its full potential, you stand at the threshold of transforming the way you work, communicate, and collaborate. By following the best practices outlined throughout this book, you have already taken a significant step towards increasing your productivity and enhancing the efficiency of your team. However, like any tool, Slack offers ongoing opportunities for growth, adaptation, and mastery. In this final section, we will reflect on key takeaways and discuss the next steps you can take to continue improving your Slack experience.

Reflecting on Key Takeaways

Slack is not just a messaging platform—it's a powerful tool designed to optimize communication, foster collaboration, and streamline workflow processes. When used correctly, it can make a significant impact on how you interact with colleagues, organize your tasks, and manage projects. By mastering Slack's channels, integrations, and communication features, you've already begun to unlock its true potential. However, real success lies in continuous learning and the application of what you've learned to your daily work life.

To recap some of the key points from this book, let's highlight a few areas where Slack truly shines:

- **Organized Communication**: The ability to create channels, both public and private, ensures that conversations remain structured and relevant. You can quickly find what you need by using Slack's robust search features, ensuring that communication is never lost in the noise.

- **Collaboration Made Easy**: Slack integrates with a wide range of third-party apps, from Google Drive to project management tools like Trello. This allows you to bring all your resources into one centralized hub, improving the way teams collaborate and work on projects.

- **Remote Work Flexibility**: Slack provides various tools for remote and hybrid teams to work together efficiently. Features like Slack Huddles, video calls, and integrations with conferencing platforms make it easy to stay connected, no matter where you are.

- **Automation and Workflows**: With the use of Slack's Workflow Builder and bots, tasks that were once manual can now be automated. By reducing routine work, you can focus on more meaningful and creative tasks.

- **Effective Notifications Management**: Customizing notifications ensures that you only receive the information that matters to you. The ability to pause notifications during off-hours or set Do Not Disturb mode can help protect your focus and prevent burnout.

These highlights illustrate the power of Slack as a workplace tool. But to truly excel, it's crucial to understand that mastery of Slack comes with continuous engagement, learning, and refining your approach over time.

Next Steps: How to Keep Improving Your Slack Experience

Even after you've gotten the hang of Slack, the journey doesn't end there. To truly harness Slack's capabilities, you must remain proactive in adapting to new features, experimenting with different techniques, and adjusting your approach based on your evolving needs and team dynamics. Here are several steps to help you continue to grow and optimize your use of Slack:

1. Stay Up to Date with New Features

Slack is a dynamic platform that constantly evolves. With regular updates and new features being rolled out, it's crucial to stay informed about the latest changes. Slack's official blog and release notes are excellent resources to track new updates. From enhanced integrations to cutting-edge AI tools, keeping an eye on these developments will help you stay ahead of the curve and discover new ways to boost your productivity.

2. Regularly Review and Update Your Slack Practices

As your team's workflow and communication needs evolve, so too should your Slack usage. Regularly review your existing channels, workflows, and integrations to ensure they are still aligned with your current objectives. Consider implementing new features or even updating your Slack etiquette guide to reflect your team's changing culture. A review session every few months could uncover new opportunities to optimize your workspace.

3. Experiment with Advanced Slack Features

Beyond the basics, Slack offers a range of advanced tools that can take your collaboration to the next level. Experiment with features like custom workflows, automation using Slackbot, and deep integrations with other tools that your team uses. By automating repetitive tasks or setting up custom alerts, you'll free up more time for high-value work.

4. Foster a Slack-First Culture in Your Team

If you are leading a team, it's important to cultivate a Slack-first culture that encourages transparency, collaboration, and efficiency. Encourage your team members to take full advantage of Slack's features, such as setting up customized notifications, using message reactions, and sharing files and resources in an organized way. When Slack is used effectively, it can create an environment where information flows seamlessly and work is accomplished with ease.

Consider hosting internal workshops or Slack training sessions to help your team get familiar with advanced Slack functionalities. This not only helps everyone work smarter but also encourages team bonding as everyone gets on the same page.

5. Ensure Your Slack Workspace Remains Secure

While Slack is a powerful tool, it's important to maintain a focus on security and privacy. Review your workspace's settings regularly to ensure that your team has appropriate access permissions and that sensitive data is protected. Take advantage of two-factor authentication, custom user roles, and secure integrations to safeguard your team's communications and files.

6. Integrate Slack More Deeply with Your Other Tools

Slack isn't just a standalone tool; it's most powerful when integrated with other tools your team uses. Whether it's project management software like Asana, file-sharing tools like Google Drive, or time-tracking apps like Harvest, integrating these tools with Slack can significantly enhance your workflow. If you haven't already done so, take the time to set up and customize these integrations to match your team's needs. This will help create a centralized hub where everything you need is at your fingertips.

7. Create and Share Custom Workflows

The Workflow Builder is one of Slack's most powerful features, and you should start using it to automate processes and tasks. Think about repetitive tasks that can be automated—whether it's managing on-boarding procedures, handling support requests, or sending reminders for deadlines. Creating these custom workflows will save time and reduce errors, and can be easily shared with your team to boost efficiency across the board.

8. Embrace the Future of Slack

As Slack continues to integrate AI and automation features, consider exploring how these innovations can further streamline your work. Slack's AI capabilities can assist with summarizing meetings, managing repetitive tasks, and even predicting trends in your communications. Stay open to experimenting with these tools as they become available to ensure you're using Slack to its fullest potential.

Final Thoughts: Embrace Slack as Your Productivity Partner

Slack isn't just about managing messages—it's about fostering a productive, organized, and collaborative environment for you and your team. Whether you are a solo worker or part of a large organization, Slack has the flexibility and features to scale with your needs and improve your workflows. But the key to unlocking its full potential is consistent, mindful use and a willingness to adapt to new tools and practices.

As you continue to explore Slack, remember that technology alone won't drive success. The real power lies in how you use it to streamline communication, boost team collaboration, and ultimately help you work smarter—not harder.

In conclusion, Slack is not just a tool; it's a way to transform your working life, making it more organized, connected, and productive. By following the strategies and tips shared in this book, you are on the path to creating a more efficient and enjoyable work environment. Now, it's time to put everything into practice and keep evolving with Slack as your trusted productivity partner.

Acknowledgments

First and foremost, I want to extend my deepest gratitude to **you**, the reader. Thank you for choosing to invest your time, attention, and trust in this book. Whether you're just getting started with Slack or looking to take your skills to the next level, I hope this guide has empowered you to work more efficiently, communicate more effectively, and collaborate with greater ease.

In a world where we are constantly bombarded with new tools and technologies, choosing to learn and master one — and doing it with purpose — is no small feat. Your decision to pick up this book reflects a genuine desire to improve the way you work, and I'm honored to be part of that journey.

Writing this book has been a labor of love, and knowing that it might help someone streamline their workflow, reduce workplace stress, or simply feel more in control of their digital environment makes every page worth it.

If you found value in this book, I would be incredibly grateful if you shared your thoughts with others — whether in a review, a recommendation to a colleague, or a conversation with your team. Your feedback not only helps me, but also helps other readers discover tools that could transform the way they work.

Once again, thank you for being part of this journey. Here's to working smarter, not harder — and to making Slack a true asset in your professional life.

Warm regards,

www.ingramcontent.com/pod-product-compliance
Lightning Source LLC
LaVergne TN
LVHW081331050326
832903LV00024B/1112